Praise for *About France*

With his keen eye and long experience as an American journalist in France, Joseph Harriss may just understand the French better than the French understand themselves. Harriss's perceptive observations, mixed with a little humor, make his writings irresistible.

—Alfred S. Regnery, Publisher, *The American Spectator*

A highly entertaining, enlightening, and idiosyncratic examination of the France of recent decades by way of the institutions, preoccupations and passions that make it the special nation it is.

—William Pfaff, Paris-based syndicated columnist

Joseph Harriss is a reporter of the old—and best—school, whose sharp insights illuminate whatever subject to which he turns his considerable talents. In this case it is France, and all who love France, that are the beneficiaries. Vive Harriss!

—Carey Winfrey, editor, *Smithsonian* magazine

Joseph Harriss combines the good journalist's zest for his subject—be it oysters, cobblestones, Simenon in his pyjamas or Malraux in his glory—with disciplined and alert research. A very useful addition to everyone's necessary shelf of books on France.

—Mary Blume, *International Herald Tribune* columnist
whose latest book is *A French Affair*

About France

Also by Joseph Harriss

The Tallest Tower: Eiffel and the Belle Epoque

Critical acclaim for *The Tallest Tower*

"Harriss succeeds admirably…This is a well-organized, exceptionally readable book; entertaining, informative, and highly recommended."
—*Library Journal*

"Fascinating and highly instructive…a book not to miss."
—Janet Flanner, Paris correspondent, *The New Yorker*

"An interesting story interestingly told, and as such it is welcome."
—*The New York Times*

"A comprehensive account…The book is written with wit and charm."
—*Los Angeles Times*

About France

Joseph Harriss

iUniverse, Inc.
New York Lincoln Shanghai

About France

Copyright © 2005 by Joseph Harriss

iUniverse books may be ordered through booksellers or by contacting:

iUniverse
2021 Pine Lake Road, Suite 100
Lincoln, NE 68512
www.iuniverse.com
1-800-Authors (1-800-288-4677)

ISBN-13: 978-0-595-34695-0 (pbk)
ISBN-13: 978-0-595-67143-4 (cloth)
ISBN-13: 978-0-595-79439-3 (ebk)
ISBN-10: 0-595-34695-2 (pbk)
ISBN-10: 0-595-67143-8 (cloth)
ISBN-10: 0-595-79439-4 (ebk)

Printed in the United States of America

For Claudie and Christopher

Contents

PROLOGUE

"I've got this love-hate thing about France." "Great country, too bad about the people." "France is too beautiful to be wasted on the French." I don't know how many times I have heard these remarks, and similar, from American friends visiting France. Ambivalence seems inevitable when the subject is France. That includes the view of that quintessential American visitor, Mark Twain, who summed up, "France has neither winter nor summer nor morals. Apart from these drawbacks it is a fine country."

Its physical charms make France the world's premier tourist destination. It is beautifully bounded by the English Channel on the north, the Atlantic to the west, and the Mediterranean on the south. Its rich, fertile soil has been carefully tended, its landscapes hand-sculpted over the centuries and adorned with magnificent cathedrals and châteaux. The whole is splendidly set off by the majestic drama of the Alps. Unquestionably, these 210,026 square miles at the western end of the Eurasian landmass make France special. Not for nothing is the proverbial German description of the good life, "Living like God in France."

On the other hand, its people—often brilliant, frequently charming, usually polite, occasionally courteous, rarely spontaneously friendly, sometimes downright wrongheaded by the lights of other nations—tend to inspire more ambiguous feelings. The one thing that can be said with certainty about France is that it leaves no one indifferent. Or, as my journalistic colleague in Paris, Roger Cohen, has put it so astutely in his column in the *International Herald Tribune*, "There are all sorts of countries and then, of course, there is France, or, to put it better, La France, a state but also a being, with its pretensions, its contradictions, its lapses and its loveliness that make us love it or loathe it or, more likely, both at once."

1

The main source of this ambivalence, the French people themselves, appear so insular and self-absorbed as to be impermeable to cultures other than their own. I know some who have spent years with international organizations in the United States without ever coming to understand the most elementary things about America. This egocentric national trait—which the French themselves term *nombrilisme*, literally, "navelism" as in studying one's own—has long been noted by better France-watchers than I.

In the 18th century the great French philosopher Montesquieu gently satirized the invincible self-centeredness of his compatriots when he asked, ironically, "How can anyone possibly be Persian?" The 19th-century Swiss writer, Henri-Frédéric Amiel, also noted this closed mindset in 1871, when he wrote, "The French always place a school of thought, a formula, convention, a priori arguments, abstraction, and artificiality above reality; they prefer clarity to truth, words to things, rhetoric to science…. They emerge from description only to hurl themselves into precipitate generalizations. They imagine they understand man in his entirety, whereas they cannot break the hard shell of their personalities, and they do not understand a single nation apart from themselves."

I myself have found France alternately fascinating, endearing, pleasurable, and maddening for the many years that I have been here. Being a Paris-based journalist gave me a privileged observation post, the opportunity to travel widely, to get to know the cities and towns, and to meet and exchange ideas with a great range of French citizens of all socio-economic circles, many of whom have become my friends.

If I had to sum up the basic attitude that runs through the French mentality at all levels, it would be a composite of preening pride, often frankly chauvinistic, in being French, and barely concealed dislike, bordering on fear and loathing, of change. As a people they advance reluctantly toward the future, eyes fixed firmly on the past, especially the glorious 17th century of Louis XIV. Noting what he calls the country's inherent schizophrenia, Denis Jeambar, the editor-in-chief of the news magazine *L'Express*, has written that France "oscillates continuously between pride and resignation, movement and immobility. More than any other European nation, it is characterized by contradictory attributes."

This fixation on the past, of course, accounts for much of France's undeniable charm. When friends ask me what I like about living in France, I sometimes reply, at least half-seriously, that I like living in the past, in a society that is usually 20 years or more behind modern trends. It often strikes me as living pleasantly in the world's biggest museum. But I would not feel that way if I were a young Frenchman starting out in life. I would feel extremely frustrated in a country where only one-quarter of those under 25 find jobs, making it the European leader in unemployment among its young people. (France also has the highest rate of adolescent suicides in Europe.) Indeed, many talented, well-educated young people are leaving France for Britain or the United States to find less elitism, a more flexible job market, and a less hidebound lifestyle.

Paradoxically, this attachment to the past exists in a society that has experienced some of the most wrenching change in its history. When I compare France with the United States, a country known for rapid socio-economic change, I find that in some ways France has changed far more in the last few decades. In little more than half a century, France has gone from an agricultural country with upwards of 20 percent of its people living on small subsistence farms without such amenities as telephones and electricity—even in Paris as recently as the 1970s, I had to wait three years to get a telephone in my apartment—to an industrialized nation with a cell phone in every pocket, high-speed trains rocketing through the countryside, and three-quarters of its electricity derived from nuclear power. But most Frenchmen are only one or two generations removed from village life and peasantry. Their mentality and manners still reflect this in their feeling for *le terroir,* or soil, their avarice and cunning, their suspiciousness of others, their distrust of modernity.

France pays a price for this inability or unwillingness to accept change, a problem that its leaders and political commentators have themselves often castigated. In the 1970s a dynamic prime minister named Jacques Chaban-Delmas despairingly called his country "the blocked society." He was not prime minister for long. The prominent political philosopher Raymond Aron once observed with regret that there was little evolution in France; from time to time there was an explosion of mass discontent, then things went back to socio-economic gridlock. As an aide to Nicolas Sarkozy, the most promising new face in French politics, and likely presidential candidate in 2007, says, "France is not eternal. If it does not reform, it will disappear."

The pieces in this book are personal, idiosyncratic looks at many aspects of France. They are certainly not, and are not intended to be, a profound or exhaustive study of the country. Not being an academic or sociologist, my credentials are that for several decades I have worked with the French, played with them, driven their roads, walked their streets, married into a French family, sent my son through mostly French schools, and observed and written professionally about them.

Some will find my tone occasionally irreverent and/or iconoclastic. While I consider myself a friend of the French—my wife is French, my son Franco-American, most of my adult life has been, by choice, in France—I try to be fair and objective. This sometimes means saying the emperor is naked. After all, if we risk being ridiculous in direct proportion to our pretensions, the French risk in this regard is rather high. I freely admit that I tend not to take the French as seriously as most of them, particularly those in government and the media, take themselves. But given the stimulation and pleasure that France has given the world, I do feel that if it did not exist, we *Anglo-Saxons,* as they call us, would have to invent it. I am sure the French would agree with that.

PART ONE:
La France Éternelle

Certain constants give French life its unchanging character. These are the things that everyone associates automatically with France and that impart its unique flavor, for better or worse. Taken together they add up to its day-to-day culture, as opposed to its rarefied high culture. I will not get into high culture, although that is certainly an important element in the overall picture, because that is better treated by specialists and has been done so copiously.

I personally tend to find *La France Éternelle*, the one always there despite political and economic changes, and even the forsaking of much of its identity and sovereignty over its own affairs to the so-called "European Union" and its 20,000 unelected, regulating bureaucrats in Brussels, in permanent areas of character I am calling, arbitrarily, *l'esprit, la gloire, la bouffe,* and *Oh la-la!*

Esprit of course literally means "mind," but also has other meanings such as wit, aptitude, and spirit in its several English meanings. The spirit, if not the soul, of France can be inferred from things like the important place it accords the notion of culture, and the prestige of its culture heroes such as the "immortals" of the Académie Française. It is also illustrated by the squabble over what finally became of the writer Antoine de Saint-Exupéry. The adventurous intellectual André Malraux was in some ways the quintessence of French spirit, but so are those meticulous master craftsmen, the Compagnons. The contradictory French cast of mind is revealed in things like the almost compulsive adoption of words from the officially despised "Anglo-Saxon" language, and the paradoxical passion, among a people so in love with intelligence, for astrology. And it culminates in that social class so peculiar to France, *les intellectuels*, which remains characteristically fecund and fractious.

The French writer and Academician Jean Dutourd once told me with his usual straightforward irreverence that France is the land of vanity. Certainly its citizens seem to have an exceptional craving for *la gloire* in one form or another. Gustave Eiffel's thousand-foot tower was built to express the country's preening pride in its 19th century industry. To a large extent, the supersonic airliner Concorde, never a commercial success, was a prestige project. And although the French army has not had a victory without American assistance since its defeat by the Prussians in 1870, the crack, non-French soldiers of the glory-laden Foreign Legion carry the French tricolor high into some of the world's hot spots.

Eternal France is also to be found, pleasantly, in its frivolities. *La bouffe* is the term of endearment the French use familiarly for their cooking when eschewing the more elegant *cuisine*. Champagne is still de rigueur at every festive occasion, and the consumption of oysters is prodigious despite their prohibitive price. But French eating habits are changing rapidly. Consumption of wine, for instance, is down by half from the 1960s. The once-national beverage is today virtually an endangered species—a parliamentary commission has proposed that wine awareness be a compulsory subject in French schools and that wine be designated a "cultural product." Fast food joints are proliferating, and restaurants where you can get a good meal at moderate price are vanishing. When I arrived many years ago, the common saying that you couldn't get a bad meal in Paris was literally true. *Hélas*, no longer.

The French talent for creative frivolity is also apparent in their take-no-prisoners approach to vacation, the number one priority on everyone's annual agenda. In fact, one sure way to start a lively conversation in France is to ask, "How about that vacation?" Your interlocutor will either be just back from one, or actively planning the next. Like food, the *oh la-la!* in France isn't what it used to be either, though the late Alain Bernardin's Crazy Horse Saloon tries hard to maintain its standards of elegant naughtiness. And that aspect of France, one hopes, will indeed be eternal.

1. L'Esprit

Culture Heroes: The Immortal Members of the Académie Française

Context: *The subject of culture holds a more important place in France than any other country I know. This does not mean that the French themselves are necessarily more cultured or better educated than others, though they certainly have a better developed sense of history than, say, we Americans. If anything embodies the French idea of culture, particularly literary achievement, it is the French Academy. Like culture itself, it serves no utilitarian purpose, unless it can be considered useful to reinforce the idea that the French have of themselves as a people that takes culture seriously. After more than 350 years, the Académie Française and its 40 "immortals" are still ostensibly trying to keep the French language pure, their official duty. I found its members an affable, gentlemanly, generally unpretentious lot who consider the Academy more a social club than a cultural bastion. Perhaps it really is one of "only three eternal things in the world."*

It happens, on average, twice a year. At 3 p.m. sharp, a group of oddly accoutered elderly figures heads down the narrow, steep staircase of a handsome, domed building that faces the Louvre across the Seine. Often steadying themselves on the banister, they wear dark, swallowtail suits embroidered with green olive leaves and carry ostrich-plumed cocked hats under their arms. They concentrate hard on not tripping over the ornate épées that brush against their calves.

When the frail little company reaches a vaulted baroque hallway where a stone Cardinal Mazarin kneels on his own red-marble casket, the silence is suddenly broken by a barked command: "*Présentez...armes!*" A 20-man detachment of France's ceremonial Garde Républicaine in képis and white gloves hoists sabers to chins as a loud drum roll, like the one that used to announce the fall of the guillotine's blade, crepitates through the vaults.

As the members take their places, 300 invited guests stand respectfully in the rotunda beneath the dome. One member remains standing at the third seat in the next-to-last row, nervously fingering a thick manuscript. For the next hour, the new member delivers a stream of fine, euphonious phrases and carefully turned past-perfect subjunctives in eulogy of a deceased, and largely forgotten, predecessor, then listens to a donnish reply describing his or her own life and work. Abruptly, the stylized liturgy is over. Members and guests file back into the vaulted hall, where there is much congratulating and kissing on both cheeks.

In much the same form, this ritual induction of a new member into France's cultural paradise, the Académie Française, has been going on for more than 350 years, come king, revolution, emperor or republic. "The Academy is the great witness of French civilization," says the daily *Le Figaro*. "What happens beneath that dome links us to all our historical and cultural tradition."

It's a tradition that pays its respects to culture heroes the way other countries revere businessmen or Stakhanovites. Paris is still the only city that I know of where until fairly recently you could list your profession in the phone book as *Homme de Lettres*. Where else do they present arms to men of letters? Or at dinner parties place them higher than government ministers and just after cardinals and princes of the royal blood?

Since Plato's Academy, which met in an olive grove, where Milton's "Attic bird trills her thick-warbled notes the summer long," many countries have had academies, including our own American Academy of Arts and Sciences. But France's, rooted in the Gallic nation's quirky idea of itself, is the most idiosyncratic and durable. In 1908 Lord Asquith, the British prime minister, was convinced that there were only three eternal things in the world: the German General Staff, the House of Lords, and the Académie Française.

Of the three, the Academy is also the hardest to define. Apart from tinkering interminably with a dictionary to keep the French language pure, it serves no visible purpose. Yet it seems to fulfill a French need for grandeur. Its coveted, theatrical uniform has long symbolized the crowning achievement of a distinguished career for the country's writers, academics, scientists, jurists and other Establishment figures. Its 40 members constitute the officially recognized *fine fleur* of French civilization, though the French themselves are hard put to say why. As Maurice Druon, the Academy's courtly Perpetual Secretary, explains, "The Academy is a complete paradox." It has a "moral authority, though no one can say exactly what we exercise it over, except vocabulary. This authority is evident, but nobody quite knows its source." No wonder the French, ever aware of the necessity of the superfluous, hold the Academy in such high esteem.

Members of the Academy have had their work cut out for them since Cardinal Richelieu granted the Academy its letters patent in 1635: "To work with all possible care and diligence to give strict rules to our language and to make it pure, eloquent, and capable of dealing with the arts and sciences." The canny cardinal, chief minister to Louis XIII, had his own reasons for offering the state's protection to the small group of Parisian writers who met informally for good conversation. Literature should be under government supervision like everything else in the strongly centralized French state: within an official academy the talk was less likely to get too political, or subversive. He stipulated that the new institution should compose a dictionary, along with works on grammar, rhetoric and poetics.

After the group spent a few years of precarious existence without any fixed meeting place, Louis XIV set it up in the former Louvre apartment of the queen mother and donated 660 volumes from his personal library, along with 40 goose quills to be sharpened into pens.

Came the revolution, and public opinion swung against the Academy for having been too close to the monarchy. Under the Terror, the Convention abolished the Academy in August 1793, calling it infected with "the incurable gangrene of aristocracy." Three members were guillotined, two committed suicide, three died in prison. But

Napoléon, who knew that men are led by the prospect of honors, revived the Academy. He gave it Cardinal Mazarin's former palace and urged it to get on with the job of sprucing up the language.

Napoléon and subsequent French leaders recognized that in a land where words often seem as important as deeds, language is a national treasure to be cherished and defended, especially against the onslaughts of English. As President Francois Mitterrand said in a speech to the Academy, "France today is threatened by English…Can a country that can build the Ariane rocket afford to lose its language?"

Clearly *non*, although French suffered a stunning setback when the journals of the Pasteur Institute, prestigious temple of French scientific research, were given English names such as *Research in Microbiology*. The French press roundly denounced Anglo-Saxon imperialism, calling English "a poor man's Esperanto" and muttering darkly about "this monstrous and unworthy event, lowering our national prestige."

Such linguistic paranoia obscures that something serious is indeed at stake. "France is, above all, the French language," said historian Fernand Braudel. Yet the people charged with protecting it, the venerable members of the Academy, have always been the most lampooned of France's *monstres sacrés*. Writer Alphonse Daudet, who never made the club, satirized them as "decrepit, broken…with leaden feet, weak legs, eyes blinking like night animals." One writer, who did get elected in the early 19th century, observed dryly, "If fame, genius or creativity were required to enter here, the seats would often be vacant." But Gustave Flaubert, another in the long list of greats who were never elected, noted with wry accuracy the true attitude of most Frenchmen: "Always denigrate it, but try to be a member."

Try they do, and once infected with the desire, some aspirants will do practically anything to get elected. Voltaire, for instance, who was in bad with the king and the church, wanted in so much that he wrote verses cravenly praising Louis XV and even denied that he had ever written the freethinking *Lettres Philosophiques*. He was elected on his third try, in 1747, with a boost from Madame de Pompadour. Victor

Hugo began campaigning for election in 1834, when he was 32, shamelessly buttering up the members. He was turned down four times before making it in 1841.

But few are chosen. Among the classics, René Descartes was not elected because he went to live in Sweden. Blaise Pascal was "only" a mathematician. Molière refused to give up the ungentlemanly profession of the theater. In the 19th century, Emile Zola was an unsuccessful candidate 24 times; the timorous members disliked his literary realism and his courage in the Dreyfus Affair. Balzac was refused, probably as much because he had financial troubles as for his rough literary treatment of the bourgeoisie, as was Alexandre Dumas *père*. Such poets as Baudelaire, Verlaine and Gérard de Nerval were too bohemian.

Who wants to be a member today? "Only about 60 million Frenchmen," says Jean Dutourd, the puckish, 69-year-old popular author of *The Taxis of the Marne* and *The Horrors of Love*, among his nearly 50 books, who has been a member since 1978. "Except for a stubborn handful, I don't know anyone who is not, secretly or otherwise, a candidate: women, children, oldsters, ecclesiastics, farmers, secretaries of Communist Party cells, street cleaners, everybody. It's the triumph of snobbery, and snobbery is one of the most powerful motivations in the human soul. Especially in France, the land of vanity."

But are Academicians really superior to common mortals? As Ludovic Halévy, a minor 19th-century novelist, once said after becoming a member, "Some Academicians are talented, others aren't. The latter are especially worthy of respect because they made it without talent."

Jean Dutourd has his own view. "I once tallied up how many really superior men had been members out of the 650 or so since its founding," he told me. "I was amazed to come up with 68. Better than 10 percent! No other group in the world has ever had as high a percentage of geniuses, and none ever will."

Academicians are now producing with all deliberate speed the ninth edition of their dictionary of purest French. Having begun work on it in 1935, they have reached the letter "I," which is about par, since each edition has taken decades to produce. The first edition was presented to Louis XIV on August 24, 1694, after some 60 years of scholarly labor. The current pace is even slower, but the 45,000-word oeuvre, with only about 10,000 new terms, is expected to be finished by the end of the century. For a rough comparison, the new Oxford English Dictionary, containing 616,500 words in 20 volumes, was completed in seven years.

At their 3 o'clock Thursday afternoon dictionary sessions, tradition requires that Immortals remain exquisitely courteous, addressing each other as "Monsieur" or "Madame," even if they have been friends since childhood, and using only the formally polite *vous*. Their conservative, purist approach to language was exemplified by the famous grammarian Émile Littré, a member whose reflexes remained true even when the flesh failed. When Madame Littré discovered him in a compromising position one afternoon with the household's *bonne*, she drew back and said, "I am surprised." Ever the man of letters, Littré, buttoning his clothing, replied, "No, Madame, you are astonished. I am the one who is surprised."

"You must remember that in France, an individual is judged and classed by the care with which he expresses himself," says the ethnologist Claude Lévi-Strauss, an Academician since 1973. "The dictionary is only the visible part of the Academy's function. But it has a symbolic role. As an honorary confraternity, it attests to the attachment the French nation has for its language. You rarely see that in other countries. Take the United States. Americans readily abuse their language by adopting terms like 'thru traffic.' I don't think Americans respect their language. For them it's just an instrument that they adapt to their needs, and use with total liberty."

"Is that bad?" I asked.

"Not necessarily. That's what gives savor to American English. There are new words all the time, an incredible creation of new words and expressions. But it's a completely different attitude from ours."

"Still," I pointed out, "the French seem in love with English words, even to the point of inventing them."

"True, the French are always inventing English words, like *tennis-man* for 'tennis player' and *footing* for 'jogging.' That's one of the main things we try to prevent when we reject new words. But," he sighed, "language always evolves too fast."

Statistics show that an Academician lasts about 20 years, and the Academy averages about two deaths per year. After a suitable period of mourning, members get down to their other main occupation, election of a replacement. This they enjoy hugely. As Paul Claudel once absent-mindedly remarked: "Elections are such fun. Why don't we have them more often?"

The main requirement to be a candidate is a certain *je ne sais quoi*, the only others being French nationality and the ability to write a letter declaring candidacy. No diplomas or degrees are necessary, nor is there any age limit. A 17th-century marquis was elected at 16 with some royal help; Cyrano de Bergerac's creator, Edmond Rostand, the youngest in the 20th century, at 33; and the oldest, historian Fernand Braudel, at 82.

If there is nothing dishonorable about being a member of the Academy, as the French say ironically, it can be humiliating to be a candidate. You have to write to each member requesting permission to visit him. Many who would be shoo-ins, like the late André Malraux, decide not to try at all because they find the very idea of the visits humiliating. Claude Lévy-Strauss didn't like the visits because he was so edgy that he was always a half-hour early and had to wait in the street. "But I understand why they're necessary," he says. "The Academy is like a club; members want to know if you're an *homme de bonne compagnie*."

Several times in recent years, the *homme* has been a *femme*. The late Marguerite Yourcenar, author of *Memoirs of Hadrian*, was elected in 1980 after President Valéry Giscard d'Estaing let it be known that the Academy ought to open its doors to women. The second woman, Jacqueline de Romilly, was a self-effacing specialist in classical Greek literature.

The election won, the new member pays a courtesy call on the president at the Élysée Palace. The next, eagerly anticipated, task is to order the Academy uniform and ceremonial épée. The elaborate uniform, designed at Napoléon's command, takes up to six months to make and costs about $16,000, but that includes a cocked hat. (An épée can be had for as little as $13,000, usually paid by the new member's friends.) Virtually the only makers today are Lanvin and Cardin, and a bespoke tailor by the name of Henri Nitlich, who crafts each suit out of—oh irony!—strong and supple *English* cloth.

"I do three fittings, and then take the whole thing apart and lay it flat to be embroidered with the olive leaves," Nitlich says. "You should see their eyes light up the first time they put the suit on with the embroidery on it. They suddenly realize that they're really members of the Academy. Their faces change completely."

The épée is a nuisance that gets in the way, for example, when entering a car or descending stairs. But it is a work of art laden with symbols from the wearer's life and work. The most famous, that of the late writer Jean Cocteau, today is insured for $50,000. At first, he wanted his friend Pablo Picasso to design it, but the incorrigible prankster responded with a sketch for a "breakfast sword," with a hilt shaped like a coffee cup and croissant. Cocteau designed his own and had Cartier, the jewelers, make it up. The hilt was in the form of a playful Cocteauian profile and poet's lyre, with a symbolic theater curtain draped around the handle. On the lyre is an impressive emerald contributed by his friend Coco Chanel, the fashion designer.

A guarantor of tradition, the Academy will probably continue to insure a subtle continuity as virtually the only French institution to survive the monarchy, the revolution, the empire, humiliating military defeats and five constitutions. Its resilience stems from its symbolic, indefinable nature. As poet Paul Valéry summed up the Academy, "We are what we believe we are, and what others believe we are, and neither we nor anyone else can say exactly what that is." In other words, if it didn't exist, the French would have to invent it. And, in fact, they did.

Update: *Recent Immortals include the former president, Valéry Giscard d'Estaing, who in March 2004 was elected to be the 706th member since the Academy's founding, and, in the same year, Alain Robbe-Grillet, a leader of the Nouveau Roman school of fiction. The latest version of its dictionary, the first since the 1930s, was published in December 2000. New words in it include* les hamburgers, le jogging, les jobs, le jackpot *and* groggy, *along with* le ketchup, le flash-back, le knock-out, *and* les girls, *as in showgirls. In another concession to modernity, the dictionary is on view at the Academy's Web site, www.academie-francaise.fr.*

André Malraux Considers the State of the World

Context: *André Malraux, novelist ("La Condition Humaine," "Les Voix du Silence") art historian, and literary adventurer par excellence, helped foment revolution in Viet Nam and China in the 1920s and later flew combat missions on the Republican side during the Spanish civil war. During the liberation of France in 1944 he met Charles de Gaulle and became an ardent supporter. After de Gaulle was elected president in 1958, he made Malraux France's first minister of cultural affairs, a position he invented and held for10 years. His charisma was undiminished by nervous facial tics and a rambling prose style that many often found incoherent.*

I found Malraux in the best form I could remember in a long time. Seated behind a vast Empire-style desk among the gilded boiseries of his office in the colonnaded Palais Royal in central Paris, the minister of cultural affairs spoke rapidly, lucidly, and to the point. His face was relatively free of the tics that often disfigure it. I was interviewing him on the occasion of the publication of the American edition of his new autobiography, whimsically entitled *Antimemoires*.

First off, he explained simply why he had dedicated this edition of the book to Jacqueline Kennedy Onassis. It was, he said, "In recognition of the way she welcomed me at the White House when I went to the United States to accompany the Mona Lisa." Asked whether the American public was likely to understand his book, which many have found typically enigmatic, he was optimistic. "I have always found the most receptive audiences in the U.S. for my books," he said. "In some countries I have found great hostility, as in England." The U.S. seemed to share this empathy with Japan, where his books were also usually "immediately understood." Relations were difficult between the U.S. and France, he admitted, but "politics is one thing, and literature is another." For his part, he had only been in America when relations were good, i.e., under the Kennedy administration.

He was already working on the next volume of his memoirs, which would have the same *esprit* but with a different *matière*. And what was the *esprit* of the *Antimemoires*, I wondered. His answer was a typically vast panorama of the state of the world.

"Right now," he said, "we are in the midst of the most extraordinary transformation of civilization that the world has ever known. Never before has civilization so changed the world in a single generation. Even the fall of Rome took a hundred or so years. Saint Augustine was very impressed by it, but it did not happen during his lifetime. With us, it is happing during a single life span. The new civilization is agnostic. Of course, there are still many believers, but the new civilization is nonetheless agnostic. Therefore the questions posed by suffering and death are posed in a very special way in our new civilization. That is the subject of my *Antimemoires*: what is the situation of an intellectual who asks himself spiritual questions in the face of an immense civilization which does not ask them of itself?"

The first volume, just published, will have been the "Asian" tome, which, despite passages concerning France, is most marked by his conversations with and reflections on Mao and Nehru. The second will be concerned with Africa and America. The parts he plans to write about America "will certainly not be published during my lifetime, because the conversations I had with President John Kennedy were confidential. I think that will be published 50 years after my death."

Malraux has no other literary ambitions at the moment. "Right now, the *Antimemoires* play the role that memoirs played in the life of Chateaubriand, though I do not compare myself to him. It is the role of an intoxicant. Personal journals and memoirs 'eat' a writer's energies for fiction. A very peculiar mental activity is set in motion, and one can write nothing else."

On other questions, Malraux sniffed at France's "May Revolution" of 1968. "When you have seen several real revolutions, as I have, you know that it does not consist only in demonstrating and promenading in the street."

On the other hand, the springtime revolt by French students represented a serious questioning of modern civilization. "Don't forget that all great civilizations have been put in question at one time or another, and that is not particularly surprising. But the questioning we are witnessing is very peculiar in that youth does not understand very well what it is questioning." The youngsters say they are revolting against the consumer society, but in reality, thinks Malraux, "It is something infinitely more profound. Proof of that is there is the same revolt behind the Iron Curtain and in China. It is something spiritual." The kids are prey to a deep malaise, he thought, noting the "quasi surrealistic" posters they plastered all over the city.

Another phenomenon of this century that Malraux found interesting is the renascence of nationalism. He noted this in connection with the Russian invasion of Czechoslovakia. "What is opposing the Soviet Union at the moment there is the nation. My feeling is that Russia is faced with a very serious problem, because if Czechoslovakia finds herself as a nation, all the Soviet satellites are going to do so too. This problem is becoming the most enigmatic and important of the 20th century." This, despite authorities as various as Marx and Victor Hugo predicting that the 19th century would be the century of nationalism, and the 20th century an international one.

Malraux declined to discuss problems in America, but did make the intriguing point that while one of the greatest Negro [this is the word he used; it was the late 1960s] contributions to modern culture is music, the greatest African music is not tom-toms or reed flutes, but Afro-American jazz.

He took the opportunity of our conversation to deny the statement often attributed to him during his talks with Kennedy. It was reported that he had asked, "How do you manage to govern without controlling television?" This, of course, reflected the state control of French radio and television at the time. (Kennedy was said to have replied, "All we ask is equal time.") Malraux snorted at this, calling it "absolutely ridiculous." Television is a useful tool of government, he said, only in a completely totalitarian state.

When I asked him what Charles de Gaulle meant to him, he replied concisely, "First, he is the man who remade France when it was no more. Second, he is an intellectual, which is very important to me. Third, and this is absolutely capital, he is the man who carried out French decolonization."

And on the subject of Mao Tse Tung, for whom Malraux has great evident respect and admiration as a revolutionary, he had this phrase, which would please makers of Chinese puzzles: "Mao is General de Gaulle if De Gaulle had been Clemenceau."

Asked to comment on rumors that he was planning to marry his companion, the French novelist Louise de Vilmorin, Malraux dismissed them with a wave of his hand: "Journalists' stuff."

Update: *Malraux did not after all marry Vilmorin, who died some time after this interview, leaving him to live and work alone in the Paris suburb of Verrières-le-Buisson. He died in November 1976. Twenty years later, in 1996, the French cultural establishment officially anointed him and his body was transferred to the Panthéon in Paris. No other volumes of his autobiography have been published to date.*

Solving the Mystery of Saint-Exupéry

Context: *His literary stature and the mystery surrounding his disappearance have made Antoine de Saint-Exupéry one of France's best-known culture heroes. His* The Little Prince *has been translated into 118 languages and dialects. But since the July day in 1944 when he disappeared along with the P-38 Lightning he was flying on a mission for the Free French, the mystery of what happened to him went unsolved. Had he been shot down by Luftwaffe fighters or ground fire? Experienced mechanical failure and bailed out? Committed suicide by flying into a mountainside (he was known to be feeling depressed)? Despite searches over the years, there was no convincing theory, much less evidence, of why he had not returned to his base in Corsica. Then, against all odds, a key—and immediately controversial—clue was dredged up from the bottom of the Mediterranean.*

It was one of those late-summer squalls that can blow up along France's Mediterranean coast, and Jean-Claude Antoine Bianco, skipper of the 60-foot, blue-and-white *Horizon* trawler out of Marseille, was soaked to the skin. "We'd been fishing since morning about an hour east of the port and the weather had turned awful," he recalls in a Provençal accent thick as the local *bouillabaisse* fish soup. "The wind and waves were tossing us around, the sky was black, and it was raining buckets. I didn't even have my slicker on. So I decided to haul in the trawl net and head home about 2 p.m."

Bianco, a stocky, balding 54-year-old, was in his cabin drying off when Habib Benamor, his Tunisian second mate, came in and announced he had found a bracelet among the usual mullet, anglerfish and squid. "I put my glasses on and scratched off some of the concretion that had built up around it," he remembers. "I saw the name Antoine. 'Hey,' I said to myself, 'This guy has the same name as me.' I scratched some more and saw Antoine de Saint-Exupéry. I thought, 'Am I dreaming or what?'" Bianco yelled excitedly to Habib, "This belonged to Saint-Ex!" But his mate just stared back; he'd never heard of anybody called Saint-Exupéry.

That made Habib a rare bird indeed. Few have not heard of the writer-aviator whose mix of Gallic derring-do and literary stature has made him virtually a demigod in France. His books *Southern Mail, Night Flight,* and *Wind, Sand and Stars* chronicled in fiction aviation's heroic era when cockpits were open and pilots delivered the mail come what may. His *Flight to Arras* was one of the first accounts of what it was like to be a combat pilot in WWII, while his *Wisdom of the Sands* laid out his chivalrous philosophy of duty and dedication to a goal higher than oneself.

His beloved *Little Prince*, about a wistful, wise young man from another planet who wonders at the strange ways of earthlings, is a world-wide best-seller translated into 118 languages and dialects, from Azerbaijani to Esperanto, Gaelic and Punjabi. The 100th anniversary of Saint-Ex's birth last year was greeted with new biographies, the renaming of the Lyon airport in his honor, a French postage stamp, a new American edition of *The Little Prince,* which still sells some 200,000 copies a year in the U.S., and an exhibit in Paris's hallowed Pantheon crypt aptly called Celebration of a Myth.

The myth's beginning can be pinpointed to July 31, 1944. Saint-Ex had shortly before rejoined his old squadron, the 2/33, a Free French outfit which was part of the American 3rd Photo Group, Mediterranean Allied Photo Reconnaissance Wing (MAPRW), under the command of Colonel Elliott Roosevelt, President Roosevelt's son. At 44 he was nine years over the age limit to fly the squadron's P-38 Lightnings—the photoreconnaissance version was the F-5B—which were then one of the fastest fighters in the sky. But Saint-Ex made deals, pulled strings, and got the slot.

Being of the old school, he didn't much like the plane, calling it "a flying torpedo that has nothing whatever to do with flying and, with all its dials and buttons, makes its pilot a sort of chief accountant." He was wrung out by missions at 30,000 feet in the Lightning's unpressurized cockpit. But he loved flying with his American comrades, whose "simple and noble courage, a sort of 'kind courage'" he admired.

On July 31 the 2/33 ops officer, Lt. Raymond Duriez, drove Saint-Ex to the field at the Borgo air base near Bastia, on the island of Corsica, helped him into his flight suit, and shoehorned his bulky form into the tight cockpit. Ground crew pulled the chocks and Sortie 33S176 took off at 8:45 a.m. for a mapping run over the Grenoble-Chambery region east of Lyon. Allied radar at Cap Corse followed him into southern France. He was due back at 12:30. He was never heard from again. A myth, and a mystery, were born.

Over the years, the search for traces of Saint-Ex, mostly desultory and unorganized, has ranged from the Alps to the Rhone Valley, the French coast around Nice-Monaco, and even Italy. One of the most determined hunts came in 1992, when a French champagne company launched a costly two-year, publicity-grabbing expedition. It engaged IFREMER, the French ocean research unit that helped find the *Titanic*, but came up empty-handed.

Amateur divers fared better. In November 1996, Marcel Camilleri, owner of a diving school on the coast, and friend Alain Costanzo found a P-38 wreck lying on its back in 40 meters (130 feet) of water in La Ciotat Bay between Marseille and Toulon. Hoping that it was Saint-Ex's Lightning, they cleaned sand off it, tamed a toothy, seven-foot conger eel domiciled in the cockpit, and started trying to identify it.

Enter Jack Curtis. A friend of Camilleri's went online and found Curtis, a former World War II P-38 pilot who flew 67 missions with 9th Air Force giving close support for Patton's 3rd Army. Now 80 and living in Rogers, Arkansas, Curtis checked his e-mail one morning and saw a message from France: "Hello! I'm scuba diver. I have found in Medditerrannée in France a P38 Lightning. I want know how to find the serial number and model."

Curtis advised looking for a small embossed plate on the instrument panel, between the artificial horizon and the gyrocompass. When the number came back, he checked his personal copies of the Air Force's

Missing Air Crew Reports, called Air Force Archives at Maxwell Air Force Base, and came up with the answer: the plane was downed on January 27, 1944. It was flown by Lt. Harry Greenup of 14th Fighter Group, 15th Air Force.

Close, but no cigar for the Saint-Ex hunters.

They're not easily discouraged. Philippe Castellano, a 42-year-old hospital technician from Cannes, is probably one of the best-informed individuals in the world on World War II air combat over the South of France. He has spent 15 years on a comprehensive list of all the 38 U.S. Army Air Force planes downed in the region, visiting U.S. Air Force records centers at both Wright-Patterson Air Force Base in Dayton, Ohio, and Maxwell. He's the proud owner of what he calls "The Bible" he got from Maxwell: the official, 1,500-page record of every American plane lost, everywhere in the world, day by day, during the war.

"I started looking for Saint-Ex in 1994," he says. "A fisherman told me about a wreck he had trawled across in La Ciotat Bay. I'd been diving around here for 20 years, but that was the first time I actually looked for a wreck. After three years, I found a P-38 in 95 feet of water, a mass of wings, booms, tailfins, wheels and cables all mixed up. For a while, I was sure I'd found Saint-Ex's plane."

He called on Pierre Becker for help in identifying it. Head of a French underwater engineering firm that works mainly for big oil companies laying undersea pipelines, Becker, 53, has been an airplane hunter for 10 years. The two found the contract number, 21222, on one of the wreck's tail-booms, meaning it was a Type J fighter, not a F-5B. Castellano wrote to Maxwell and they traced it to Lt. James Riley, who had been shot down on the same day as his wingman, Harry Greenup. Escorting a big 15th Air Force bombing raid by B-17s and B-24s of German bases in the South of France prior to the Allied landing at Anzio, they had been jumped by some 40 Messerschmitt 109s and Focke-Wulf 190s.

Then, on September 7, 1998, Bianco netted the bracelet. "That was the find we've waited 50 years for," Becker says. "First, it proved that Saint-Ex crashed in the Mediterranean, not in the Alps or anywhere else. Second, it showed us that the crash site was farther west, toward Marseille, than anybody had thought. As for its authenticity, I know what objects look like after spending a long time in seawater. There's no doubt about it."

Henri-Georges Delauze agrees. As the biggest name in French underwater engineering for decades, he was the man Bianco took the bracelet to after finding it. "I know a thing or two about marine archaeology," he says. "I've brought up enough silver pieces of eight from sunken sailing ships to know how salt water corrodes silver. That bracelet is authentic."

Financing the operation with his own money, Delauze immediately launched a three-week, $200,000 secret search of the area with his sophisticated research ship, *Minibex*, with side-scanning sonar, a mini-sub, and a remote-controlled robot explorer. "Bianco showed me where he had trawled," he says. "My idea was to find the wreckage quickly, then announce that we had found both the bracelet and the plane. I told Jean-Claude, 'Then we'll go and have some champagne with President Chirac.' But all I found was a German Junker 88 bomber whose sonar image was so good I was sure it had to be the P-38. Then I had to stop because Big Brother butted in."

Word of Bianco's find had leaked out. French authorities, acting under a law covering archaeological sites of historical interest, ordered Delauze to cease his search and told Bianco to turn over the bracelet. (This being France, there are *lots* of authorities involved. Locally there are the Maritime Affairs Office and the Department of Subaquatic and Underwater ((*sic*)) Archaeological Research, in Toulon there is the Maritime Prefecture. But the final authorities are the ministries of culture and defense in Paris.)

Saint-Ex having been an air force officer, the controversial bracelet went to the French Air Force, which tossed the hot potato to the

Musée de l'Air et de l'Espace at Le Bourget airport. The museum, in turn, tossed it to France's national research and restoration service, which normally authenticates and restores art for the country's museums. It did a quick exam under an optical microscope and, with the descendents of Saint-Ex clamoring for possession, diplomatically declared it couldn't say one way or the other.

The descendents, represented by a great-nephew of Saint-Ex, Frédéric de Giraud d'Agay, got the bracelet and had it analyzed two more times. They have kept the results secret. "This whole affair of the bracelet has been surrounded by mystery, and we would like to clear it up," says Giraud d'Agay. "Saint-Exupéry was not known to have one [a bracelet like the one found], so we wonder what's going on." (In *Saint-Exupéry: A Biography*, author Stacy Schiff reports that the aviator did own a gold one.)

Some who have seen it believe the bracelet might well have belonged not to Saint-Ex himself, but to his wife, Consuelo. That would account for her name being engraved on it in parentheses. They also say it was too small to fit the wrist of a hefty man like Antoine. Still, the distinction may prove a minor one. "I think Saint-Ex might have carried [Consuelo's bracelet] with him as a sort of keepsake, in a bag or pocket or even hanging on his instrument panel," says Castellano.

Divers now knew where to look. One was Luc Vanrell, the 41-year-old owner of a diving equipment shop in Marseille. Son of one of France's diving pioneers in the 1940s, he had for years searched for a plane wreck his father had mentioned. Vanrell started mixing with aviation buffs like Castellano, and found the invaluable Jack Curtis on the Internet. By last May he had located the left landing gear, part of a tail-boom with its peculiar oval air intake for that model's turbo supercharger, and a Lightning wheel. He examined the gear sufficiently to see that it had the telltale rectangular fulcrum attached to a side strut.

Then he sent Castellano an e-mail asking innocently whether any modifications had been made to P-38 landing gears. "I knew then that he'd found it," says Castellano with a grin. "I told him straight, 'If you've found a P-38 landing gear with a rectangular fulcrum, it can only be Saint-Ex's plane, because all the other F-5Bs have been accounted for.'"

Vanrell officially declared his find to the Maritime Affairs office in Marseille on May 12, which duly forwarded the report to the local Department of Subaquatic and Underwater Research, a branch of the Ministry of Culture. At first, French authorities were ready to excavate the wreckage, hiring Vanrell, Delauze and others for ten days of cartography, photos, videos, and raising parts for examination. "We were ready to go," recounts Delauze, "but suddenly the culture ministry said they'd had a call from the prime minister's office: don't touch it." Admits one official at Underwater Research, "I can't tell you what the government's position is on this because it hasn't declared one yet, and I think it'll be quite a while before it does. It's all very Latin."

Besides bureaucratic inertia, another factor is the opposition of Saint-Ex's descendents, who apparently have the ear of the authorities. "That plane is a sepulcher that must be respected," says Frédéric de Giraud d'Agay. "It's such a beautiful myth, disappearing over the ocean the way the Little Prince disappeared from the earth. Those divers are just trying to make money from selling photos." He and the family hold rights to royalties from Saint-Ex's books, and also sell Little Prince products ranging from pens and watches to stuffed animals and cosmetics.

The situation is blocked for the moment. "Unless there's a surprising, high-level political decision, I don't believe this excavation is going to happen," says Philippe Grenier de Monner, assistant director for archaeology at the ministry of culture. "The defense ministry is against it, partly because the descendents of Saint-Exupéry are. For us at the culture ministry this is not a scientific priority, and it would be very expensive. And if we did excavate it, that could lead to requests by families who lost members during the war for us to do costly excavation of other wrecks. We don't want to encourage that."

At stake is whether the myth of Saint-Ex—and small-minded bureaucratic blockage—is stronger than the right to know the historical truth of what happened to him. Such a simple question for most countries has produced a very complex French *affaire* with unpredictable developments probably ahead. As Philippe Castellano says, "This has now gone too far for anybody to stop it."

Update: *In the summer of 2003, exactly five years after Jean-Claude Antoine Bianco found the I.D. bracelet, French authorities finally gave permission to excavate what remained of the P-38. As Philippe Castellano tells it, "On September 27, about 3 p.m., we found the numbers 2734 on one of the pieces. That was the Lockheed serial number. By putting it together with the Army Air Force serial number, we were able to confirm beyond doubt that this was Saint-Ex's Lightning F-5B." The affaire over the bracelet, however, continued, with Bianco suing the heirs, who refused to confirm that it was authentic, to have them release it back to him.*

Quel est Votre Signe?

Context: *The French passion for astrology comes as a surprise to many foreign observers, this one included, but it goes back a long way. The great cathedrals of the late Middle Ages often have astrological symbols sculpted into their columns and porticos, and featured in their stained glass windows. Michel de Nostre Dame, known as Nostradamus, famous in the 16th century as now for his book of predictions, was a regular at the court of Marie de Médicis, where he served as royal physician to King Charles IX. French astrologers are still doing very well.*

The French claim to have coined the term "intellectual" as applied to a social class. Certainly *les intellectuels* have traditionally cut a wide swath here, from René *("cogito ergo sum")* Descartes to Jean-Paul ("hell is other people") Sartre. It is the land of the 18th-century Enlightenment, the first encyclopedia, and schools that force-feed the young with certified High Learning.

How is it, then, that the French are so crazy about the benighted pseudo-science of astrology? January is the season when astromania becomes pandemic in France, as otherwise solid bourgeois folk snatch up horoscopes at news kiosks and make appointments with astrologers to find out how their health, money and love lives will fare in the New Year. How much they believe of the Delphic predictions is imponderable, but the fact is that they are willing to pay hard cash for them.

A consultation with an astrologer with an exotic name like Lutezya, Chandrane or Madame Soleil can cost upwards of $50. They and some 30,000 other French astrologers will have no less than 6 billion paid sessions this year, prompting one consumers' organization to suggest that astrology is a big enough business to be considered a consumer good and regulated accordingly.

Besides practicing astrologers, the business includes horoscopes in all the mass-circulation newspapers and magazines. One paper known for its particularly convincing horoscopes boosts its print run by 20 percent in January, and a slick new astrology magazine called *You and Your Future* is a rising star, as it were, of French publishing. Radio stations vie for the astrology audience. The well-known Madame Soleil outlines the implications of the zodiac every morning on one station; another counters with a call-in horoscope program that receives over 12,000 calls daily.

Thus it is that American visitors expecting rarified political and artistic discussions at Paris dinner parties are often nonplused when a French table companion turns and asks, *"Quel est votre signe?"* He who does not know his sign of the zodiac and its ascendant is an instant wallflower.

The French are convinced that it all goes back to Nostradamus, who came from Aix-en-Provence. The most famous seer of the Renaissance, he made prophecies that fell on fertile ground in France, where astrology was at a peak. Queen Catherine de Médicis invited him to the court of Henry II as official astrologer. To this day many Frenchmen believe he foretold historical events, such as the martial reign of Napoléon, and they continue to scrutinize his cryptic writings for clues to the future.

But Colbert, the energetic chief minister of Louis XIV, banned astrology from the Sorbonne in 1666. Luminaries like La Fontaine, Voltaire and Diderot fulminated against "charlatans who make horoscopes." Astrology went into eclipse in France, only to shine again in the 20th century, legally tolerated, along with other concessions to human foibles, like prostitution.

Today much of French astrology is computerized. Something called Astroflash on the Champs Élysées squirts out 500 computerized horoscopes a day at $15 each. But many French still prefer a long, confidential chat with the likes of Madame Soleil, who boasts a clientele ranging from veteran Communist Party members to priests, along with a sampling of politicians and cabinet members. Indeed, the political traffic in her salon gets so heavy that she has to reserve certain days for right-wingers and others for the left to avoid conflict.

Which might help explain how France got into the politico-economic mess it's in today. Be that as it may, astrology is also taken seriously by the personnel directors of a number of big French companies. Some have fired their resident psychologists and hired astrologists, insisting that a study of the stars is as valid as looking at Rorschach ink spots to see if a new executive will fit in with the management team.

That attitude is consistent with the French rejection of most of 20th-century psychiatric theory, starting with Freudianism. While a minuscule minority has gone in for psychoanalysis, most Frenchmen have had other ideas of what a couch is for. And if they want to pay to talk about their unhappiness, they prefer to base the conversation on the heavens rather than on toilet training. Such tenacious wrong-headedness is enough to give one pause, but only briefly. Surely, 50 million Frenchmen can't be *right*.

Update: *The advent of computers and the Internet have vastly broadened the range and variety of horoscopes now consulted by the French. Many have a personalized horoscope delivered by e-mail every morning, to read along with their café au lait and croissant. Recent studies show that astrological sites are the most visited Web sites in the country. The latest twist for French believers: Chinese astrology.*

Intellectuals in Crisis

Context: *The French esprit is literally embodied in its intellectual class. More than any other nation, France certifies, recognizes, and adulates its thinkers, placing the likes of mere businessmen and physicians comparatively below the salt. Graduates of the Grandes Écoles such as Polytechnique and the École Normale are ipso facto intellectuals, while informal intellectual status is conferred on just about anyone who can pick up a pen—even journalists—or wield a polysyllabic vocabulary. Twentieth-century French intellectuals were long in thrall to Marxism, a situation that started to change when the truth began to emerge about the world's premier Marxist state, the Soviet Union.*

A specter is haunting today's French intellectuals, the specter of Red Fascism.

Perhaps more than any other nation, France is influenced by that class of thinkers, writers, and endless café conversationalists known collectively as *les intellectuels*. Sometimes the term is uttered with derision, when they get too far out of touch. But in this book-reading land, they set the tone of public discourse.

For the last 50 years that tone has been almost uniformly Marxist.

The Communist prophet's words fell on fertile ground in a country with rigid class lines, a self-conscious industrial proletariat and a frankly money grubbing bourgeoisie. During the war, the Communist Party took the moral high ground by working hard in the Resistance, though most people overlooked that it did so only after Hitler broke his pact with Stalin and invaded Russia.

In the postwar era, the French intellectuals' moral/philosophical position was embodied by Jean-Paul Sartre, who was a provocative thinker, a good writer and a lousy political theorist.

All self-respecting intellectuals had to be on the left, he decreed. "Don't make them despair in Billancourt" was his slogan, referring to a communist-dominated working-class Paris suburb he presumed to be hanging on his every polysyllabic word.

What appealed especially to French intellectuals was that Marxism developed into an all-encompassing general theory. As such it could be used to replace the worldview of Catholicism, for centuries identified in France with the monarchy and the moneyed class.

By the 1970s, French thinkers had elaborated theories not only of Marxist economics, but also of Marxist sociology, Marxist urbanism, Marxist psychiatry and Marxist aesthetics. Marxism had become the opium of the intellectuals. As long as they could puff on it, they didn't need to think.

Then came Alexander Solzhenitsyn and *The Gulag Archipelago.*

"He is the Shakespeare of our time," writes Bernard-Henri Levy, one of the few prominent French philosophers to dare question Marxism openly. "He is the one who forced us to see the horror and the evil. Our Dante too, for he shows us the hell of the Gulag." Stalinism, Levy concluded unfashionably, was not an aberration of Marxism, but its essence.

But fashions die hard, and Marxism is still the orthodox mode of thought in France. Thus the surprise and scandal, when those who have soldiered on the left for decades start breaking ranks.

One such is Jean-Marie Domenach, a writer who was in the wartime Resistance and who generally followed the leftist line for 30 years. Now he is pointing out that the French Socialist government insists on bending facts to fit ideology, on continuing to fight "the lost battles of the 19th century," of refusing to see that social classes have evolved since then.

The shocker came when Domenach said in a recent book, "In the past, we defended freedom with the Stalinists. Tomorrow I will, if necessary, defend it against the Stalinists with the extreme right."

Another former leftist trying to wean French thinkers from their Marxist opiate is Yves Montand, the 62-year-old actor and singer.

Though not a card-carrying intellectual, Montand has long been the popular symbol of conscientious, petition-signing socialism.

Appearing on a TV talk show, Montand said flatly that the danger today was not capitalism but Red Fascism. "We've got to defend democracy," he said. "It's all we've got, guys."

The show was flooded with callers saying *merci* for speaking the truth as he—and they—saw it. "He is saying out loud what we have all been thinking," wrote a nominally leftist columnist the next day.

Slowly, tentatively, a radical new philosophy is taking shape in the Left Bank cafes. Its theme: Intellectuals of the world, unite. You have nothing to lose but your blinders.

Update: *Since the fall of the Berlin wall it gets harder every day to find any support for Marxist ideology, and certainly not in Eastern Europe, where they know it all too well. But many French intellectuals are letting go of it reluctantly if at all. A university professor in Nice recently took pains to assail the Harry Potter book/movie series as a nefarious portrait of the capitalist universe, "a caricature of the excesses of the Anglo-Saxon social model." Harry Potter as capitalist tool? Now who but a French* intellectuel *would have thought of that? In any case, France's professional thinkers have fallen on hard times: 40,000 of them recently signed a petition accusing the government of waging "war on intellectuals" by cutting research budgets. A French newspaper headlined, incredulously, "The end of intellectuals?"*

Schools of Thought: Ferment in French Philosophy

Context: *The ferment among French intellectuals that resulted in the open revolt against Red Fascism had been bubbling beneath the surface for some time. Partly prompted by the new method of structuralism, French philosophers had begun questioning the dilemmas posed by the Marxist ethic, as well as the very foundations of Marxism as a system of thought. In terms of research and debate, the 1960s were one of the most fertile periods in the post-war history of French philosophy. To savor what follows, readers might want to look again at the quotation from Henri-Frédéric Amiel in the Prologue to this book.*

What, exactly, do French philosophers have on their finely honed minds today? To test the waters, I started with a visit to Nicos Poullantzas, an amiable young assistant professor of political science at the law faculty of the University of Paris and a leading Marxist theorizer. He writes philosophical essays for the magazine *Les Temps Modernes*, which has the distinction of being edited by Jean-Paul Sartre. His latest conclusion is quite simply that traditional moral questions are false and empty of meaning. That does not, however, mean there are no moral questions and that Marxist philosophy does not grapple with them.

"For a Marxist, moral questions are secondary," he explains. "Traditional Christian moral dilemmas are private and individual, and were typical of 19th-century liberalism when the individual was the center of the cosmos. They are always a question of intention, not really of action; something is a sin if you think it is, but the act itself is not necessarily sinful. They are defined by transcendent values and categorical imperatives that are supposed to govern in detail the individual's life. All that really ended with Hegel, when we became conscious of the primary importance of the totality rather than the individual.

"Marxists believe that what counts is whether an action conforms to the march of history and the requirements of the revolution. The results of my actions are thus good or bad insofar as they are good or bad for the revolution. But the completely individual question such as what kind of food I eat or how and with whom I choose to make love have nothing to do with that and therefore are meaningless. That is where Marxism and Existentialism join: they both believe in the importance of engagement in a collective action to give life meaning, but it doesn't matter how individuals live their private lives."

The Marxist ethic poses its own peculiar dilemmas. "Our problem is that we don't really know how we must act in order to advance the revolution. How are we to know? In Christianity the moral system is rigidly defined: the individual always knows whether he is doing right or wrong. We Marxists cannot tell whether our acts are good or bad—really whether we are criminals or not—until the revolution comes and we can see if we contributed to it. You can see what happened in Russia. Stalin was a saint and then suddenly a criminal. Right now, Marxism is undergoing a crisis because the revolution is not imminent. It seems that we will never know whether our acts are good or bad, and so moral problems even in the Marxist sense are also more or less false."

Poullantzas does not pretend to know what then shall do we do, as Lenin once asked. "In any case, it is clear there can be no absolute criteria. After the wars we have seen, after the church's self-serving attitude, after the impersonalization of the individual due to industrialism, no one can take a theory of absolutes seriously. Marxist humanism, with its concern for the well-being of all, is still our best hope of maintaining human dignity."

The two main currents in French philosophy today are Marxism and structuralism, though the two are not directly opposed as such: Marxism is a body of more or less well-defined ideas, whereas structuralism is an intellectual method. Structural analysis, which has become fashionable in the 1960s, sees all elements of a question as roughly of equal importance. Marxists see a key element, economics, that they think structuralists neglect. Structuralism is a functionalistic method concerned with being as scientific as possible and based on the belief that all societies are built on structures of thought, customs, and so on, that can be clearly defined and ultimately synthesized into a whole body of knowledge. Its followers understandably view Marxism as a loose, perhaps well-intentioned set of ideas woefully lacking in rigor.

The Marxists themselves are aware of their lack of philosophical system. Louis Althusser, whose Marxist structuralism differs from the anthropological structuralism of the anthropologist Claude Lévi-Strauss, is France's foremost Marxist precisely because the 47-year-old secretary general of the École Normale Supérieur is making the most serious effort at defining Marxism. Nicos Poullantzas calls him "the greatest Marxist thinker in France, and perhaps in the entire world Marxist movement." Althusser's book, *Pour Marx*, just out, is his third.

Pour Marx is a collection of Althusser's essays which he calls "a search for the philosophical thought of Marx, indispensable for getting out of the theoretical impasse where history has left us." In his preface he deplores what he calls "the *misère Française*: the tenacious, profound absence of a real theoretical culture in the history of the French worker movement." Citing the theorists of other European countries such as Marx, Engels, and Kautsky in Germany, Rosa Luxembourg in Poland, Plekhanov and Lenin in Russia, Labriola in Italy, he observes that "French intellectuals accepted their condition and did not feel the vital need to look for their salvation at the side of the working class.... The domination of the bourgeoisie for a long time deprived the French worker movement of intellectuals indispensable to the formation of an authentic theoretical tradition."

Not only does French Marxism not have a solid theoretical base, but after the passing of the dogmatism of the Stalin era, Marxist philosophers everywhere suddenly realized their philosophical poverty, he notes. "The end of dogmatism made us face this reality: that Marxist philosophy, founded by Marx in the very act of founding his theory of history, still largely remains to be formed." The questions to be posed are the most basic, Althusser believes: "What is Marxist philosophy? Has it theoretically the right to existence? And if it has the right to exist, how can its specificity be defined?"

One of the most original, influential, and provocative French thinkers today cannot be said to be of any particular philosophical school. Michel Foucault, the 39-year-old professor of philosophy at the University of Clermont-Ferrand is the author of the important *Madness and Civilization: A History of Insanity in the Age of Reason.* Although it sounds more like a treatise on psychology than a philosophical reflection, the work goes to the heart of defining the human by studying the relationship of civilization to madness. Its theme is that attitudes toward mental disorder change with the times, and thus with the varying notions of what it means to be human. "If Don Quixote lived today," he likes to say, "he would be in a psychiatric clinic."

Foucault traces attitudes toward madness from the end of the middle ages, when Bosch, Brueghel, Erasmus, Shakespeare and Cervantes made the voice of madness virtually a form of poetry, through the 17th century, when Europe began putting up cruel madhouses, to the present day when the mad are literally alienated. His book is a compassionate look at mental disorder and an important work, but Foucault, perhaps to his credit, is out of the present mainstream of the Marxist-structuralist debate: he rejects Marxism as a valid philosophical system.

French philosophy today is marked more by looking backward than forward, if the way it is taught is any indication. At the prestigious Collège de France, for example, the two chairs of philosophy are occupied by historians of philosophy rather than philosophers. According to François Châtelet, philosophy professor at the heavyweight lycée Louis-le-Grand, "This produces a certain discouragement of new ideas and experiments. Historians have invaded philosophy."

Châtelet, who has written four books on philosophy, points out that present-day philosophy must be viewed against the triple modern currents of Marxism, existentialism, and liberal Christianism as exemplified by Teilhard de Chardin. "Those three currents are our real intellectual institutions, and all philosophical discussions include them. When the communists hold a philosophical debate, they invariably invite existentialist and Christian spokesmen. Like many of our institutions today, they are completely rigid, impossibly out of date."

Châtelet, himself a Marxist in good standing, outlines the change in French philosophizing over the last decade this way: Philosophy students were always very politically oriented and engaged, and that usually meant communist or at least leftist. Then came the 20ᵗʰ Communist Party convention in Moscow in 1956 with the dethronement of Stalin, followed by the anti-Soviet revolt in Budapest, which upset the faithful. Also disillusioning was the failure of the French Left to react vigorously against Charles de Gaulle when he took over in 1958. It was all too much for most French philosophers who had believed in communism, and many broke with it.

When they did, they were left without an ideology. To fill its place they turned to the social sciences: psychology, ethnology, psychoanalysis, sociology. They represented a refuge for those trying to get back into contact with something concrete. At the same time, some began trying to renew Marxism, using the social sciences. They came to realize that 1) Marx was not always right, and 2) Marxism sometimes falsified Marx. Three thinkers particularly left their mark on the new sciences: Levi-Strauss in ethnology, Raymond Aron in sociology, and Jacques Lacan, whom Châtelet calls "perhaps the best theorist of psychoanalysis since Freud," in psychoanalysis.

"I think we are watching the death of traditional philosophy," Châtelet told me. "I mean systematic philosophy that lines up everything neatly and resumes all the world's problems in one book of 500 to 600 pages. There are all sorts of philosophical currents running through Paris right now, particularly German and English. Philosophy will end up taking one of three possible routes. First, it can become more positivist than ever, throw out abstract theory and turn entirely to specialized social sciences where all knowledge could be empirical.

Second, it can follow the lead of Nietzsche and Heidegger into a poetic transcendentalism. Third, it can try for a synthesis of the social sciences, attempt to shape their diverse results into a coherent new vision of man and his existence. That is what Sartre favored in his *Critique de la Raison Dialectique*.

"The first of these options seems to predominate now, and I think it will prevail. At least I hope so. There is a new realization among philosophers that the social sciences are valid even if they are not as exact as the natural sciences. They are losing their inferiority complexes about that. I believe philosophy can be renewed only through a very precise examination of these sciences. It must be done with absolute scientific rigor."

And Sartre? Is the most famous existentialist French philosopher of his age still relevant to French philosophy? "Sartre," Châtelet replied after a moment's pause, "is still important precisely because he is no longer an existentialist."

Update: *French philosophers no longer cut the wide swath of celebrity they did in those days. Few achieved the international star status of Jean-Paul Sartre, who anyway was a better writer than thinker, and whose best work was, for me, his touching autobiography,* Les Mots. *Sartre, who died in April, 1980, was awarded the Nobel Prize in 1964 and managed to cause a brief stir by childishly refusing it. The most famous French philosopher of the latter 20th century was the Algerian-born Jacques Derrida, whose deconstruction technique was so impenetrable and murky that top scholars at Cambridge University, for instance, called it absurd, vapid and pernicious. Far more popular in the United States than in France itself, where academics gave up trying to make sense of it, deconstruction was adopted for their own reasons by American activists of many stripes, from feminists to advocates of homosexual rights, and academics surfing on the latest vogue. Derrida's own explanation that deconstruction "takes place as the experience of the impossible" was not much help to the rest of us.*

The Masterful, Medieval Brotherhood of the Compagnons

Context: *Steeped in ritual and craft guild methods inherited from the Middle Ages, these painstaking artisans are an anomaly in an era of "quick 'n' easy." Their professional ancestors were the stonecutters and carpenters who built medieval France's cathedrals and tens of thousands of parish churches and other structures. Today they keep alive that flame in the French* esprit *that still values craftsmanship.*

When he reflects on it, Jean Wiart still seems astonished by a discovery he and his group made in the New World. "We suddenly realized," he says, "that there was no one in this big country that could do what we do."

What he does is things like renovating the Statue of Liberty's huge, 13-foot bronzed torch with its golden flame. Or fashioning an extra-tall steeple for Manhattan's Fifth Avenue Presbyterian Church, not to mention restoring the city's 2,900-pound *Civic Fame* statue atop the Municipal Building. It was Wiart's people who repaired the splendid, copper-domed Borough Hall in Brooklyn. Lately, they also have made decorative wrought-iron gates and stair railings by hand for some of the country's fanciest homes, among them Chez Ralph Lauren and Chez Madonna.

Wiart's team does such things so well that he has won awards from the likes of New York's Art Commission, the Classical America Society, and the National Trust for Historic Preservation. A self-effacing but supremely skilled metalworker from eastern France, he has a simple explanation for why he and his small team of craftsmen, based in Paterson, New Jersey, have succeeded so well in this country within a single decade. "Here in America it's unusual for talented young people to choose work with their hands," he says. "My people and I are experts at our craft, because we are all products of France's best apprentice program."

They are in fact Compagons (the companions), spiritual descendants of a French craft tradition many centuries old. As such they are heirs of the rigorous, fanatically demanding craftsmen who, as members of secretive medieval guilds, festooned France with its crown of cathedrals and châteaux. Along with the redoubtable French Academy, the Compagnons are one of the rare institutions of ancient France to have survived revolutions, the Terror, communes, religious persecution, Vichy secret police and, perhaps most remarkable, modern time-and-motion studies.

These lovers of *la belle ouvrage* literally worship manual work. To hear them tell it, they jump out of bed every morning rubbing their hands with relish at the prospect of another hard nut to crack. "For us it's never a chore to go to work," says Serge Mory, a young Compagnon carpenter in Paris. "The tougher and more complex the problem on the job, the more we look forward to solving it." Some call them the world's finest craftsmen.

Their professional ancestors, stonecutters and carpenters who practiced the royal art of construction, helped build some 80 cathedrals, 500 large churches and tens of thousands of parish churches from about 1050 to 1350. Later on—a certain July 14, 1789, to be exact—a band of Compagnon carpenters at the Bastille put together a sturdy wooden bridge over the moat so rioting Parisians could storm it.

With the advent of industrialization in the 19th century, traditional trades changed radically, often leaving the Compagnons caught in a kind of time warp. At first, that is. When Gustave Eiffel was ready to hurl his unprecedented thousand-foot tower at the Paris sky in 1887, he chose a 27-year-old Compagnon carpenter, Eugene Milon, as foreman. Many of Milon's colleagues considered iron beams a betrayal of tradition. But he finally found 40 good men willing to switch from wood to metal, despite the repugnant fact that the iron beams were—*quelle horreur*—prefabricated, requiring none of their proud skill at shaping them.

Since then they have adjusted. For decades now, Compagnon locksmiths have worked all kinds of metal. Boilermakers bang away at sheet metal in myriad ways. Coachbuilders do automobile bodywork. Saddle makers are happy to stitch upholstery. Compagnons leaven most of France's big projects, both renovation and innovation. They painstakingly restore the towers of Notre Dame de Paris, chisel artfully at the Arc de Triomphe and the Louvre, and refurbish the romantic winged horses atop the Paris Opera and the vertiginous statue high above Mont-Saint-Michel on the Normandy coast. Compagnons also helped bore the Channel tunnel, build the Louvre's new transparent entryway pyramid, and shape engines for the Ariane rocket, which launches satellites from faraway French Guiana.

Today the three Compagnon societies that comprise France's craft guilds train young people in nearly a hundred trades, from chocolate makers and photographers to fashioners of false teeth. What they all have in common, besides uncommon command of their trade, is an idea: manual work, the transformation of matter by man's hand, is a noble calling.

Members include the world-renowned chef Joel Robuchon, whose Paris restaurant, a three-star gastronomic summit, sports craft guild symbols even on its napkins and menus. Robuchon, also known by his guild name, "Poitevin la Fidelité," started out to take orders as a priest, then shifted from ecclesiastical to culinary pursuits and to that other monkish order, the Compagnons. "I owe them a lot," he says; "they taught me the love of work." They also taught him one of many trades that can pay handsomely if the individual is good enough and backed by a well-connected organization.

Pierre Deschamps, president of the Ateliers Sainte Catherine, France's leading maker of special-order trucks, semi-trailers and other hauling equipment, regards the Compagnon's apprenticeship as *"formidable."* "I hire all the Compagnons I can get," he says. "A dozen of our 100 employees are Compagnon coachbuilders, and we'd have 20 if we could find them." Painted in giant black letters on a big yellow I-beam above the shop floor is a text from French writer Charles Peguy that could be the Compagnons' creed: "'Working with your hands teaches you the value of the things of this earth."

The text points up the craft guilds' insistence on the dignity of manual labor and its right to equal prestige with white-collar work. The idea is hardly new. In the fifth century B.C., the Greek philosopher Anaxagoras held that "man thinks because he has a hand." But it gets overlooked in an era when for many of us, work consists of tapping little plastic buttons to make electrons whirl.

"Anybody who joins the Compagnons just to find a job is on the wrong track," says Laurent Bastard, curator of France's Guild Museum, which sits beside the Loire River in Tours. "Being a Compagnon is about brotherhood and sharing. If the Compagnons thrive today, it's not only because they teach a trade better than anyone else, but because they inculcate a moral reference point that's lacking among most young people."

Grandiose sentiments, and very French. But somehow in keeping with a group that claims such an ancient pedigree. Yet Compagnons are thriving today, even in a country that has a 12.5 percent unemployment rate, and close to 25 percent among the young. With some 30,000 Compagnons plying their trades and another 6,000 apprentices learning theirs, "not one of our Compagnons is unemployed," says Jean Champigny, a guild official in Tours. "They're snapped up by employers as fast as we can train them."

One guild, the Association Ouvrière, does an ongoing study of what becomes of their Compagnons after they complete their masterwork. Forty-five percent own their own businesses, 30 percent are shop foremen, 10 percent technicians, 6 percent architects or engineers, 6 percent teachers, 3 percent miscellaneous. Zero percent on the dole.

Their success is all the more remarkable because it depends on training steeped in ritual and organization, basic craft guild methods inherited from the Middle Ages: one-on-one oral transmission of trade secrets from master to apprentice; years spent working under different masters at guild houses in a succession of cities in the four corners of France (known in the trade as the "Tour de France"); and finally the creation of a masterwork, followed (if it is approved) by formal initiation with a secret ritual.

The would-be Compagnon can apply as young as 15. Ordinarily, if he passes a test of general knowledge and manual skill—only about half do—he has to spend a week in a guild house, observing and being observed. "The first thing we look for in a youngster is whether he's motivated, modest, accepts criticism well, and is patient and persistent," says Michel Lamarque, the provost at the Federation headquarters in Paris. "If he has the right character, only then do we follow up to see if he's a good worker."

The guilds place new apprentices with cooperative local firms who teach them the rudiments of their trade while paying $600 a month, about half the French minimum wage. Usually after two years, if they're doing well, they set out on the sine qua non of the Compagnon experience: a six-to-eight-year Tour de France.

In a romantic novel about the Compagnons, the 19th-century writer George Sand describes the tour as "a poetic phase, an adventuresome pilgrimage, the artisan's period of errant knighthood." A typical tour starts in Paris, variously follows the valley of the Seine, Saone and Rhone rivers south to the Mediterranean, then up the Atlantic coast to Nantes, then straight east through the Loire Valley. (The guilds now also have houses in Germany, Switzerland, Belgium, the Netherlands and Canada.) Lodging in one of the 147 *maisons* throughout the country at a cost of about $500 a month for room and board, aspirants normally spend six months in each town. A local Compagnon takes the new boy under his wing and supervises his learning new techniques, new jobs, new tools, new materials. Each day after work the candidate grabs a quick dinner, then takes night courses in his trade.

Aspiring Compagnons work at firms like the Ateliers Sainte Catherine that are glad to be part of the program. "The great thing about the oral tradition of learning," says Damien Roussarie, a curly-headed apprentice metalworker at Sainte Catherine, "is that I'm not picking up my trade from textbooks and a shop teacher, but every day from a master."

For a look at the variety of experience the tour gives a Compagnon, consider the itinerary of stonemason Patrick Kalita. After an initial apprenticeship in Marseilles, he went up north to the champagne country where he helped restore Reims cathedral with its famous smiling angel. Heading southwest to Bordeaux, he learned sandblasting techniques while cleaning a series of ancient building facades. Again crisscrossing the country, he spent months building stone wine cellars in Strasbourg. Next stop was Paris, for restoration of the Arc de Triomphe, changing stones in the great vault over the Eternal Flame and cleaning grime off the monument's statuesquely turbulent tribute to the Revolution, *La Marseillaise.* Then it was down to Provence to learn fresco work in Avignon, and across the Atlantic for his last stop, Montreal, where he produced his masterwork.

Kalita is a freelance mason now, doing everything from chateau restoration to a hand-sculpted stone model of a Ferrari sports car for a Paris auto showroom, but he still glows when recalling his tour. "Where else but with the Compagnons," he asks, "could I have traveled like that, got that much experience, met that many good people and learned how the world works?"

Where, indeed? On the other hand, in their dedication to their craft, these young apprentices voluntarily forgo some understanding of "how the world works." According to medieval tradition, Compagnons are supposed to stay celibate during the Tour de France, and Compagnon guilds remain closed to women. François Icher, a French writer who has studied the Compagnons at length, calls the craft guilds "a school, a family, and an ethic articulated around the practice of a manual trade." Male bonding born of shared professional skill and living together in a succession of guild houses is an essential part of the experience.

Having girls around is regarded as a distraction. If there were females in the group, as Icher rather obliquely puts it, "Free time traditionally devoted to research and personal work would be used differently." Stephane Pouessel, the young provost of a guild house in Tours, prefers to take the long view. "It's true that we don't admit women," he says, "but then women have really only been in the work force for about 50 years, haven't they? We go back 2,000 years. There's still time."

There is one woman, however, who definitely is part of craft guild life, the local guild housemother, *la Mère*. Every guild house has one, often the wife of an established Compagnon, who makes sure the house is in good order, and the meals are well prepared. She also sees that the young apprentices toe the line according to The Rule. Posted prominently in the dining room and read aloud to every new arrival, The Rule prohibits "reading at table, using gross expressions, criticizing those absent, starting quarrels or engaging in loud discussions, staining the table or floor, wasting bread or any other food." Any apprentice caught violating The Rule pays a fine on the spot. "We never have much trouble with our boys," says Marie-Claude Bardolo, Mère at a Paris maison. "They're pretty tired from working all day and then taking courses for two hours after dinner. I love to watch them bloom as they start mastering their trade."

The final hurdle before initiation is the *chef d 'oeuvre*, the craftsman's PhD "dissertation," which is presented to a jury of veteran Compagnons. In creating a masterpiece, candidates don't strain for esthetic effect. Instead they pile on intricacies of structure and design, making the project as demanding as possible. Case in point: the masterwork of a young metalworker, Frederic Signoud, who did his at a shop 25 miles south of Paris. Signoud kept a diary of his project, complete with photographs, detailing every step in its making. The deceptively simple-looking sculptural object is in the form of an omega about six feet tall. But the omega is also a subtly stylized anvil. "I discussed ideas with my Compagnon tutors for three months," Signoud explains, "before I got the green light for something they found difficult enough."

Though you can't tell by looking, the ring is actually hollow, involving an intricately welded inner shell. This meant Signoud had to shape the rectangular portion with four flat faces joined by internal ribs, while he formed the round part by stamping semicircular sections and joining them to make a tube. "When I started, I expected to spend about 350 to 400 hours on it, he says. "But in the end it took 700 hours, all in my spare time. It was worth it, though, because the jury decided it made me a full-fledged Compagnon."

"The guiding principle behind the masterwork is to show that the candidate knows his trade inside out," explains Laurent Bastard. We are exploring the museum in Tours, which holds a collection of masterworks from many trades. Stopping at a showcase containing a bijou of a miniature staircase by one Agricol Perdiguier, a 19th-century joiner and guild hero who became a member of Parliament, he directs my attention to its underside. "You can slide the curving bottom piece out. There's no reason for that except to show he could do something so devilishly difficult."

He points out other scale-model staircases that swirl up in a paean to a perfectly solved equation, the angle of curve changing constantly as when—a favorite Compagnon stunt—the stairs are built around the curve of a wine bottle. Treads fan out from curving stringers, their width changing minutely with each step. Carpenters' masterworks, twisting and turning beyond the mathematical ken of most of us mortals, are mazes of joists and rafters reaching upward to the culminating spire or finial.

In the locksmiths' section we pause before a whimsically complex masterwork. Hidden behind a steel door, the lock's secret keyhole can be opened only by simultaneously moving three different elements. Once the safety is set, any false move sets off a Rube Goldbergian chain of events to thwart the thief: the bolt touches a trigger that releases a tiny steel boot that kicks a firing pin and shoots a round from a minute pistol barrel. The slightest additional movement of the lock's handle sets off a steel trap that grabs the thief's hand.

No doubt Emile Ottia, creator of that lock in 1860, was soon going through the centuries-old initiation rite at his local maison. But little is known of the secret ritual, even among Compagnons themselves; it varies not only from one guild to another, but from one trade to another. A stonemason doesn't know what goes on at the initiation of a baker or a carpenter.

The mystery surrounding their initiation rites used to cause trouble for the Compagnons. In 1539 King François I, fearing a cabal, the growing power and secret ceremonies of the Compagnons, banned "all brotherhoods of craftsmen in the Realm." In 1655 the Sorbonne's Theological Faculty condemned alleged "impious, sacrilegious and superstitious practices" in Compagnon initiations. The liberal free-thinkers of the French Revolution were just as repressive: one of the new republican government's first acts in 1791 was to ban the Compagnons. So much for *liberté, égalite, fraternité.*

By all accounts, anyone looking for "impious, sacrilegious and superstitious" goings-on in today's guilds would be disappointed. Now the initiation amounts mostly to verbal consciousness-raising, a sort of secular baptism in which the candidate receives a new ceremonial name, usually combining hometown and dominant characteristic (Provençal le Résolu, for example). He also receives a cane and a colored ribbon or sash corresponding to his trade. Some scholars link it to Masonic rites—French guilds and Freemasons share the compass-and-square symbol, and both refer to God as the "Great Architect of the Universe"—but the Compagnons reject any close historical connection to Freemasons.

The pride of every Compagnon is his bulrush cane with an ornamental pommel of horn, ivory, silver or wood engraved with trade emblems, his name and date of receipt. At home he will hang it on a wall in a place of honor; at weddings he and his peers will hoist their canes to form a vault above bride and groom. At death it will be beside him in his coffin.

He will break it out, too, to celebrate the guild's frequent feast days. Each trade has its patron saint, and many trade-saint pairings bear a touch of whimsy: Saint Joseph for carpenters, Saint Catherine for coachbuilders (she was martyred on a wheel). As for roofers, the big day is, *naturellement,* Ascension Thursday. Bakers fete Saint Honoré, which also happens to be the name of a popular French cream pastry.

When I looked in on a maison in Paris where Compagnon bakers were honoring their saint, everyone was in full cry. Traditional guild songs, often melancholy with the kind of nostalgia for the Tour de France that American alumni feel for good old Ivy, resounded off the coffered wooden refectory ceiling. Golden loaves laden with wheaty garlands stood on tables, including one four feet high in the hexagonal shape of France. All in jacket and tie, not a glazed eye, slack jaw or long lock of hair among them, the young Compagnons were the most squared-away bunch you could find this side of Marine boot camp. The singing went on until midnight, when they joined hands and formed a ring around the Mère before turning in.

Medieval manuscripts refer to the Compagnons. When France's wily King Louis IX drew up statutes for the trades in 1270, he forbade workers generally to leave their masters without permission. Compagnon masons were the only exception: they alone had the right to travel from one worksite to another and cockily wore a gold earring as sign of their free status. During the crusades they joined the Knights Templars as a sort of corps of engineers to build fortresses and Christian churches; the oldest known image of the Compagnons, in a Renaissance manuscript in Paris's Bibliothèque Nationale, shows them being received with pomp during the Muslim siege of Rhodes in 1480.

They would have been well received indeed, for they alone possessed the esoteric construction know-how taught them by Cistercian monks. It was only plane and solid geometry, but at the time it amounted to a powerful trade secret. Compagnons handed it on orally from master to apprentice to make sure it stayed that way. That explains why, even today, Compagnons are such a discreet bunch. They discuss their activities only up to a point, then politely decline to go further.

For centuries French craft guilds were France's only form of organized labor. By the early 19th century they had such a hammerlock on the labor market that they could shut down a recalcitrant employer just by banning work there. No worker dared scab against the Compagnons. It took massive industrialization, with its machines and an urban proletariat indifferent to craftsmanship, to thoroughly undermine the Compagnons. By 1940 craft guild membership, up to 200,000 in the mid-19th century, had fallen to less than 5,000. Since World War II, in an age of increasing technology, the Compagnons have made a strong comeback. One reason, as Paris's heavyweight daily *Le Monde* recently noted, is that "young people with university degrees are having real difficulty entering the job market." Craft guilds "increasingly appear as the guarantee of high-quality training, a virtual passport to the future."

Increasingly, too, France's guilds are opening to the outside world. Though they have not yet taken in women, they are beginning exchange programs with craftsmen from other European countries. The French government has asked them to look into setting up training programs in Eastern Europe to help artisans there regain the skills their grandfathers knew before communist rule. They've even been asked to set up a chapter in the United States. "The problem is," says a guild official at a maison in Tours, "Americans tend to see manual work as just a dull job to make a living."

Compagnons lately have been showing up, Superman-like, to help America save its national heritage. At the request of the Historic Charleston Foundation, a handful of them flew to South Carolina in August 1990 to help repair the damage wreaked by Hurricane Hugo, putting new roofs on stately homes and restoring damaged antique furniture. Before that, ten Compagnon metalworkers set up shop at the foot of the Statue of Liberty in 1984 to rebuild the torch, so corroded by decades of leakage it was in danger of falling off.

One of the toughest jobs of Liberty's $40 million restoration, the repairing of the torch was made harder because all the original drawings for the flame were lost. To arrive at a working maquette of its complex geometry, the Compagnons used an age-old device called a measuring frame to plot the flame in three dimensions. Then they fabricated steel molds over the maquette and hammered 23 copper sheets into shape with wooden mallets, repeatedly annealing each to keep it malleable. The final touch was 5,000 squares of gold leaf applied by a specialist father-and-son team from Paris, Robert and Fabrice Gohard.

After finishing that job, half a dozen of the Compagnons decided to stay on and, with Jean Wiart, create the LMC Corporation. They are glad they did, and so are their customers. As a pleased member of the New York architectural firm Swanke Hayden Connell wrote to Wiart, "You have set a precedent for specialized metalwork not seen in this country for many years…and set a standard which other metal craftsmen should follow."

American craftsmen take note. But to meet that standard it would help to have about 1,800 more years of tradition under your belt. Plus a few spent doing a Tour d' Amérique. And forget about girls.

Update : *France mandated a 35-hour workweek a few years ago, ostensibly to stimulate job creation, largely as a sop to hard-line Socialists and those who much prefer vacation to work. It did nothing to help employment, with the jobless rate staying around 10 percent. But today's 9,000 or so Compagnons still love work, and still have their choice of jobs. They are especially appreciated on high-tech projects like the new Queen Mary2 passenger ship and the Airbus A-380 super-jumbo airliner.*

2. La Gloire

France Raises The Tallest Tower

Context: *The French, it need hardly be said, are a proud people. I myself believe that the best single symbol of their sometimes irritating pride, their constant need for* gloire, *is an utterly superfluous thousand-foot structure called the Eiffel Tower. When France decided to hold a world's fair in 1889 to celebrate the centennial of the Revolution, officials wanted a thousand-foot tower as its proud centerpiece to show the world what it could do. Gustave Eiffel, possibly the greatest engineer of the 19th century, who constructed innovative bridges and train stations in Europe, Asia and South America, as well as the interior bracing of the Statue of Liberty, was chosen to build it.*

The notion of a thousand-foot tower was not particularly new. In fact, it was in the air on both sides of the Atlantic as the nations that had been the first to realize the early potential of the Industrial Revolution looked for ways to dramatize their new prowess and prosperity. It was as if they were obeying a compulsion constant throughout history to thrust mighty structures toward the sky in moments of special pride: in legend the Tower of Babel, in reality the Great Pyramid of Cheops and the medieval cathedrals.

As early as March 1833, the British railroad engineer Richard Trevithick had proposed a thousand-foot tower for London to commemorate passage of Britain's First Reform Act, which had created a more equitable distribution of seats in Parliament and added half-a-million voters to the lists. The structure was to have been of cast iron, 100 feet in diameter at the base and 10 feet across at the top, surmounted by a colossal statue. Trevithick died in April of that year, however, and his idea was not acted upon by King William IV.

The idea continued to fascinate engineers. In 1874, two Americans, Clarke and Reeves, drew up plans for a thousand-foot iron tower for the Philadelphia Centennial Exposition of 1876. The cylinder was to be only 30 feet in diameter, braced by cables attached to a circular masonry base. The exposition's organizers rejected what must have resembled a glorified factory chimney.

The most ambitious tower actually to be erected before 1889 was the Washington Monument. But this 555-foot, all-masonry obelisk completed in 1884 was far smaller than the thousand-foot tower that had become a virtual obsession of 19th-century engineers. Therefore when French officials considered how to give the Paris Exposition of 1889 special éclat, a thousand-foot tower was the obvious choice.

On January 8, 1887, the City of Paris signed a contract with Gustave Eiffel. The engineer agreed to construct a thousand-foot tower in time for the opening of the Exposition of 1889. To anyone but the supremely confident Eiffel, the undertaking would have appeared foolhardy, questions of the basic wisdom of creating such an eccentric structure aside. For one thing, a scant two years remained in which to construct the tallest tower ever conceived. No guiding precedent existed. The Washington Monument had taken no less than 36 years from cornerstone to capstone, including time lost due to financial and technical problems. And the subsidy granted by the French government covered less than one-fifth of the tower's projected cost. Eiffel was to provide the remainder, the equivalent of $1.3 million, with the possibility of recovering his investment if the tower turned out a financial success.

But there was no question now of turning back. France had announced to the world the most complete, the most dazzling world's fair ever held. Its symbol and centerpiece had to be the thousand-foot tower that seemed the inevitable technical apotheosis of the century.

The final decision made, workers began digging the tower's foundations on January 26, 1887. There was never any doubt in Eiffel's mind that he was engaged in a historic enterprise. It was his intention, he said, "to raise to the glory of modern science, and to the greater honor of French industry, an arch of triumph as striking as those that preceding generations had raised to conquerors."

The tower's immediate symbolic importance for France and, in particular, for the Exposition of 1889, was spelled out by Alfred Picard, official historian of the fair: "This colossal work was to constitute a brilliant manifestation of the industrial strength of our country, attest to the immense progress realized in the art of metal structures, celebrate the unprecedented progress of civil engineering during the course of this century, attract multitudes of visitors, and contribute largely to the success of the great peaceful commemoration of the centenary of 1789."

But before its construction got underway, the tower was to make a number of people angry. Self-appointed tastemakers in this nation that prided itself on being beauty's most devoted acolyte rose up in rage. Forty-seven of the most righteously indignant, artists and writers, penned a letter of protest to the minister of public works to argue against "the erection in the heart of our capital of the useless and monstrous Eiffel Tower."

Considering this hostile reaction to his tower by part of the artist community, Eiffel viewed the matter with solid Burgundian equanimity and a sure grasp of aesthetics. "I believe that the tower will have its own beauty," he declared in an interview published in the serious daily, *Le Temps*. "The first principle of architectural beauty is that the essential lines of a construction be determined by a perfect appropriateness to its use. What was the main obstacle I had to overcome in designing the tower? Its resistance to wind. And I submit that the curves of its four piers as produced by our calculations, rising from an enormous base and narrowing toward the top, will give a great impression of strength and beauty.

"Besides," Eiffel continued, on another tack, "there is an attraction and a charm inherent in the colossal that is not subject to ordinary theories of art. Does anyone pretend that the Pyramids have so forcefully gripped the imagination of men through their artistic value? What are they, after all, but artificial hillocks? And yet what visitor can stand without reaction in their presence? The tower will be the tallest edifice ever raised by man. Will it not therefore be imposing in its own way?"

He concluded on the note that had come to be the leitmotif of the Exposition of 1889, France's emotional need to be taken seriously in the community of nations. "It seems to me that the Eiffel Tower is worthy of being treated with respect, if only because it will show that we are not simply a frivolous people, but also the country of engineers and builders who are called upon all over the world to construct bridges, viaducts, train stations and the great monuments of modern industry."

France had come a long way since its humiliation by Prussia in the War of 1870, and it intended to prove that to a skeptical world—and coincidentally to itself—with the 1889 world's fair and a tower so tall that other nations had only dreamed of building it. The country was riding the crest of the first wave of industrialism. In a broader sense, the iron tower that was to symbolize France's soaring pride of accomplishment would also signal that a new era, full of incalculable portent, had begun.

"These are indeed glorious times for the Engineers," exulted James Nasmyth, the Scottish inventor who designed the first steam hammer. His euphoric mood was echoed throughout the industrializing world. Gustave Eiffel, an engineer living the "glorious times" of his profession, was at the peak of his career. Contemporary photographs show him at 55 to have been small but well proportioned, with large, thickish hands, close-cropped, graying beard and hair, and heavy-lidded light blue eyes. If anything was remarkable about his appearance it was his serene, hooded gaze, which gave him a look of complete self-possession free of interior conflict of any sort: dull company, perhaps, but you would feel safe crossing one of his bridges.

Professionally, Eiffel had a self-confident mastery that led him to disdain secrecy. He routinely published the blueprints and calculations of his projects once they were completed. He was an engineer through and through, scorning superfluous embellishments. When exasperated by a bad design, he was often heard to mutter, "Stupid as an architect." In the rapidity and sureness with which he overcame technical problems, he appears to fit poet Paul Valéry's description of the great builders of the age, who "conceived their structures visibly as a complete whole, rather than in two mental phases, one relating to form and the other to matter…they *thought* in materials."

The one thing Eiffel lacked on the eve of the 1889 Paris World's Fair was fame, for he remained relatively unknown outside engineering circles. And it may be true, as the internationally famous Swiss architect and city planner Charles-Edouard Jeanneret, better known as Le Corbusier, has suggested, that "He was pained by not being seen as a creator of beauty…His calculations were always inspired by an admirable instinct for proportion, his goal was elegance."

The thousand-foot tower he had proposed for the Exposition would make his name a household word in many lands. It would even be considered beautiful by some.

Eiffel went to work on the tower in his usual methodical fashion, basing everything on meticulous computations. He had his draftsmen turn out blueprints for every piece of metal to be used in it: 5,329 mechanical drawings representing 18,038 separate items. These drawings alone took 30 draftsmen 18 months to produce and covered 14,352 square feet of paper.

Eiffel's greatest difficulty derived from the tower's odd angles. If it had been only an "assemblage of iron ladders," as some critics called it, a few basic elements could have been designed and then copied thousands of times, as they had been for Eiffel's portable bridges. But the tower's curved, weight-bearing edges describe irregular arcs and the trussing of its 28 panels varies gradually from bottom to top.

Each piece therefore had to be designed separately, taking into account the variable inclination of columns and braces along every foot of the tower's height. In addition, every rivet hole had to be drawn in at precisely the right spot, so that all the on-site workers would have to do was to place one-third of the 2.5 million rivets, the rest being placed at the shops in advance. The Eiffel Tower was one of the first examples of large-scale industrialized construction; all calculations had to be accurate to one-tenth of a millimeter.

When it came to determining the strength of the tower, Eiffel paradoxically ignored the weight of visitors, despite the fact that the structure was designed to accommodate a maximum of 10,416 persons at once on its three platforms. Their total weight, he figured, at an average of 154 pounds, would be 800 tons, or less than 10 percent of the tower's total weight. "The violence of the wind that we estimated in determining the tower's strength," Eiffel explained later, "was so great that it would make visiting impossible. Besides, the visitors' weight produced negligible stress compared with that created by the weight of the tower itself and high winds."

The real problem was the wind. Eiffel knew his old enemy well and had outsmarted it in every one of his tall bridge piers. In designing the tower, he adopted two extreme hypotheses to simulate wind force. In the first, he took into account a wind of 134 miles per hour exerted evenly over the tower's entire surface from top to bottom; in the second, a wind of 148 miles per hour at the top, diminishing gradually to 105 miles per hour at the bottom. Never had such winds been observed in Paris. In addition, the surface to be struck was deliberately exaggerated. The upper half of the structure was assumed to be a solid surface taking the wind full-face; the intermediate area, where the open spaces are much greater, was figured to be four times its actual surface; below that, the four piers were assumed to be solid surfaces rather than open trusses.

Then coefficients for vertical weight and wind force were combined to give a total working coefficient for the entire tower and each of its 28 truss work panels. The figures showed that the mathematical center of the wind's action in the first hypothesis would be at a height of 278 feet, and in the second, 323 feet. The wind's total force, or overturning moment, was then compared with the tower's predetermined resistance to overturning, or moment of stability, considering its weight, height, and base area. The moment of stability was greater. (In reality, the tower would sway only about 4 ¾ inches in a strong wind; due to dilatation of its iron, on a sunny day the top slowly describes an ellipse of seven inches as the sun strikes it at different angles.)

The tower would stand because of Eiffel's grasp of a paradox: victory over wind is achieved not through an accumulation of brute force, buy by reducing the supporting elements of an openwork structure until the wind has virtually nothing to seize. In other words, the Eiffel Tower's real strength is in its voids as much as in its iron.

Work proceeded swiftly. The second level was reached in early July 1888, and on the 14th, Bastille Day, a fireworks display was shot off from the new height to the pleasure of crowds gathered across the Seine at the Trocadéro. That day, Eiffel held a banquet on the first platform for the Paris press. He took the occasion to deliver a pep talk.

"Judging by the interest that the tower seems to inspire both in France and abroad," he declared, champagne glass in hand, "I believe it is fair to say that we are showing the world that France continues to be the leader of progress, and that she is realizing a project which has often been tried or dreamed of. Only through the advancement of science, metallurgy and the art of engineering that distinguish the latter part of our century have we been able to surpass the generations that preceded us. Construction of this tower will be one of the landmarks of the modern industry that made it possible."

At the end of March 1889, the tower topped out at 312.27 meters, including flagstaff, or 1,025 feet. Technicians were still tinkering with the worrisome elevators, but Eiffel's structural work was finished, two years, two months, and five days after it began. The tower was the world's tallest manmade object by far, making the runner-up Washington Monument look stubby by comparison. It would remain the tallest structure until completion of New York's Chrysler Building decades later.

Eiffel's execution had been marked by a deftness unique in the annals of great engineering projects until that time. His clockwork precision had enabled him not only to meet his deadline, but also to build the vertiginous structure with the loss of only one life, that of a worker who fell from the first platform while apparently showing off for his girlfriend after the bell had sounded ending the working day.

Such a safety record was phenomenal compared with other contemporary monumental works. The Brooklyn Bridge took some 20 lives including that of its designer, John Roebling. The death toll at the Forth Bridge was 57 workers, at the Quebec Bridge 84. And in a time when cost overruns plagued big projects nearly as much as they do today—the Brooklyn Bridge, for instance, cost twice the original estimate—Eiffel built his tower for exactly the equivalent of $1,505,675.90, or 6 percent *less* than the initial budget of $1.6 million.

"Fruit of intuition, of science, of faith, daughter of courage and of perseverance," as Le Corbusier later called it, the tower was ready to be christened in that gusty early spring of 1889. Eiffel invited a few dignitaries such as Prime Minister Pierre Tirard, members of the Paris Municipal Council, and the Exposition's directors, Adolphe Alphand and Georges Berger, to a simple ceremony.

Promptly at 1:30 p.m. on Sunday, March 31, he led the way up the north pier stairs. Most of the group dropped out, winded, at the first and second platforms. Eiffel and a few others, among them his veteran colleagues Emile Nouguier and Jean Compagnon, and the president of the Municipal Council, Emile Chautemps, reached the top a bit after 2 p.m. There Eiffel unfurled an appropriately grand French tricolor, 15 by 25 feet, emblazoned with the golden initials *RF* of the *République Française*, and ran it up the flagpole. Fireworks were set off on the second platform to resemble a 21-gun salute, rather as if the tower were a visiting sovereign.

Eiffel and his party descended, and he addressed the guests and about 200 workers. Toasts were proposed as champagne flowed, an excited Emile Chautemps crying, "*Gloire à Monsieur Eiffel et à ses collaborateurs! Vive la France! Vive Paris! Et vive la République!*"

In keeping with the unstated theme of the Exposition of 1889, Eiffel's speech was frankly patriotic, from the "great satisfaction" he felt at flying the French flag from the tallest edifice ever built, to the final moral: "You will remember always the great effort we have made in common to show all that, thanks to her engineers and her workers, France still holds an important place in the world, and that we are always able to succeed where others have failed, to the great honor of France and the Republic."

Holding his top hat against the growing wind, Prime Minister Tirard made a brief reply, declaring that Eiffel was being promoted to the rank of officer in the Legion of Honor. The City of Paris awarded a silver commemorative medal to all workers who had been on the site during the last months of construction.

Shortly after the ceremony, a violent spring storm swept across Paris from the northeast, lashing the city with rain, hail, and gale-force winds. Those who had tarried for a second glass of champagne scurried for shelter beneath the tower's arcades. Far above the Seine, the immense tricolor thrashed and whipped on its lacy, thousand-foot iron mast, but held.

Update: *After falling into disrepair in the 1970s, the Eiffel Tower was thoroughly refurbished in time for its centennial in 1989. To date, over 200 million people have visited it since its construction. Year in, year out, it is the most visited monument in France, easily topping the Arch of Triumph, Notre Dame Cathedral, the châteaux of the Loire Valley, and Mont-Saint-Michel in Normandy. It also outdraws comparable attractions in the United States such as the Washington Monument and Statue of Liberty. Managed by a private company, the Société Nouvelle d'Exploitation de la Tour Eiffel, the tower generates a turnover of some $50 million annually, including admissions, concessions for several restaurants, and rental of its 116 antennas—which now bring its total height to 318* *meters, or 1,043 feet—by six television channels and 28 FM radio stations. In 2004, two American mathematicians, Patrick Weidman of the University of Colorado and Iosif Pinelis of Michigan Technological University, finally broke Eiffel's mathematical code for the tower's shape: it is, they say, a nonlinear, integro-differential equation yielding an exponential profile. Eiffel, of course, knew that in 1887.*

Concorde: A Plane for Prestige

Context: *Pride and the search for national grandeur have led France in many directions. Just as a thousand-foot tower was something that had to be done because it could be done, so a supersonic airliner was the dream project of aeronautical engineers in the 1960s. It was, therefore, just the prestige symbol that the France of Charles de Gaulle wanted. British engineers, too, were ready to do it. Thus it was that the French and British governments spent some $3 billion to develop "the superplane, the symbol of progress, the icon of invention, a totem," as a London newspaper put it. The French considered Concorde their own, and references to British engineering were rare in French media. But prestige alone is not enough in the airline business: no company except the captive, state-owned airlines of France and Britain ever bought it.*

Normally you don't want a tailwind on takeoff. But André Turcat, the laconic, 47-year-old test pilot of this particular flight, was willing to trade that for the advantage of a crash barrier at the other end of Runway 33 at France's Toulouse Blagnac airfield. Eager to get going after being blocked by two days of bad weather, Turcat sighted down the runway's centerline, smoothly spooled up the four monster Olympus engines to a bone-shaking roar, switched on afterburners, and released the brakes. As Concorde Prototype 001 swiftly accelerated and rotated off in its patriotic blue, white and red livery, an odd little scene was taking place just outside the field's perimeter fence: many of the onlookers standing there were not just watching the maiden flight of a new airplane, they were excitedly chanting *Allez France! Allez France!* as if it were an international soccer game and France was winning.

No matter that those Olympus engines were mostly British, as was roughly half the plane, or that a few weeks later, with less chauvinistic fanfare, Prototype 002 would make its first flight at Fairford, England. When the French plane landed in Toulouse 35 minutes later at 4:10 p.m. after a gear-down, subsonic flight, it was clear not only that aviation history had been made on March 2, 1969, but also that France had a proud new symbol. As the Paris newspaper *Le Monde* once noted, Concorde "was created largely to serve the prestige of France...[it was] the expression of political will, founded on a certain idea of national grandeur."

Concorde prototypes went on to become the world's first Mach 1 airliner on October 1 that year, and made Mach 2 a year later. After the longest and most costly development program in the history of aviation—5,540 hours of flight testing over nearly seven years, of which 2,000 hours were supersonic—Concorde began service in January 1976 with simultaneous takeoffs from London to Bahrain by British Airways and Paris to Rio de Janeiro by Air France, with takeoff clearance given at precisely the same moment.

The airplane instantly became an aeronautical icon. With its spindly, 13-foot-high landing gear and droop nose, Concorde on the ground looked slightly forlorn, ungainly and out of its element. But once in flight with gear and visor up, it became the sleek "beautiful white bird," the French invariably called it, covering a mile every 2 ¾ seconds at Mach 2, faster than a rifle bullet. Not bad for an aircraft designed when engineers still used slide rules and log tables to figure out supersonic aerodynamics.

It operated in a weird environment. At Mach 2, about 1,150 knots, and 60,000 feet, the air temperature is around minus 67 degrees F., but atmospheric friction heats the fuselage skin to the boiling point of water, expanding the metal and making the plane about half-a-foot longer. Shock waves stress the airframe, atmospheric pressure is only one-tenth that of sea level. Today its flight deck instrumentation, which has never been modernized, is considered old technology, the equivalent of a first-generation Boeing 747. Concorde pilots laboriously read electro-mechanical dials instead of glancing at the comprehensive, computer-generated displays of a contemporary "glass cockpit."

"It's not an easy plane to fly, you have to be constantly alert," says Peter Duffey, a retired British Airways Concorde pilot and author of *Comets and Concordes*. "Things happen more quickly. For example, its takeoff time is only half that of a 747. At Mach 2, 22 miles a minute, you're always thinking about where you can land in event of an emergency, and there are about 50 reasons besides engine failure why you would have to take it down to subsonic flight."

But the hard, paradoxical fact about this aeronautical triumph is that nobody wanted to buy it. Grandeur and prestige alone won't keep airline shareholders happy. After the French and British governments sank some $3 billion dollars in development costs in it in the 1960s, no airline other than their two captive, state-owned national carriers ever flew it. To be sure, commercial success looked possible at first, with original sales estimates for 240 Concordes by 1978. But the first oil shock hit, sending fuel prices up—and Concorde consumes four times as much fuel to carry one-quarter as many passengers as, say, a 747. Moreover, the plane's unsettling sonic boom on the ground, like the crack of a high-velocity rifle shot coming with no warning, made lucrative overland routes like New York to Los Angeles impossible.

All prospective buyers except British Airways and Air France, who got the plane at bargain prices from their governments, cancelled their options. Finally only 20 Concordes were built, including prototypes and pre-production models; 14 entered service. "The economics of Concorde never made sense and there was never a market for it," contends Ronald Davies, curator of air transport at the National Air and Space Museum in Washington, D.C. "For every hour it spends in the air, it spends 14 on the ground. And for every seat transported across the Atlantic, it has to carry one ton of fuel; two tons if it's only half full, which often happens. It's so inefficient it's unbelievable." And all that money spent on the development of this prestige project? "Taxpayer funded executive air transport," Davies says flatly. "It's one of the biggest scams ever perpetrated."

Concorde's reputation for invincibility—it had no fatal accidents in 24 years of service—ended at 4:44 p.m. local time on July 25, 2000, when Air France Flight 4590 blew a tire on takeoff from Paris Charles de Gaulle Airport. Trailing a long sheet of flame from its left wing, the plane lost power in its two left engines and, unable to retract its gear, struggled barely 200 feet into the air before crashing onto a hotel, killing all 100 passengers, three flight crew, six flight attendants and four persons on the ground. Newspapers compared the crash to the sinking of the Titanic, the Hindenburg bursting into flames, the Challenger space shuttle exploding.

Both Air France and British Airways immediately grounded their Concorde fleets. On August 16, France's Bureau Enquêtes-Accidents (BEA) declared that the blowout caused the crash, and took the extremely rare step of recommending suspension of Concorde's certificate of airworthiness. Aviation circles around the world were shocked. And yet, several omens had indicated that not all was well with the aging beautiful white bird. The very day before the crash, Air France had discovered cracks in the wings of four of its six Concordes, though not in the one that crashed.

Perhaps more ominous was the long series of incidents and warnings that came to light as crash investigators and the media delved into Concorde's past. For example, several had lost parts of their elevons (the combination elevators and ailerons on the trailing edge of delta-wing aircraft) and rudders several times in flight, but were able to land safely. The Olympus 593 engines were the subject of a 1998 study that found 152 problems concerning hardware design or other factors, 55 of which were considered "significant risks." The Federal Aviation Administration issued airworthiness directives ordering additional X-ray and ultrasonic inspections of the engines. As the engine study warned presciently, "A major technical event would probably end Concorde operation."

But the scariest scenario to come out was the French BEA's list of 57 tire-related incidents from 1976 to 2000, 30 of which were on Air

France flights and 27 on British Airways. Of those, 32 blowouts damaged the aircraft's structure, engines or hydraulics, and six resulted in penetration of one or more fuel tanks.

Worst of these occurred on June 14, 1979, when Air France Flight 054 to Paris blew its two rear tires on the left main landing gear on takeoff from Washington Dulles Airport, hurling high-speed rubber and wheel rim debris at the left wing and engines. The flight crew knew about the blown tires and were diverting to News York, but they were unaware of the true extent of the problem until an American passenger convinced the mostly indifferent cabin attendants to bring a crew member back to examine a 12-square-foot hole in the top wing skin.

"I took the gentleman who had come back from the flight deck to my seat and virtually held his head to the window so that he could look down and see the hole in the wing," the passenger wrote in a statement to the National Transportation Safety Board. "When he saw the hole, he exclaimed, 'Mon Dieu!'" The flight crew managed an emergency landing at Dulles with highly flammable Jet A1 fuel streaming from a dozen holes in fuel tanks, damage to the number two engine, severed electrical cables, and the loss of two out of three hydraulic systems.

All Concordes were later modified to include tougher roll-on wheel rims, strengthened tires and a tire failure warning in the cockpit. But even after the chairman of the U.S. National Transportation Safety Board (NTSB), James B. King, wrote to his French counterpart on November 9, 1981, expressing his "serious concern" about "the repetitive nature of these incidents," they continued, with their constant threat of catastrophe. As a former NTSB chief, Jim Burnett, points out, "Concorde could have been certified with a design flaw nobody noticed at the time. If there were as many Concordes flying as Boeing 737s, I suspect that we would have seen this problem many times."

Two official French enquiries were set in motion following the July 25 crash, the BEA searching for its causes, and a judicial investigation headed by three magistrates, aided by gendarmes, to determine legal responsibilities. The most controversial finding concerned a spacer that, due to an Air France maintenance error, was missing from the oleo/bogie coupling on the left main landing gear. The BEA ruled out the missing spacer as a cause of the crash. (Air France, which was sued by families of the crash victims, declined repeated interview requests for this article.)

Meanwhile, about 100 engineers with the original Concorde builders BAE Systems, successor to British Aircraft Corporation, and EADS Airbus, along with the original Olympus constructors Rolls Royce and Snecma, began searching for solutions that would satisfy the authorities that Concorde could resume service safely. They quickly focused on modifications to the fuel tanks to cut the risk of fire from a fuel leak, and armoring electrical cables in the plane's wheel wells, which were suspected of igniting the fire with a spark.

Armoring the electrical wiring in the wheel wells was the easy part. It was shaped into "looms" of 15 to 20 cables each, protected with stainless steel braiding and Teflon, replacing the aluminum tubing used before. To protect the fuel tanks, engineers decided on flexible liners of Kevlar and Viton, derived from existing technology used in tanks of military helicopters and Formula One racing cars. Five times stronger per weight than steel, the thin sheets of Kevlar (best known for use in bulletproof vests) were sandwiched between layers of Viton, a heat-resistant rubberized sealant. This, the reasoning goes, will reduce any shock wave produced by debris and limit the flow of fuel by being sucked down into a hole. This sort of modification has never been tried before.

Can Concorde come back? "I have always said that Concorde would fly again," French Transport Minister Gayssot declared, reflecting official French optimism about the plane's future. When Concorde entered service in 1976, its original lifespan was expected to be 6,700 flights, which would have meant ending operations in 1993. Since then, structural modifications, changes to inspection and maintenance programs, and other alterations have stretched that to around 2010, depending on usage. But Concorde's comeback is not just a question of technology. Only time will tell whether it can again occupy the same mythical place in the public mind that it has held since the cheering French were thrilled by it over 30 years ago.

Update: *After modifications costing tens of millions of dollars—prestige has its price—Concorde did come back, but only briefly. After barely a year in service, it was grounded for good and the remaining planes sent to museums in the autumn of 2003.*

Rogues of Peace: Today's French Foreign Legion

Context: *With its glory-filled tradition of iron discipline and dedication, the Foreign Legion is a unique unit of 8,500 professional soldiers from some 120 countries, practically a mini-United Nations in itself. After a century and a half of swagger,* Beau Geste *myth and artfully cultivated mystery, it has adopted a new humanitarian role as international rescuer and peacekeeper. Although French citizens are prohibited by law from joining its ranks unless they are army officers—a rule often observed in the breach—it is a permanent source of* gloire *for Frenchmen. They always give the Legionnaires the loudest applause on Bastille Day when they come marching, with their special slow cadence, down the Champs Élysées. It was certainly not the Legion that General George Patton had in mind when he said, "I would rather have a German division in front of me than a French one behind me."*

Amid fire-blackened buildings and looted shops pockmarked with bullet holes, the stench of death hangs over Brazzaville. For weeks the besieged capital of the Congo Republic has been a battlefield for armed factions supporting either the former Marxist dictator, General Denis Sassou-Nguesso, or President Pascal Lissouba. Now clouds of flies feed on bloated corpses littering the streets as rival Cobra and Zulu militias, drunk and drugged, wildly fire heavy mortars and machine guns at everything that moves. Thousands of terrified residents, many of them victims of random violence and rapine, hole up behind barricaded doors and hope for rescue from certain massacre. Then in the early hours of June 5, 1997, they hear a heartening rumor: *The Foreign Legion is coming!*

Armored personnel carriers of the 2nd Foreign Airborne Regiment are rumbling up Avenue Charles de Gaulle. Mounted with .50-caliber machine guns, manned by Legionnaires in full combat gear, the olive drab vehicles suddenly run into a roadblock. A wild-eyed Cobra militiaman charges up. "All right," he shouts with a wave of his machine gun. "Everybody out of those vehicles, and fast!" A second Cobra, pockets stuffed with grenades, joins him, followed by others spoiling for a fight. For a tense moment the two groups eye each other, fingers on triggers. Then 31-year-old Captain Jean-Michel Trotignon flashes a cool, Clint Eastwood smile. "We're not looking for a fight, but we're going evacuate any foreign civilians who want to leave," he matter-of-factly tells the militiaman. The Cobras blink, look over the 15 crack Legionnaires with automatic assault rifles and fixed bayonets, and think again: "Okay, okay, go ahead," their leader mutters.

The unit goes on to rescue several foreign residents, including a Chinese woman whose French is limited to a sincere *merci* and a Korean diplomat, and takes them to Maya-Maya airport to be flown out to safety. Despite repeated skirmishes that costs them one killed and eight wounded, the Foreign Legion methodically combs for endangered civilians and leads them to safety under armed guard, saving 5,265 persons of 52 nationalities, including nearly 100 Americans. When it's over, one of the Legion's last tasks is to escort U.S. Ambassador Aubrey Hooks to the airport. "They did an absolutely superb job in a very difficult situation," he said later. "They were extremely professional and took a humanitarian approach, going back repeatedly into areas to be sure they had gotten everyone out."

The operation shows what a changed outfit the Foreign Legion is. Long known for the macho mystique of its roguish, glory-filled past, today's Legion has become a familiar, and welcome, sight in the nasty, ambiguous little conflicts of the post-Cold War era, from Beirut to Bosnia, Cambodia to Somalia. With its 166-year tradition of iron discipline and dedication, it is a unique band of 8,500 professional soldiers from some 120 countries. Now it has adopted a new humanitarian role as international rescuer and peacekeeper.

But it's still the only place in the world where men from any country can get a new start in life. Oddly enough, these tough guys demonstrate daily that people who apparently have nothing in common—neither nationality nor language nor religion nor even the same sense of humor—can live and work together in mutual respect. What these men without a country do have in common is a near-fanatical dedication to an ideal: the Legion itself. It's their home and family all in one. Their motto: *Legio Patria Nostra* (the Legion is Our Homeland).

This ideal creates an almost supernatural bonding. Legionnaires never leave a wounded comrade on the battlefield, in combat they often shield officers with their bodies—and officers serve their men breakfast in bed on the Legion's annual day, April 30. "This camaraderie is no myth," says Captain Joel Bonis with the Legion's 13th Foreign Demi-Brigade in Djibouti, on the sandy, sun-blasted Horn of Africa. "The other evening I was in a bar with a civilian friend and he pretended to throw a punch at me. Suddenly a Legionnaire was pinning his arms behind him, growling 'Nobody lays a hand on a Legion captain!'"

Put that esprit de corps with the Legion's unique multi-national diversity, and you have one of the best-suited combat units for the difficult, demanding task of international peacekeeping. "Traditionally the Legion has been designed for all-out combat," explains the Legion's commandant, General Dominique Piquemal, "but today full-fledged war operations are increasingly rare, so we've adapted to a new mission of crisis management in trouble spots."

Wherever the trouble is, the Legion always has ready-made interpreters and guides in its ranks. When it went into war-torn Beirut, for instance, interposed between fighting Syrians and Israelis, the Legion got its first taste of house-to-house urban combat, complete with booby-tapped buildings, snipers, checkpoints, and UN bureaucracy. "It was a challenge," says General Piquemal, "but we could do it partly because our Lebanese Legionnaires knew the city, spoke Arab and were perfectly at ease there. Obviously that's an enormous advantage."

It was an advantage too in Sarajevo, where Legionnaires in the UN Rapid Reaction Force insisted on deploying in camouflage to make the point they were a fighting force, not just peacekeepers. They forcibly drove the point home in August 1995 after the Serbs surrounded a Legion observation post: Legionnaires of Serb origin disguised as Serb troops infiltrated a headquarters, cut the sentries' throats, and made the commander withdraw his men.

In Sarajevo's confused cauldron, Legionnaires often acted beyond the call of duty. One night, when a 14-year-old Bosnian boy desperately tried to run across the airport runway, Serb snipers callously shot him in the chest. Witnessing the tragedy, Legion Sergeant Bruno Chaumont dodged bullets for 40 yards, picked the boy up, and carried him to safety. And when a young Bosnian woman needed post-natal medical attention, Legionnaire Ratislav Benko went and delivered her to a clinic. Minutes later, hot shrapnel from Serb mortar fire ripped through his blue UN helmet, killing him instantly.

The peacekeeping missions of recent years, so different from the Legion's legendary last stands, seem to bring out Legionnaires' heroism and humanism. This can take the form of burly, booted Legionnaires in combat fatigues gently teaching robed Cambodian monks the finer points of French so they can vote in the country's elections. Or routinely delivering medicine to African villages and treating natives in Legion dispensaries. Often the Legion's surprisingly big heart beneath the tough exterior comes out in the most horrific circumstances.

In the hell of in Rwanda, for example, where Legionnaires distributed food and medicine, disarmed Hutus and Tutsis trying to slaughter each other, and opened a 300-km corridor so refugees could get out. They also had the emotionally wrenching task of burying the dead in mass graves. One day in June 1994, Lieutenant Arthur Da Silva Santos, a 22-year Legion veteran from Portugal, saw a small arm move amid a pile of dead bodies in Goma, Zaire. Ordering bulldozers to halt the grisly operation, fighting back nausea as he clambered through decomposing bodies, he pulled out a 6-year-old Hutu boy. "I decided this one, at least, wasn't going to die," Da Silva recalls.

He put the limp body in his jeep, drove to a military hospital, and spent weeks following the boy's progress back to life, fighting cholera and multiple parasites. When the boy could leave the hospital, he took him for bouncy, joyful rides in a Legion jeep. Da Silva and his wife, Marie-Reine, considered adopting him until a relief agency finally located the boy's family. Later the boy's father sent his heartfelt thanks to "the white soldier."

Who are these men, most of whom live under false names, many of whom came to the Legion for one last chance, 36,000 of whom have died serving it? How do they merit such accolades as that of American military historian Douglas Porch, who writes, "There can be few, if any, units that have produced such a sustained record of combat performance"?

Over the years, many kinds of men have been Legionnaires. Besides the occasional defrocked bishop or gentleman running from gambling debts, its ranks have included the likes of Sivori Peshkoff, adopted son of Russian writer Maxim Gorky, and another escapee from the Bolshevik revolution, Georgian Prince Dimitri Amilakvari. The Legion's who's who also includes Henri Bourbon-Orleans, the Count of Paris and Pretender to the throne of France, who enlisted as Swiss citizen Henri Orliac, and Prince Napoléon, both of whom joined in 1939 as privates. The Prince of Bavaria, Albert Frederick von Hohenzollern, Prince Louis II of Monaco and Ali Khan, son of the Aga Khan, did tours. The arts were represented by German painter Hans Hartung, American songwriter Cole Porter and Hungarian author Arthur Koestler.

Instead of royalty, today's Legion is getting a lot of eager Slavs, who compose fully one-third of its ranks. They come mainly due to the economic conditions in Eastern Europe and the large number of ex-soldiers looking for jobs. One employment agency in Budapest put an ad in the papers saying the Legion was hiring and proposing to arrange transport to the nearest recruiting station in France. Manpower figures for the 2nd Foreign Airborne, for instance, show the largest contingent by far to be from Central and Eastern Europe, with Poles, Rumanians, Hungarians and Czechs predominant. Also included are a number of former officers from the Red Army. They say a Legion general reviewing new troops one day thought he recognized one of the enlisted men. "What were you before joining the Legion, soldier?" he asked.

"A general, General," the recruit replied, snapping to attention.

In any case, the Legion's perennial appeal remains basically the same. South Korean Kim Leshan, a former parachutist with the Korean Army, told me he joined because he wanted "lots of action and travel, and the money's not bad." Sergeant Jim Morrison, from Cambridge, England, an eight-year Legion veteran who instructs sniper marksmanship, wanted something special in soldiering. "This is the way soldiering should be, highly trained and disciplined," he says. "Give a Legionnaire an order and it's done and done right. Other outfits today are too lax."

Hungarian Oliver Busanszski had a good education and worked in computers until he lost his shirt in the Budapest stock market. "So I bought a ticket to Paris and asked the first policeman I met where I could enlist in the Foreign Legion," he recalls. "My French was so bad I couldn't even understand the drill sergeant when he called my name, and I hated the strict discipline. Sometimes at boot camp I thought I couldn't take it any more. But the other guys helped me and I kept going. Now I want to stay in 15 years and become a sergeant."

Captain Zlatho Sabljic, a 23-year Legion veteran of Croatian origin, fled Yugoslavia when he was 17 to escape communist persecution for his Catholic faith. "When I got to France I had no ID papers, no money, and couldn't speak a word of French," he recalls. "Communist propaganda said the Foreign Legion was a bunch of robbers and other criminals, but I figured that was just another commie lie so I decided to give it a try." Summing up his feelings for the outfit, Sabljic says simply, "The Legion gave me a life."

Becoming a Legionnaire starts at Aubagne, the Legion's headquarters near Marseilles, where new applicants are put through two weeks of rigorous testing. Anonymity is still the Legion way of life, and it attracts more than its share of adventurers, men down on their luck, guys with girl trouble or family problems. Some have been hooked on the Legion ever since they saw Gary Cooper striding across Saharan dunes in the film version of *Beau Geste*. Or since they heard Edith Piaf's famously poignant song about starting over from scratch, "Je ne regrette rien," which she dedicated to the Legion.

Some candidates frankly need the money—though it's only standard French army pay—while others want the experience. "Oddly enough, some Japanese recruits enlist because they think it looks good on their CV," says a Legion captain. "We have information that some are even encouraged by Japanese employers to take a five-year sabbatical with us to get toughened up."

And some, to be sure, are petty delinquents, though the Legion never, ever, says who. "We prefer that they come in with an ID card," says Lieutenant Colonel Patrick Munoz, chief of recruitment. "If not, we push our background checks harder. We have people who can question candidates in their own languages, and they are very good at finding out their pasts. If necessary, we check with national police forces and Interpol." Candidates also take intensive psychological tests, along with medical and physical checks. Sure to be rejected are those guilty of violent crime, child molesters, drug traffickers and addicts.

And women. "Impossible," says General Piquemal flatly. "There has never been a woman in the Legion and there never will be. What sets us apart is our camaraderie; the day you introduce women, that disappears. Besides, we're an assault force and that's not women's work." Being politically correct is definitely not one of the Legion's many traditions.

This being the *Foreign* Legion, French citizens are also legally forbidden to join, unless they are already officers in the regular army. But it's one of the Legion's worst-kept secrets that French recruits enlist all the time under the "declared identity" of Swiss or Canadians. Which might explain why none of the "Canadian" Legionnaires I met, some of whom looked me in the eye and claimed to be from Montreal, had a trace of Canuck accent. In all, an average of 8,000 candidates knock on the Legion's doors annually; only about 1,000 will make it even as far as boot camp. "In the past, when we had five times as many troops and big combat losses, we had to take more questionable recruits," says one officer. "Now we can be choosy. We take only the biggest and the smartest."

The chosen few will be sent to the 4th Foreign Regiment at Castelnaudary in southwestern France. There they get four months of tough boot camp, twice as much training as in the regular French army, several more weeks than the U.S. Marines. "I don't know anything about these men's pasts, where they come from or what they might or might not have done," says Captain Emmanuel Gastine, a lanky, muscular company commander. "All I know is they want to be Legionnaires, and that's what I'm going to make them."

Making them into Legionnaires means days, and many nights, filled with miles-long marches, shooting assault and sniper rifles on the firing range, hand-to-hand combat, bayonet practice, and what seems like hundreds of push-ups a day. Instead of staying in the relative comfort of conventional army barracks like ordinary soldiers, Legion recruits are immediately shipped out to the boondocks where they rough it for a month. This "cohesion phase," a complete break with civilian life, is when recruits bond together. They realize they must count on each other for survival, whatever a new buddy's national origin or mother tongue.

Besides the intensive instruction in basic soldier's tradecraft, they spend weeks learning to march at the Legion's majestic slow cadence—88 steps a minute, vs. the usual 120 for other armies—a pace that gives the impression they are still unconsciously tramping through the Saharan sands where the Legion was born. And while marching, they have drilled into them the Legion's traditional songs: slow, melancholy chants that refer to suffering and solitude as the Legionnaire's lot.

Above all, they discover that they are no longer Polish, Australian, German or Japanese, but citizens of a country called the Legion, with its uncompromising Code of Honor, which states: "Every Legionnaire is your brother in arms, whatever his nationality, his race, or his religion." And there's no doubt left in anyone's mind where his first loyalty lies: all recruits take an oath to serve not France but the Legion itself. "We try to teach recruits the values they don't find in today's way of life," says one of the Legion's top officers. "Things like unselfishness, fidelity, fraternity and generosity toward each other. That's what makes the Legion different."

Once he is awarded his white képi, the new Legionnaire signs his life away for five years of monkish dedication and self-denial that few monasteries, much less armies, require today. He is forbidden to get married. Or have a bank account. Or own a car. Or have a room off-post. Or wear civvies, making it easier for the military police to spot them in town. In return, the Legion gives him a new identity complete, if he wants it, with a new name, birthday and nationality, and the possibility of French citizenship when he completes the contract.

But for many foreign recruits the hardest hurdle is the French language itself. The first phrase they learn is, "Those who can understand French, sit down." Those still standing quickly learn survival French, with every instruction session a language lesson: *"La crosse,"* a sergeant bawls, pointing to a rifle butt. A typical after-hours scene at Legion boot camp is a Swede helping a Japanese with his French, if only so they can go out together to order a beer and chat up a girl. Any time left over is spent ironing the proud uniform, complete with large, red-fringed epaulets and blue cummerbund. The shirt comes in for special treatment: it must have no fewer than 15 precisely placed creases to pass the drill sergeant's inspection.

In today's Legion, officers work hard at developing close rapport with new recruits. "Although we are very firm with our men, this is the last great institution where the Christian ideal of fraternity exists," insists Captain Jean d'Escayrac-Lauture, who traces his family back to the 11th century. "It's true that many of our men are rogues, but most have noble hearts. It's up to us to bring that out." On Camerone Day last April 30, he served his men breakfast in bed and swept out the barracks, an old Legion tradition. And at Christmas he left his wife and children at home and spent it with his company, like the other officers.

But a close relationship between leaders and led doesn't mean the Legion has gone soft. Its discipline is still famous for being tough and swift, though it too has changed with the times. No longer is an officer likely to run his saber through a Legionnaire's chest for murmuring in the ranks, as one did in the 19th century. "They know if they do something wrong, they'll be punished," says one officer. "But then it's forgotten."

After boot camp, training goes on permanently at Legion bases in the South of France and at its far-flung outposts: Djibouti in Africa; Mayotte, a rocky speck in the Indian Ocean; Hao atoll, lost in the Pacific 700 km. from Tahiti; Kourou on the fringe of the Amazon jungle, where Legionnaires guard the launch pad for Europe's Ariane space rocket. It can be mountain climbing or military skiing in the Pyrenees, or commando workouts in the Amazon that push men to their physical and psychological limits. At the Equatorial Jungle Training Center in French Guyana, Legionnaires not only run and swim through devilish obstacle courses, but learn to live on the jungle and manhandle giant boa constrictors.

Legion combat training starts early, ends late, and hones men to a sharp edge, as I saw at the elite 2nd Foreign Airborne Regiment on the Mediterranean island of Corsica. This outfit is the Legion's crème de la crème, priding itself on jumping at lower altitudes, higher speeds and more tightly bunched than any other airborne troops in the world. Briton Christian Jennings, a former member of the 2nd, writes of the regiment's atmosphere: "Everything moved at the double, and there was no sense of slackness or lack of direction. The camp was impeccably tidy, the insides of the buildings spotlessly clean with everything in place, and underneath the differences of rank was the shared feeling of belonging to an elite regiment."

At dawn one morning I was packed in with 80 troops in full combat gear, heavy backpacks and two parachutes aboard a noisy, cavernous military transport. When the jump master raised his arms like an orchestra conductor, columns of men on both sides of the plane sprang up, hooked their static lines to overhead cables, and crowded toward the open rear doors. Suddenly the plane was over the drop zone. A red signal light changed to green, a piercing klaxon shrieked, and the assistant jumpmasters at each door began screaming "Go! Go! Go!" The hard-charging Legionnaires piled out almost on top of each other at dizzying speed—two per second according to my stopwatch. After landing they gathered up their chutes, reassembled on the double, and got into combat formation.

We climbed to 8,500 feet and the Legion's elite commando jumpers in fluorescent red helmets repeated the operation with "flying wings." As I watched, they went into free fall for long, breathtaking seconds before popping their chutes. Circling above the drop zone, deftly controlling direction and speed, they landed on a small bull's-eye in the middle of the zone. "On a commando operation we can drift like that for miles into enemy territory at night without being seen or heard," explained their chief, Captain Benoit Desmeulles.

After landing, I drove to a rugged, remote area in the shadow of the island's hulking, 6,000-foot Monte Rosso peak. There a squad of Legionnaires, uniforms dark with sweat, was practicing patrol tactics over rough terrain. Faces streaked with green and brown grease paint, helmets and rifles camouflaged with branches, they dived to take cover when "enemy" fire crackled just ahead. Suddenly a hand grenade came out of nowhere and landed beside the point man. He was reaching down to throw it back when it exploded—covering him with white flour. "You're lucky that was a practice grenade," his sergeant bellowed. "They only throw grenades back at the enemy in war movies, you dummy. In real combat you hit the ground as far away as you can jump." After hours of training in the thorny scrub, the tired squad spent the night marching back to camp with weapons and full back-packs.

Today's Legion professionals are a far cry from the original ragtag bunch of scoundrels on the run from the law. Their initial reputation grew up after the Foreign Legion was created by French King Louis Philippe in 1831 to conquer new colonies in Africa. It was, after all, much easier politically to send foreigners out to get shot at by ungrateful natives than the sons of French *mamans* (and it still is). For decades it slogged through the deserts and jungles of France's colonial empire, often manned by the dregs of society thanks to the Legion's policy of enlisting all comers, no questions asked. Thieves and drunks, anonymous adventurers, and romantic aristocrats who wanted to forget their pasts, they took on new names and new lives in return for fighting the dirtiest of wars. They weren't always covered with glory. In 1842 the disgusted French governor-general of Algeria wrote in a report, "They fight badly, they march badly, they desert often."

But slowly the Legion found itself. Sent to Mexico in 1863 to prop up the shaky government of Emperor Maximilian, a French puppet, the Legion's rascally rabble began to show the mettle that would set them apart among the world's fighting forces. When a unit of 65 men led by Captain Jean Danjou was attacked on April 30 by a wave of 2,000 Mexican troops, they held out all day in a dilapidated hacienda in the village of Camerone. Rather than surrender, the last five standing fixed bayonets and charged. "These are not men," the awed Mexican commander exclaimed, "but demons!" A legend was born.

The Legion would go on to create the longest combat record of any elite unit in modern history. In the First World War, it garnered more distinguished service citations than any other regiment. This was the great period of American enlistment. So many U.S. citizens joined that the Legion's 1st Regiment was practically an American outfit. They were a mixed lot: there was Bob Scanlon, a black boxer from Ohio, and Charles Sweeney fresh out of West Point. David King, Victor Chapman and Andrew Champollion were Harvard graduates, Algernon Sartoris was a grandson of Ulysses S. Grant. Then there was Alan Seeger, a poet who joined the Legion in 1914 and was killed at Belloy-en-Santerre on July 4, 1916, at the age of 28. His poem, "I have a rendezvous with death," was found on his body. Today the church bell that rings out over the village is a commemorative gift from Seeger's family.

Proving the validity of *Legio Patria Nostra*, many German Legionnaires unhesitatingly fought against Germany in the Second World War. The Legion lost nearly 9,000 men and carried out spectacular actions from Narvik, Norway, to Bir Hakeim in Libya. But as France's colonial era wound down, the Legion, which had served for 72 years in Indochina, found itself tragically trapped at Dien Bien Phu in May 1954. Besieged by the communist Viet Minh, Legionnaires held out for 56 days, often calling for their artillery to pound their own positions as human waves swarmed over them. When it was over, the decimated Legion unit had suffered more than 10,000 casualties. Another heroic legend was born.

On the last day of my visit to the 2nd Foreign Airborne I was studying a display of Legion mementos—battle flags, bullet-holed helmets, the inevitable paintings and photos of glorious but tragic last stands at Camerone and Dien Bien Phu—laid out in a small, carefully composed museum near the post entrance. The pitiless Corsican sun beat down on the immaculate parade ground. Squads of Legionnaires in green berets marched by, singing their strange, dirge-like marching songs. I turned to Captain Yann Talboudel, a graduate of France's Saint Cyr military academy who requested Legion duty "because of its mystique, and because it's the most professional outfit in the world." "Camerone, Dien Bien Phu," I mused aloud. "It's funny how the Legion celebrates its defeats instead of its victories." He reflected a moment. "Yes, but those are the most sacred actions for us," he replied thoughtfully. "They symbolize our ideals of maximum effort and ultimate sacrifice."

Update: *The Foreign Legion keeps on doing its unique job, recently protecting the Ivory Coast capital of Abidjan, and the 20,000 French nationals living there, from invading rebels. And it still gets high ratings from its peers, like that other elite fighting outfit, the U.S. Marine Corps, whose official* Gazette *concluded an article, "No combat unit surpasses the Legion in wartime exploits, professionalism, and courage." But not even the Legion wins them all. Despite General Piquemal's warning that "Women would mean the end of the Legion," the French government, in an access of misguided political correctness, decreed in 2000 that the Legion must open its ranks to females. Somehow, no woman has yet become a combat Legionnaire.*

The Divine Sarah

Context: *She was the first international superstar, dazzling audiences in Europe and America as she pioneered the cult of personality. As the most adulated and celebrated woman of the Victorian era, Sarah Bernhardt during her prodigious 62-year career gave a new definition to the term* la gloire.

It was the kind of surreal mob scene New York reserves for showbiz celebs, with frenzied fans gathered at the stage door for a glimpse of the famous foreign star. When she finally appeared, late after 29 curtain calls, they went wild. Everyone was shouting to her, reaching for her, trying to snip a lock of her hair or snatch an ostrich plume from her hat. One wild-eyed woman tore a gold brooch from her own coat and nearly knocked her down pinning it on her. Men pulled their cuffs out of their sleeves and noisily begged her to autograph them. A hysterical girl brandished an autograph book, then realized her pen was out of ink; she plunged her teeth into her own wrist and dipped the instrument in her blood. With the mob out of hand, the frightened star beat a retreat back to the theater. She tore off her hat, veil and chinchilla cloak, put them on her sister, and sent her out to impersonate her while she slipped out by another door.

It could have been yesterday's rock star event. But it was 1880 and the star was Sarah Bernhardt, The Divine, The Eighth Wonder of the World, and the most celebrated woman of the Victorian era besides—and maybe including—Queen Victoria herself. Arguably the first international entertainment icon, The Bernhardt, as Americans called her, personified stardom carried to outsize, mythical proportions; when *Variety* ran a story on the 100 top stars of the 20th century, she was number one on the list as "the first superstar-diva."

It is difficult today to imagine the spell she cast over admirers as different as Sigmund Freud, who kept a photo of her in his waiting room, and philosopher William James, who called her "the most race-horsey, high-mettled human being I've ever seen." Mark Twain observed there were five kinds of actresses: bad, fair, good, great—"and then there is Sarah Bernhardt."

Her myth traveled throughout the pre-cinema, pre-television world via paintings, photos, posters and newspaper stories. One biographer calculates that if pasted end-to-end, the articles about her during her 62-year career from 1861 to 1923 would stretch around the earth, while a pile of her printed photos would reach the top of the Eiffel Tower. She promoted that myth with panache, eccentric behavior and in-your-face attitude. She made sure everyone knew that she slept in a coffin. And when an American reporter exclaimed during an interview, "Why, New York didn't give Dom Pedro of Brazil such an ovation!" she purred, "Yes, but he was only an emperor."

Despite her modest origins, Madame Sarah wasn't very impressed by emperors and their ilk. Many had been at her feet—and even closer, with Britain's Prince of Wales a very dear friend indeed, and her only son fathered by Belgian Prince Henri de Ligne. Europe's crowned heads visited her backstage, and she gave command performances in their palaces. Austrian Emperor Franz Joseph placed an antique cameo necklace around her neck, while Archduke Friedrich insisted she stay at one of his palaces while in Vienna. Italy's King Umberto gave her an exquisite Venetian fan, Spain's King Alfonso XII a diamond brooch, France's Emperor Louis-Napoléon a magnificent pin with the imperial initials in diamonds. In Saint Petersburg, where they ran a red carpet over the snow to the stage door, Czar Alexander III called on her after a command performance at the Winter Palace. As she was making a deep curtsy, he stopped her: "No, Madame," he ordered, "it is I who must bow to you." And so he did before his entire Court.

The Divine continues to fascinate. A New York theater recently presented *The Divine Trilogy of Sarah Bernhardt*, while Connie Clark, an actress based in North Carolina, has done her one-woman show, *Sarah*, tracing her life and career, at the Lincoln Center, summer theaters, and in Europe. Paris paid homage to her this year with a sumptuous exhibit at the ornate old Bibliothèque Nationale, just a short walk down Rue de Richelieu from the Comédie Française theater where she starred and stormed.

The show presented paintings, costumes, playbills and photos recalling her life, loves, and many of the 125 plays she acted in. There were pearl-covered, floor-length gowns, a spectacular pectoral collar and belt of stage turquoise she wore in *Cleopatra*, an imposing faux diamond necklace from her most famous role, the repentant, languishing courtesan Marguerite in *La Dame aux Camélias* (known oddly in America as *Camille*, though there is no character by that name in it). On the walls were flowing Art Nouveau posters of her by Alphonse Mucha. Recordings from 1906 of her vibrato voice gave a faint idea of the dramatic power and intensity of her delivery. "She was really the first media star of our era," says Noelle Guibert, director of the Bibliothèque's Department of Theater Arts, who curated the show. "She incarnated the fantasies of the Belle Epoque. She was the one everybody admired, the one to whom they attributed the wildest passions, eccentricities and perversions."

Quite a symbolic load to bear for a pathologically skinny girl whom doctors expected to die before 20. Henriette-Rosine Bernard was born on October 23, 1844, in Paris, the illegitimate daughter of a Dutch Jewish woman of dubious morals from Amsterdam and an unknown, probably French, father. She was an emotionally unstable, sickly child who seemed to run a constant temperature and frequently spat up blood. Doctors diagnosed a wasting disease like tuberculosis and prescribed snail soup for strength.

Her mother Julie, a high-flying courtesan, had little time for her. She left Sarah with a succession of nurses until sending her to a girls' school in suburban Paris, where she learned to read and write and throw memorable tantrums. After that it was a convent school in Versailles, where her tempestuous, headstrong behavior drove the nuns to distraction. Altogether she received only six years of formal education. She tells us in her memoirs, *My Double Life*, an artful mix of fact and mythmaking, that when she was nine she adopted her spunky lifelong motto, *"Quand Même,"* meaning in spite of everything. She had jumped over a wide ditch on a dare, landing painfully on her face and spraining a wrist. "I'll do it again if they dare me," the willful child screamed through tears at her mother and aunt as they doctored her. "And I'll do whatever I want all my life!" Sighed the aunt prophetically, *"Quelle enfant terrible!"*

At 15 she overheard doctors telling her mother that she had only a few years to live. Death became an obsession, and she asked for a pretty coffin so she could get used to it. (The resulting rosewood and satin model became one of the stage props in her life; countless postcard photos of her reclining dramatically in the flower-strewn casket were sold in Europe and America.) About this time, too, the influential Duc de Morny, one of Julie's wealthy lovers and Emperor Napoléon III's half brother, advised the family to send the *enfant terrible* to the Paris Conservatory of Music and Drama. When Morny got her a box seat at the Comédie Francaise, France's prestigious national theater, Sarah sobbed uncontrollably at the heroine's plight. That did it: the girl who would become the last of the great Romantic actresses was hooked on the theater.

She threw herself into her lessons at the Conservatory, then considered the world's finest drama school, even if she later mocked it in her memoirs. "We learned to walk on stage with the nobility and solemnity of camels," she recalled mischievously. She also rattled off senseless elocution lessons and learned to sit with body language that said "Speak, Sir." It was solid training, but mostly a bore for Sarah, who always relied on her instincts and raw emotion for effect. "I worked hard at forgetting it all," she wrote later, "nothing is so useless."

Still, it got her into the august Comédie Francaise—with a little more pull from Morny—at the age of 18. Her first performance on August 11, 1862, was nearly a catastrophe due to a bad case of teeth-chattering stage fright, which would nag her all her life. The critics were indulgent but unimpressed. "Mademoiselle Bernhardt...is a tall, attractive young woman with a slender waist and most pleasing face," wrote one. "She carries herself well and pronounces her words with perfect clarity. That is all that can be said for the moment."

In any case, the high-strung, rebellious young woman felt uncomfortable among the stuffed shirts of the French theater establishment. Within a year she was fired for slapping a leading lady who had been rude to the younger sister Sarah doted on, Régine.

Out of work except for occasional roles, Sarah turned to her mother's trade to make ends meet. It was a time when "actress" was virtually synonymous with courtesan/kept woman, and the toffs expected their favors as a right. One day, for example, the Prince de Joinville, Emperor Louis-Philippe's son, sent a cryptic note to Rachel, one of France's great leading ladies: "Where? When? How much?" She zinged back a succinct, practiced reply: "Your place. This evening. No charge."

In 1864, after a particularly bad performance in a second-rate play, Sarah took off for Brussels. There she had an affair with Prince Henri de Ligne, got pregnant, and gave birth to a son she named Maurice, whom she adored and indulged the rest of her life. If anyone had the bad taste to enquire about his paternity, she would assume a pensive pose and reply evenly that she could never make up her mind whether it was Prime Minister Léon Gambetta, Victor Hugo, or General Georges Boulanger.

Two years later her slow, erratic acting career took a turn for the better when she joined Paris's Left Bank Théatre de l'Odéon. There she honed what would become her trademark technique: extravagant, florid acting in the grand style. Favoring improbable, whole-hearted, three-hanky drama, she became the consummate tragedienne, running the emotional gamut of tigerish passion, melting seduction, excruciating loss and unbearable sorrow.

Moving with feline grace, she didn't walk across the stage, she glided. Something as simple as descending a staircase she transformed into magic: "It was as though she remained immobile and the staircase turned around her," marveled French writer Jules Renard. Her very curtain calls were worth the price of admission. Instead of bowing, she would stand with hands clasped under her chin or palms on cheeks, panting with exhaustion, then stretch her arms straight out to the public as if to embrace the house with the last of her strength.

Such technique compensated for being no great beauty. Her hair was hopeless, a frizzy, unruly, reddish-blonde mop. She hid her low brow beneath a tumble of curls, which also had the advantage of enlarging her small eyes. And in a day when the cannons of beauty called for opulent, Rubensesque women, she was not only thin, she was skeletal—"A Madonna's head stuck on a broomstick," as the writer Alexandre Dumas *fils* called her. She never needed an umbrella, boulevard wits said, she was so skinny she could walk between the raindrops. "An empty carriage pulled up at the stage door and Sarah Bernhardt got out," went one caricature.

It was at the Odéon that a star was born on the evening of January 16, 1872, when she played the love-stricken Queen of Spain in Victor Hugo's *Ruy Blas*. Backstage visitors included HRH the Prince of Wales, who stepped aside respectfully when the white-maned, bewhiskered author, by then a French monument, entered, dropped to one knee, kissed Sarah's hand and murmured "*Merci, merci.*" Outside a cheering crowd filled the streets, while excited students unhitched the horses from her carriage and pulled it themselves, shouting "Make way for our Sarah!"

Shortly thereafter the Comédie Française invited her back. At first she played only minor parts in the House of Molière and again chafed under rules that rotated leading roles, operated on strict bureaucratic seniority and permitted no stars—a stifling atmosphere for an actress with her temperament. As playwright Maurice Rostand said, she could be "unjust, angry, capricious, unbearable, contradictory, provocative, rebellious, intransigent." She threw so many tantrums, slammed so many doors that the theater's exasperated director called her *Mademoiselle Révolte*. Once during rehearsal in which she played a supporting role, he decided not to shine a spotlight on her for a moonlight scene because the leading lady was supposed to get the moonlight. "I won't act without the moon!" she shrieked. "I want my moon!" They did the play with *two* moons.

But even French bureaucracy could not prevent Madame Sarah's star quality from shining in another Hugo tragedy, *Hernani,* in which she played a Castilian noblewoman who loves the bandit Hernani and takes poison with him at the end. So moved was Hugo this time that he sent her a box with a note in it next day. "Madame," he wrote, "when the public, touched and enchanted by you, applauded, I wept. This tear that you caused me to shed is yours. I place it at your feet." The tear in question was a single perfect diamond on a gold bracelet.

Hugo loved what he termed her golden voice. Not powerful or deep, it was a highly musical voice that writers vied to describe: "As sonorous as pure crystal," wrote Alphonse Daudet, while Jules Lemaitre called it "a caress that strokes you like fingers, so pure, so tender, so harmonious." British man of letters Maurice Baring, who saw Sarah act dozens of times over 20 years, rhapsodized that it was "a symphony of golden flutes and muted strings; silver dawn lit by lambent lightnings, soft stars and a clear-cut crescent moon."

But beyond that, the lady could really *act.* "Acting is all internal, but must be externalized," she said, building her characters from the inside out and practicing The Method long before Stanislavsky and the Actors Studio got credit for it. As a young woman she could transform herself into an 80-year-old crone, simulating blindness by showing only the whites of her eyes. As a 56-year-old grandmother, she could convincingly play the 20-year-old Duke of Reichstadt, Napoléon's consumptive son, dying in the last act "as angels would die if they were allowed to," said one critic. And in *Joan of Arc,* when the judge demanded her age, she invariably brought the house down when she deliberately turned to face the audience, who knew she was 65, and declared triumphantly, "Nineteen!"

Both her memory and stagecraft were the stuff of legends. She could memorize a part merely by reading it through four times, blocking out her moves as she went; after the fifth reading she had it down pat, and performed without a prompter. When playing Cleopatra, she often used a real snake for the final scene. And she captivated audiences at *La Tosca* with her stage business of placing lighted candlesticks around the body of Scarpia and a crucifix on his chest after stabbing him, then slowly backing off in horror, her gown's long train trailing along the stage until the curtain fell. (It was her acting that inspired Puccini to compose his opera based on the play.) She bewitched many, including English novelist D.H. Lawrence. "Take care about going to see Bernhardt," he warned. "Her winsome, sweet, playful ways… her terrible panther cries…and the despair and death. It is too much in one evening."

Inevitably the time came for her to decide whether to stay in safe repertory at the national theater with its stilted acting style, or try an independent career. She resigned from the Comédie Francaise in 1880, formed her own troupe and headed to London's Gaiety Theater to begin her life as an international star. It was the first stop on foreign tours that would, over the next 40 years, take her throughout Europe from Britain to Greece, Spain to Russia, and to North and South America.

After London, where rumors were rife—she was said to hold a Witches' Sabbath certain nights, smoke cigars in the morning, take boxing lessons, even dress in men's clothes—Sarah sailed for New York for a six-month tour. She landed on October 27, 1880 amid all the fanfare her canny impresario for the tour, Edward Jarrett, could muster with spicy advance publicity, perhaps the first campaign to deliberately create an international star. The public was dying to learn more about The Bernhardt, who they believed had had four illegitimate sons, one by the Czar of Russia, and had seduced every crowned head in Europe, not to mention the Pope.

Her first New York performance, *Adrienne Lecouvreur* at Booth's Theater, was declared off-limits to children because it dealt with an unmarried actress's affair with a rakish aristocrat. Despite, or perhaps because of that, she played to a packed house that broke into roaring applause after Adrienne died in the final scene, and went on for 27 curtain calls. It was at Booth's that same month of November 1880 that she created her signature role, Marguerite Gauthier in *La Dame aux Caméllias* by Dumas *fils*, that for the next 45 years she would play more than 3,000 times all over the world. On a later U.S. tour, the New York *Globe* confirmed the play's endless popularity in a piece of doggerel entitled "Boo Hoo": "Who's done *Camille* in ev'ry clime/From here to Zanzibar,/And trickled briny tears enough/To float a man-o'-war?" it asked. "Why Bernhardt The Divine!" And indeed, railway magnate William Henry Vanderbilt attended every one of her performances that season, weeping openly into a large handkerchief. When Sarah returned to France, he gave it to her as a souvenir.

Then it was on to Boston. Proud of its open-minded appreciation of culture, the city welcomed her more warmly than New York. The critics were ecstatic: "Before such perfection, analysis is impossible," wrote one. Sarah returned the feeling. "Boston belongs to women," she declared. "They are in the majority there, they are intelligently puritan, and gracefully independent."

After Chicago, where the bishop conveniently thundered against her, she boarded the Sarah Bernhardt Special for a grueling series of 156 appearances in 50 cities and towns from New Orleans and Mobile to Toledo and Buffalo. She rode in her own private Palace Car with walls of inlay wood, overhead brass gas lamps, Turkish carpeting, lounge area with sofas, upright piano and potted palms. The dining room table seated 10 and was laid with linen and china with her *Quand Même* crest. Two cooks prepared meals. On another tour, in Louisiana, she bought a small alligator she named Ali-Gaga, which made itself comfortable beneath her bedcovers at night. It finally died, they say, from too much champagne.

Americans fell in love with Sarah, and vice versa. "I adore this country, where women reign," she said. In eight more tours—four of them billed as "The Farewell Tour of Mme. Sarah Bernhardt"—she crisscrossed the country. She did *Camille* in huge tents in Missouri and Texas, cornstalk stubble tearing the dresses of women spectators. At one Texas stop a cowboy rode up and asked for a seat. None was available until he pulled his six-shooter. Entering the tent, he drawled in passing, "Say, what does this Bernhardt gal do anyway, sing or dance?"

An interesting change of image from her own self-description as "that anxious, strange, morbid being named Sarah Bernhardt." At home in her Paris townhouse on Boulevard Péreire, her furnishings included a skull on her desk and an anatomical skeleton named Lazarus, plus the famous coffin in which she often studied her roles and, gossips said, received her lovers. She liked to welcome other visitors dressed in a long white gown and reclining on a cushion-strewn divan on a raised platform, canopied with oriental hangings supported by velvet-covered spears. She kept a menagerie that could include her enormous wolfhound Osman, a friendly lynx on a leash, a baby tigress named Minette, and a tame lion until it started smelling too bad. Visitors never knew what to expect. When Alexandre Dumas *fils* called one day to show Sarah a new play he had just written, a pet puma calmly devoured his straw hat.

None of which deterred her devoted admirers, known as *sarahdoteurs*, from flocking to her. Her Court, as she called them collectively, ranged from writers like Hugo, Zola, Dumas, Flaubert, D'Annunzio and Oscar Wilde, who wrote the play *Salome* especially for her, to statesmen like Gambetta, the Prince of Wales, U.S. Ambassador Myron T. Herrick, and Theodore Roosevelt. She could be very funny, often mimicking some of them wickedly, and regaling them with catty remarks. Of an actress who tried to play the male lead she had made her own in *L'Aiglon*, she said, "The poor dear isn't man enough to make us forget she's a woman, and not woman enough to be appealing."

That wasn't her problem. Sarah played some 25 male parts, from Prince Charming to Cyrano de Bergerac, Judas and, most controversially, Hamlet. She liked men's roles, she said, because they were generally more tormented and intellectual than women's. She first did Hamlet in a four-hour French translation in May 1899, doing the "To be or not to be" soliloquy sitting down. It was a hit in Paris, but reaction in London was predictably mixed when she took it there. British wit Max Beerbohm ironically called it "Hamlet, Princess of Denmark," finding her unbelievable as a man, but admitting she did it with class. Maurice Baring disagreed, finding her Hamlet "natural, easy, lifelike and princely."

Certainly she had courage enough for several men. When Jewish Army Captain Alfred Dreyfus was unjustly sentenced to Devil's Island in 1894 on trumped-up, anti-Semitic charges of treason, Sarah took his side against most French popular opinion. Though many of her friends and her son Maurice stopped talking to her, she helped persuade Emile Zola to write his famous *J'Accuse* article that turned the tide in Dreyfus's favor.

And when spreading gangrene struck her right leg in 1915 as a result of painful, longstanding osteoarthritis of the knee, she pleaded with two doctors to amputate it, threatening to shoot herself in the knee if they refused. They declined because she was 71 and suffering from chronic uremia. Finally a surgeon agreed, and she hummed the Marseillaise as she was wheeled down the hospital corridor. Later she tried an artificial leg but found it too cumbersome. Also refusing to use a wheel chair, she opted for a specially designed litter chair in Louis XV style with gilt carving, and was carried around like a Byzantine princess. She altered her stage business so actors were gathered around her, seated, and kept on acting. For ovations she stood on one leg, held on to a piece of furniture, and gestured with one arm.

Shortly after the amputation, she visited the WWI front lines near Verdun to perform for French troops in mess tents, hospital wards, open market places and ramshackle barns. Propped in a shabby armchair, she recited a patriotic piece to war-dazed men fresh from the trenches. When she ended with a rousing *"Aux armes!"* clutching the French tricolor, they rose cheering and sobbing. "The way she ignored her handicap was beautiful," wrote an actress who accompanied her. "A victory of the spirit over the failing flesh."

Despite failing flesh, Sarah flung herself into silent movies, making eight in her waning years, including her biggest hit, *Queen Elizabeth.* She was shooting a film on location in her townhouse for an American producer in the spring of 1923 when she collapsed. She died in the arms of Maurice on March 26 at the age of 78. That evening all Paris theaters observed two minutes of silence. Parisians lined the streets as her funeral procession wound its way to Père Lachaise cemetery, where Molière and her admirers Marcel Proust and Oscar Wilde were buried. There she was interred in the rosewood coffin. In contrast to the famous cemetery's ornate tombs with handsome sculptures and long inscriptions, only two words were deemed worthy to decorate the simple granite tomb of The Divine: Sarah Bernhardt.

Update: *More than 75 years after her death, Bernhardt is still virtually alive in France. A recent revival of the play* Sarah *about her writing and autobiography got rave reviews. Every production of Racine's* Phèdre *is inevitably compared with how Bernhardt would have done it, and new biographies of her continue to appear. The small fortress ("Inaccessible, uninhabitable, uncomfortable and therefore enchanting" as she called it) that was her summer residence on the Breton island of Belle-Ile, and which is visited by tens of thousands yearly, is now being restored by the government as a historical monument. A gilded crown she wore in a play written for her by Edmond Rostand was auctioned off in 2004 for $22,500.*

3. La Bouffe

Champagne: The Brilliant Soul of France

Context : *If much about a people's national character is revealed by their approach to food, then* La France Eternelle *as reflected in its cuisine has traditionally been complicated, meticulous, and epicurean. In some ways that approach to life culminates in champagne. It is only white wine with bubbles, but champagne, like France itself, manages to be more than the sum of its parts and attain mythical status. It can rightly be called the country's national drink, one that, Voltaire believed, "Reflects the brilliant soul of France."*

The French may slyly have invented champagne to bring out national characteristics, just as it gradually reveals an individual's hidden personality traits. The British and the Italians, for example, though they would seem to have little else in common, drink it just for the fun of it. The careful Swiss, on the other hand, are reputed to drink it only with a mistress. The prudent Dutch take it only a little at a time. Americans, despite rumors of changing mores and tastes, still have it only on special occasions. The French, predictably, drink it more than anybody.

In vino veritas indeed, but this is not just any *vino*. It is the most lovingly tended, the most intensely scrutinized, the most thoroughly codified, the most famous and, *naturellement,* the most expensive wine in the world. It is also the most universally appreciated and quite possibly the least understood.

Of the millions of bottles of bubbly produced annually in the legally defined vineyards of France's Champagne district, the French buy one-and-a-half bottles for every man, woman and child among them before letting the rest go to export. That probably says more about them than any displays of mulishness at international conference tables. But a look at who takes the rest gives a revealing picture of the world as seen through a champagne glass. "Champagne is a sort of *baromètre du bonheur*, a barometer of happiness," says Robert-Jean de Voguë, head of

Moët et Chandon, France's biggest producer. "When things are going well, sales always go up. It's a universal sign of good times."

Thus despite periodic news reports that their island is sinking into a sea of economic and political chaos, the British generally pop more corks than anyone outside France. And coming up fast on the giggling Brits are those hardy survivors of another often-troubled country, the Italians, even though it costs far more than their own *spumanti*. "They have a bottle whenever they feel like one," explains a spokesman for the Comité Interprofessionnel du Vin de Champagne (CIVC), the champagne makers' organization in Epernay, 87 miles east of Paris. "They don't worry about the pleasure-seeking image of champagne, unlike the Swiss. In Geneva, for example, a bottle of champagne on a restaurant table is usually taken as a sign that a man is with his mistress, not his wife. The Dutch are uptight about champagne too, only ordering a glass at a time so no one will see the bottle." And Americans? "For them it's only a wine to drink on big occasions like weddings. It doesn't occur to them to drink it sheerly for the pleasure."

With millions of bottles of this subversive liquid lubrifying the world's social relations, the temptation is strong to paraphrase Dorothy Parker: If all the girls who drank champagne were laid end to end.... The days are past, alas, when amorous gentlemen quaffed it from milady's slipper. But the atmosphere of happy expectation engendered by the sharp pop of a champagne cork and a gush of silvery foam still works its magic. As an executive at the great old house of Veuve Cliquot Ponsardin once told me over a bottle of perfectly acceptable *brut*, "Let's face it, for most people champagne means an orgy. It has no taste for them, really. What they like about it is an ambiance, a feeling of gaiety." Women seem especially attracted to it, perhaps because it connotes wealth and well-being, perhaps because it is a generally accepted pretext for doing whatever comes to mind, and perhaps because, as Madame de Pompadour is said to have observed, champagne is "the only wine that leaves a woman beautiful after drinking it."

The wine of the ancient Province of Champagne has been cultivated from time immemorial. Caesar's legions were fond of it until A.D. 92 when Emperor Domitian ordered the vines destroyed out of fear that they might compete with Italian wines, and perhaps to keep his troops sober up on the Gallic frontier. Fortunately the wise Emperor Probus abolished this decree two centuries later, to the undisguised delight of everyone: "It was a wonderful sight," wrote a contemporary historian, "to see the dwellers on these slopes, drunk with joy, consecrating them with religious rites to the God of Wine."

Troubadours sang of champagne in the middle ages, and it became a court favorite. Reims, capital of Champagne, was also the royal city of France where kings were crowned. A 16th-century French physician observed in a treatise that Champagne wine was "subtle and delicate, with a taste which is extremely agreeable to the palate; it is the wine par excellence for kings, princes, and great lords." Pope Leo X, Charles V, François I, Henry VIII of England and Henry IV of France all owned vineyards in Champagne to insure a steady supply.

At that time and until the early 18th century, champagne was mostly a still wine, albeit with a mystifying propensity to undergo a frothy second fermentation in early spring. The winemaking friars at the Benedictine abbey at Hautvillers, near Reims, studied this diabolical *vin diable* that mischievously popped corks almost as soon as bottles were filled. They tinkered until they found how to control the second fermentation and to produce a consistently excellent wine by blending the *crus*, or growths, from several different vineyards.

Many friars joined in the research, but Dom Pierre Pérignon generally gets credit today for champagne's successful formula, thanks largely to the special bottle named for him and that James Bond, according to his official biographer, so relished. The first champagne houses, Ruinart, Chanoine and Moet et Chandon, were founded around 1730. The bubbling wine's popularity grew apace, some seeing it as the quintessentially French drink. Voltaire, for one, wrote, "This wine where sparkling bubbles dance/Reflects the brilliant soul of France."

It's important to define exactly what we mean by champagne. Sparkling wines are made in nearly every country where grapes are grown. It's no trick to put bubbles into wine, either by a second fermentation in the bottle as in France, or by inducing one while the wine is still in vats, or even by simply injecting still wine with a shot of carbon dioxide gas. The distinction between true champagne and its imitators, therefore, is one of authenticity. The real thing is made from special grapes grown in a special place, using special techniques. With vintners from New York to California and Japan to Spain making sparkling wines and frequently calling them champagne, this may sound like an exercise in semantics or arrant snobbery, or both. It is neither.

Wine, any sort of wine, is basically the product of a fortuitous fusing of soil and climate. Its distinctive personality is formed by the earth that nourishes the vines, the amount of moisture that wets them, the degree of sunshine that warms them. For elementary ecological reasons, these conditions cannot be duplicated at two different spots on the globe.

Champagne's soil and climate are special indeed. The only grapes permitted by law, hearty black Pinot Noir and Pinot Meunier and elegant white Chardonnay, grow on gently undulating slopes of solid chalk formed by deposits of sea shells during the Tertiary Era a hundred million years ago. The vines' roots plunge through the thin layer of soil, often no more than eight to 20 inches thick, and penetrate 10 to 12 feet into the chalk bed. The chalk gives champagne its light, dry, slightly acid character; it also provides excellent drainage for the roots and reflects the sun's warmth back on the vines. The latter function is especially important here, for these are France's northernmost vineyards. Annual mean temperature is 50 degrees F., the absolute minimum required for vine cultivation.

Add to this unique ecological setting a code of rules that only a French bureaucrat could lovingly conceive—length of vines, maximum quantity of juice from each pressing, alcohol content, duration of aging—and you have the framework for a special wine. But champagne's pedigree also includes the people who make it.

The 16,500-odd growers of champagne grapes cultivate an average of two to three acres each, a scale more akin to backyard gardening than big-time agribusiness. The entire 54,000 acres now planted, about 70 percent of the champagne zone defined by law in 1927, comprise only one percent of all France's vineyards. But these tiny parcels of land bordering the somnolent Marne River are among the most valuable farmland on earth: one pound of genuine champagne grapes is worth up to 10 times as much as grapes from most other French vineyards. Champagne growers are reputedly the most prosperous *vignerons* in the country, a reputation many reinforce by tooling along vineyard roads between villages with delightfully suggestive names like Bouzy and Dizy in luxury cars.

From March, when he does the first close pruning of an average 4,000 vines per acre, until the harvest in late September, the grower painstakingly nurtures, protects and nurses his crop with one eye on the weather and the other on the all-governing Law of 1927. He is the first of a series of skilled workers who will care for the embryonic wine during the critical period from flowering bud to finished bottle. Champagne is, in economic jargon, the most labor intensive of all wines, which explains, along with its mythic status, its high cost in wine shops.

Once the harvest is in—an operation that mobilizes every able-bodied citizen in the 300-odd classified villages of the district plus a goodly number of miners from the coal mines of Lorraine who come over to help—the bunches are gone over one by one to eliminate unripe or damaged grapes before loading them into the press. By law, again, exactly 8,800 pounds of grapes go into each pressing, which may yield no more than 704 gallons of must. The tag-end of the pressing is considered unworthy of champagne and may be used only for other products such as distilled *marc*. The must is run off quickly into vats to avoid contact with the skins, so that a white wine results from black grapes.

At this point enter the aristocracy of the Champagne district, the roughly 145 major champagne houses, or shippers, which buy most of their wine from the growers and ferment it in their own Gargantuan vats of glass-lined concrete or stainless steel. (Oaken casks, while considerably more charming and folkloric, are awkward in handling great quantities and have been abandoned today by all but a few arch-traditionalists such as Krug and Bollinger.) Even the giants with multi-million-bottle production lines own only a small fraction of the vineyards necessary for their output. This tempts many *vignerons* to make and sell champagne under their own labels. As a result, there are in fact more than 1,000 brands of champagne on the market, accounting for over one-third of sales in France. Their small-scale production, while often excellent, is not exported.

After a few weeks of tumultuous, boiling fermentation in winter rooms warmed to around 75 degrees F., the wine settles down. Then begins the unique and crucial rite in champagne making, the "marriage" or blending of crus. Other great wines such as Bordeaux and Burgundies are the product of a single vineyard; the glory of champagne is that it is a subtle mixture of wines from up to 50 different vineyards of the Champagne district.

The setting is invariably the same. In February or March a few gentlemen gather in a neat, laboratory-like room where everything—walls, ceiling, floor, tabletops—is white. After an exchange of pleasantries they turn gravely to a long table where dark green bottles and half-filled, tulip-shaped glasses are waiting. They raise the glasses, look closely at the pale golden liquid to check its color (hence the absence of any other color in the room), sniff it thoughtfully and then sip with a gurgling sound. After a moment they spit it into a ceramic or stone basin, scribble their reflections on a note pad, and turn to another glass. The wine at this stage is rough and bitter, but these men, usually the head of the house with a few close assistants, and the *chef de cave*, can predict what it will taste like with three years of aging.

After several mornings of this (taste buds are sharper before lunch), they draw up a formula for mixing the crus so that the lightness of one enhances the body of another, one's sweetness counters another's acidity, high alcohol content boosts weakness. Normally "reserve" wines from previous years will be blended in to obtain exactly the right *cuvée*; the characteristic personality of each house will be faithfully reflected year after year in this mix. Some years, no reserve wine will go into the formula. All the crus will be from that year's harvest—a vintage bottle.

The question of vintages goes to the heart of many misunderstandings about champagne. Opinions differ even within the industry itself about them. For if the peculiar genius of champagne lies in its being a blend to achieve great consistency, what's the point of claiming that one year is better than another?

"I would be in favor of doing away altogether with vintages," says Rémi Krug, the handsome young scion of the champagne house of the same name in Reims. "In fact, if I have my way, we might just stop putting vintage labels on a bottle." Krug is a loner, still using only oak casks for fermenting and real cork instead of modern crown caps while the bottles are aging. This makes a bottle of Krug nearly as expensive as another house's vintage.

Other big names in champagne tend to agree that vintage champagne is largely a sales gimmick. "The *less* you know about champagne, the more a vintage label counts," says François Philippoteaux, head of Laurent Perrier. "In countries where buyers are generally ignorant of what makes a good champagne, they feel more secure if it has a year marked on it." His superb blend of mainly Chardonnay crus, Grand Siécle, costs twice the price of a Laurent Perrier vintage, yet never bears a vintage label. Some houses produce a vintage bottle especially for American consumption even in years when a blend is a better wine. In a typical year, only a small percentage of total champagne production will be vintage, mainly to satisfy the snob market.

Once the jealously guarded formula has been drawn up for each house's blend, the wine is bottled. It is still non-sparkling at this point. To get the bubbles in, a short shot of natural fermenting agents and high quality cane sugar dissolved in wine goes into each bottle to trigger the second fermentation. This fermentation would probably take place anyway, but adding a catalyst gives champagne makers positive control over the process. It takes place exactly when and as it should, the sugar converting into a predictable amount of alcohol and carbonic-acid gas. Pressure within the bottle rises to about 90 pounds per square inch, triple that in a typical automobile tire. Houses used to lose thousands of gallons of champagne annually due to exploding bottles, and workers in the cellars wore iron masks for protection. Today the glass industry makes a far more reliable product and five explosions per thousand bottles is average.

Second fermentation complete, the bottles are left lying in the vast, cool cellars that honeycomb the soft chalk subsurface beneath Reims and Epernay. The cellars of all the major houses together total 120 miles of galleries, enough storage area for some 150 million bottles. The houses need that much stock on hand, for champagne must by law be aged at least one year, and no reputable maker puts his brand on the market with less than three years' aging. Thus a bottle of champagne is ready to be drunk immediately when bought. It is at its peak and will not improve by further aging. Indeed, maximum life of the average bottle is about 10 years; older, it tends to maderize, lose its sparkle and become heavy.

The second fermentation leaves a sediment in the bottle, and thereby hangs the tale of another series of punctilious operations peculiar to champagne. Bottles are placed obliquely on racks, neck downwards so the deposit tends to gravitate toward the cork. Skilled workers called *remueurs* (literally, stirrers) visit each bottle daily to give it a rotary twist and tilt it slightly more toward the vertical. After two to three months of this—a man with a good pair of wrists can handle

30,000 bottles a day—the bottle is standing upside down in its rack with the sediment against the cork.

The tricky problem now is to get the sediment out without spilling valuable champagne or losing gas. The tricky solution is to immerse the neck of the bottle in a vat of super-cooled liquid that freezes the cork, sediment and a bit of wine. The cork is pulled and the little block of ice containing the sediment pops out. The worker performing the *dégorgement* sniffs the bottle to insure the wine is still in good shape, then doses it with about a tablespoonful of *liqueur d'expédition* made of reserve wine and cane sugar. How much sugar depends on whether the champagne is to be an extra-dry *brut* or a sweeter *sec* or *demi-sec*. Tastes vary, but champagne has followed the worldwide trend to lighter and dryer drinks; production now runs around 86 percent brut, six percent sec and eight percent demi-sec.

Admittedly, not everyone finds the foregoing convincing evidence that only wine from France's Champagne district deserves to be called champagne. Makers—and drinkers—of imitation champagne are numerous. The CIVC can do nothing about drinkers, but it has sued makers and won court injunctions against labeling a sparkling wine champagne. "We didn't act quickly enough to get exclusive rights to use the name in the United States," mourns Joseph Dargent of the CIVC, who carries the fight around the world, "but we've done better elsewhere."

A few years ago Old Bailey banned "Spanish champagne" from the British market, terming it dishonest trading. "Japanese champagne" was worrisome for a while, despite analyses revealing that it was not made from grapes, and a bouquet suggesting a pharmaceutical product. A new Franco-Japanese trade agreement has taken care of that, and the offending bottle no longer bears a label printed in French or using the magic name.

The stakes are high, like the price of a typical bottle, for champagne is very big business. To drink it is to go first class, and it seems unlikely that the lords of the Champagne district of France will ever cater to mass man. "I would not like to see champagne vulgarized," confides François Philippoteaux of Laurent Perrier. He is echoed by Louis d'Harcourt of Veuve Cliquot Ponsardin: "Champagne should not be available to everyone. Fortunately, I don't think there is any danger of that."

Snobbery? Perhaps just a trace, and in that, too, champagne reflects the *esprit* and soul of France. On the other hand, champagne makers around Bouzy and Dizy like to explain away the cost of this special wine with a neat, impeccably logical formula. "Champagne is not really expensive," the local saying goes. "It only seems so in proportion to the rapidity of consumption."

Update: *French champagne makers, still concerned about non-French sparkling wine in the U.S., recently launched a branding campaign in upscale American magazines, ridiculing the notion that anything but French champagne could ever be authentic. "Washington apples from Nevada?" it asked. "Gulf shrimp from Nebraska?" But they seemed to have little cause for financial worries. They are selling some 300 million bottles a year, on average, with Britain still the biggest foreign market but the United States now number two, with 19 million bottles.*

Oysters for Openers

Context: *"Oyster dear to the gourmet, "wrote the Roman statesman/philosopher Seneca, "beneficent oyster, exciting rather than sating, all stomachs digest you, all stomachs bless you." Roman epicureans agreed with him 2,000 years ago, as do millions of Frenchmen today. A festive meal in France often opens with a dozen sea-fresh Belons or Portugaises, accompanied with a chilled white wine from the Loire. During the winter holiday season oyster stands proliferate outside Parisian restaurants and cafes to cope with the demand. French oyster growers sell nearly 100,000 tons of the bivalves annually and gross something over $175 million.*

The French won't eat just any oyster, of course. Although the ones reaching Paris from the extensive beds out in Brittany and down near Bordeaux are not all of French origin—many nowadays are the descendants of recently imported Japanese seedlings—they are the product of an art and a science at least as complex and exact as wine making. Oysters are usually bred in one specialized area, then delicately rebedded in another for a couple of years of maturing, being taught to close their mouths for travel. When they reach the stands, they are divided into nine categories, ranging from 000 (the largest and most expensive) down to number 6. A dozen medium-size oysters served on a bed of crushed ice are guaranteed to leave the stomach comforted, the palate titillated, and the pocketbook considerably lighter.

Today, Parisian oyster fanciers are having to look a little harder for their oysters: the number of stands, and the thick-wristed oyster openers who man them, are decreasing. While nearly 150 stands lined Paris streets in 1960, there are fewer than 60 today. The *écaillers* who slip their stubby knife into an oyster and pry it open faster than you can say conchologist have declined in roughly the same proportion: 800 then, fewer than 300 today.

And thereby hangs a surprising socio-economic tale. For contrary to what most people assume when they see a Paris oyster opener dressed in Breton fisherman's togs and looking for all the world like an old salt, most of them have traditionally come from the French Alps. Or to be more precise, from the three villages of Montaimont, Mongelafray and Montpascal in Savoie. Just as Basques emigrated to Idaho to become shepherds and Bretons sailed to New York to start French restaurants on the West Side, so sons of Savoie left their hardscrabble hamlets to open oysters in Paris. Long Alpine winters hardened them to withstand a cold outdoor job in Paris that began at 10 a.m. and ended at 2 a.m. next day. Peasants by the dozen would bid their families farewell in September for the trip to Paris, then return to Montaimont, Mongelafray and Montpascal in May to work on farms during the summer.

Usually a beginner worked with a friend or relative who had already set up his Paris stand. The first year was spent as an apprentice, learning not only to wield a knife without losing fingers, but also acquiring the knack of telling oyster quality and freshness at a glance without having to sniff its odor. An experienced *écailler* can make a good living. Beyond that, it's not a bad life. "You see a lot of people," explains one. "Foreigners like to take photos of us as souvenirs of their trip to Paris. It's more fun than working in an office."

But a way of life is passing. It began with France's ski boom, which inversed the migration by sending Parisians to Savoie. Ski resorts sprang up to mine the new white gold, creating winter jobs for the mountain men. Whereas the three villages used to provide some 15 *écaillers* a year, lately they have become an endangered species in Paris. Even with the decline of oyster stands due largely to skyrocketing prices, that is insufficient to man them. So the Savoyards are gradually being replaced by immigrants from Algeria. Still, one aspect of the tradition is being preserved: most Algerian oyster openers come not from the Mediterranean coast, but from the rugged mountains of Kabylia.

Update: *French researchers recently tried to find the chemical secret of oyster aroma. They whipped oysters into a slurry, heated it to 240 degrees C., and examined it with a gas chromatograph. Going beyond pure laboratory* *techniques, nine human ``oyster noses" were given odor detection training at the National School of Food Industries and Technologies in Nantes. The humans identified 42 distinct odors, including cucumber, butter, garlic, boiled potato, lemon, almond, and mushroom from a single kind of oyster, but the technicians could link only a dozen of those smells to specific chemicals such as hexanal, octanal, 2,6-nonadienal and nine others. The rest, mercifully, are still a mystery. Meanwhile, worried French health officials warned that sharp oyster shells cause citizens "numerous severe accidental injuries" to the fingers and hands every year. Some 20 percent of France's oyster-related injuries require emergency-room treatment.*

How Fast *Le Food?*

Context: *Old Paris hands will tell you, ad nauseam, that it used to be impossible to get a bad meal in France. And they are right. From working-men's bistrots to raucous brasseries, you could, if need be, just point to something on the menu and be sure of a copious, well-prepared meal at a fair price, if nothing fancy. But French cuisine could not resist the Decline of the West. Now it is all too easy to get a bad meal in France. Careful diners have to practice defensive eating, trying to decide which item on the menu is least likely to be botched or phonied up with the latest fad like mango chutney in the pot-au-feu.*

"Hey, anybody want a hamburger?"

I did a double take. True, I was sitting in a news bureau of the Associated Press, the sort of hurried place where hamburgers tend to be ingested more frequently than, say, Tournedos Rossini. But this particular AP bureau was in Paris, where the standard sandwich sent out for, if one came to such a gastronomic pass, was savory paté or salami between long halves of crusty *baguette*.

Then a long-suppressed, painful memory surfaced: There were now several hamburger joints on the Champs Élysées, along with other new emporia specializing in what the French call *le fast food*.

Unfortunately, they are doing exceptionally well, as French eating habits sadly begin to catch up with the rest of the world. Indeed, the day may not be far off when, as one French food critic sourly predicts, the only restaurant food available in Paris will be hamburgers and Chinese take-out.

Both are spreading here so fast that the traditional French meal should be classified an endangered species. In 1976, a recent study says, there were only 15 known fast-food outlets in the whole country. At latest count, there were well over 1,000.

As evidence of how things are going, the same study notes that already one Frenchman out of five no longer goes home for the traditional lengthy lunch with his wife, presumably sneaking off for a quickie at Burger King.

Other statistics show that while meat consumption, reserved for the aristocracy at the turn of the 20th century, is up by 30 percent over the last two decades, and sugar and butter are up by comparable amounts, the French are eating less of the longtime staples like potatoes, cheese and bread. Neither do French housewives any longer do their daily food shopping at the local butcher's, baker's, fishmonger's and cheese shop.

Instead, they are following the American model and stocking up once a week at the hypermarket, some of which are larger, with 40 or more checkout counters, than most in the United States. And what do they buy there? Frozen and canned foods, *naturellement.* And bread wrapped in plastic and tasting much the same.

In fact, one of the surest signs of the decline of eating in France is the sorry state of French bread, long admired and imitated around the world, and emblematic of the French way of life. Bought fresh each morning at the local *boulangerie,* a good French loaf always had a yeasty aroma and crisp crust that made its safe arrival home problematic: many were half-eaten en route, especially if *maman* had sent her youngest out for it.

Today, however, French bakers often cheat by oxygenating the dough with ascorbic acid for faster rising, and add extra salt to sharpen flavor. Many mix loaves made from frozen dough with those freshly made, and few customers spot the difference.

Though some 85 percent of bread eaten in France comes from 39,000 small, family-run bakeries, some say there are no more than 300 honest bakers in the country. First-rate restaurants no longer buy their loaves from such unreliable sources, but bake their own bread to ensure quality. But such restaurants are themselves becoming a rarity, victims of the *nouvelle cuisine* fad, a scam that restaurant owners and chefs use to convince eaters that less is more.

True, there are still a few temples of *haute cuisine,* where a lamb chop will be presented on a special morsel of toast called a *croustade* sculpted in the form of a Corinthian pedestal, garnished with chopped liver paté and vegetables cut with military precision. Classical French cookery can still be an unforgettable experience for eye and palate. But it takes a big, and expensive, kitchen staffed with a brigade of 20 or more skilled cooks and apprentices. It also takes customers with the time, money and taste to appreciate it, all of which are increasingly rare. So restaurateurs cut their overhead and set out to convince us that a raw sardine marinated in lemon is actually far better than anything August Escoffier, king of chefs and chef of kings, ever cooked up for his princely patrons.

It was only a step from that debasement to *le fast food,* which at least has the advantage of being unpretentious and less expensive. No one is trying, so far, to sell hamburgers as *nouvelle* anything.

And they are still of proven effectiveness at sustaining journalists on the run, a problem Escoffier never faced.

Update: *The current gastronomic debate in France: is wine a food or a condiment? It's purely academic, since the French are abandoning wine in favor of sodas with their hamburgers; wine consumption has plunged from 130 bottles per person a year in the 1960s to less than half that today. The latest fad,* le fooding, *views restaurant atmosphere and background music as more important than great food. The French have coined a new word for the poor quality of their food today:* la malbouffe, *literally, bad grub. And that old tourists' question, "Is it safe to drink the water?" is as pertinent as ever: The European Court of Justice has twice found France in violation of European Union guidelines for drinking water safety, due to excess nitrite from agricultural pollution.*

Taking Mustard Seriously

Context: *Cheap and relatively easy to make, mustard has become an affordable luxury for consumers, and a cottage industry in many places, including the U.S. But in France, where mustard is still taken seriously, it has to come from Dijon, where it was first codified in the 14th century.*

Enticed by the fragrant white smoke wafting down Mount Horeb's East Main Street from an outdoor grill covered with sizzling bratwursts, I accept a free hot dog from a friendly man in a bright-yellow T-shirt. Then comes the hard part: what to put on it. Eschewing mustards on the table such as Bertman's Ball Park, Plochman's Spicy Peppa, Mamma Rap's Garlic and French's Classic Yellow, I opt for a hearty dollop of Mike's Magic Mustard. "You'll like that one," promises Jim Thompson, the man in the T-shirt and proud creator of this blend of mustard flour, two kinds of mustard seed, red wine vinegar, whole eggs, and sugar. "Welcome to National Mustard Day!"

Munching the dog—I find Mike's Magic, like many of today's new mustards, a tad sweet for my taste—I head past blue-haired Skippy the Clown and a five-foot-tall French's squeeze bottle that waves at me, and enter the Mount Horeb Mustard Museum. I quickly see why this small Wisconsin town just west of Madison has become the epicenter of America's burgeoning mustard mania. Jars of the stuff in all shapes, sizes and colors fill the show window, line the walls and stack on display tables. Mustards from more than 40 countries, from Italy to Iceland and Belgium to Brazil, are on display, along with a handsome collection of crockery, porcelain, silver, and crystal mustard pots.

"One of our rarest is a Yak mustard powder from Nepal," says Barry Levenson, a puckish former lawyer in the Wisconsin Attorney General's office who created the museum-cum-boutique in 1992. "In all, we've got about 3,400 varieties of mustard. As far as I know, that makes this the world's largest collection." People send him mustards they find during their travels, such as a jar from Sri Lanka that Wisconsin State Chief Justice Shirley Abrahamson brought back. Besides the collections behind glass, some 500 kinds of mustard are on sale here. That includes, believe it or not, chocolate fudge mustard made in—where else?—California.

Today is the first Saturday in August, making it National Mustard Day according to Chase's Calendar of Events, which keeps track of noteworthy moments in our nation's life. No doubt about it, mustard's on a roll. With mustard seed now the world's most heavily traded spice, an unctuous river of creamy yellow paste is spreading across the world's platters and palettes. It's as if gourmands everywhere have come to agree with 16th-century English poet Thomas Tusser's recipe for good cheer: "Good bread and good drink, a good fier in the hall,/ Brawn pudding and souse and good mustard withal."

Today's mustard mania has led to dozens of Websites run by small specialty and regional mustard makers hawking their wares. Mustard flowing via the Internet is one measure of how far the spice has come since the days of Alexander the Great, who once used it as a sort of primitive telegraph during a battle in 331 B.C. Alexander figured he would knock off Persia in an easy afternoon's work, but Persia's cocky emperor, Darius III, sent him a saucy warning: a bag of sesame seeds symbolizing how numerous his troops were. Alexander coolly replied with a similar bag—but filled with much more numerous mustard seed to show not only the number of his warriors but their hot ferocity as well. Alexander won.

All the great ancient civilizations, from Greece and Egypt to China and India, cultivated and consumed mustard seed. The Greek dramatist Aristophanes wrote in the fifth century B.C. of mustard-spiced stews, while Pythagoras, perhaps looking for ways to help people remember his theorem about right triangles, held that mustard improved memory. Bronze Age sites in Greece and Anatolia have yielded the seed; Indian and Sumerian texts going back to 3,000 B.C. mention it.

The ancients held that mustard was good, and good for you, if not a virtual panacea. The Greeks credited Aesculapius, son of Apollo and god of medicine, with creating it. Dioscorides, the first-century A.D. Greek physician whose *De Re Medica* was the standard pharmacological text for 1,600 years, prescribed mustard for everything from swollen tonsils to epilepsy, and as a tonic against "feminine lassitude." The Roman scholar Pliny the Elder ground mustard seed with vinegar and used it as a poultice for snakebite and scorpion stings, while the Greek physician Hippocrates favored mustard poultices for treating bronchitis, pneumonia, rheumatism and neuralgia—ample precedent for today's folk medicine remedy of a mustard plaster for many of the same ills.

Persian noblemen, they say, used to show off their swordsmanship by putting a mustard seed on a block and slicing through the minuscule orb with a single stroke of their scimitar. No mean feat when you consider that a brown seed is only 0.064 inches in diameter, and it takes some 26,500 of them to make one jar of Dijon mustard. That's why Saint Matthew, when searching for a metaphor to show how powerful even a tiny bit of faith is, wrote, "If ye have faith as a grain of mustard seed, ye shall say unto this mountain, Remove hence to yonder place; and it shall remove."

We know the Greeks and Egyptians chewed mustard seeds with meat, probably to disguise its gamy taste. But it was the Romans who used it most widely and creatively, mixing it with vinegar, honey and oil, and pickling meats with it. Lucius Junius Moderatus, also known as Columella, wrote of mustard in his 12-volume reference work *De Re Rustica*, giving detailed recipes for making the condiment with things like saltpeter and hot coals.

It appears that the Romans also gave us, at least indirectly, the condiment's name. Savants disagree, as they will, over the origin of the word "mustard," but the consensus seems to lie with the Latin *mustum*, or "must," because the condiment has often been prepared by mixing with unfermented grape juice. Add the Latin *ardens*, "hot" or "fiery," and you have it. But some hold for a Celtic derivation from *mwstardd*, meaning something that emits a strong odor.

The conquering Romans took mustard seed to their province of Gaul, where it took root and formed the basis of France's traditional preeminence in mustard making—and consumption. By the ninth century, French monasteries were already making a good revenue from their mustard preparations. In 1336, the Duke of Burgundy supplied no less than 70 gallons of it for a single day's feasting.

In medieval Paris, hundreds of sellers, wearing a blue apron and red cap, trundled wheelbarrows of mustard through the streets, housewives popping out their doors for a daily refill. French king Charles VII fortuitously discovered a new mustard recipe in 1422 while fighting the Hundred Years War. Blowing into the village of Sainte Menehould in eastern France between battles, he demanded dinner, but most local cupboards were bare. Finally one obliging housewife threw together what she could find: four pig's feet. She prepared them in a batter of breaded herbs and mustard sauce. The king was delighted and *voilá*, a traditional French recipe was born, *pied de cochon à la Sainte-Mene-hould*. His successor, Louis XI, also was fond of mustard but feared being poisoned. Solution: he always carried his own personal mustard pot with him when he traveled, breaking it out when he pitched up unannounced to dine with his subjects.

By the mid-19th century, mustard was becoming so popular in France that gastronomic authority Grimod de La Reynière commented that mustard had become "such a primary necessity that without it at least two-thirds of the stomachs in Paris wouldn't be able to digest." And not only in Paris. Most self-respecting French cities have had their local mustard, but France's supreme center of mustard making has long been the Burgundian city of Dijon. This seemed so obvious to writer Alexandre Dumas *père* that when he stopped at the city's Hotel du Parc for dinner one evening, he was taken aback when the waiter asked what mustard he wanted with his two lamb cutlets and half a cold chicken. "*Parbleu*," the author of *The Three Musketeers* exploded, "*moutarde de Dijon!*" But the waiter politely explained that Dijon mustard then existed in both a men's and a milder ladies' version. He hesitated, then took some of both. "At just the sight of the beautiful yellow color of this admirable stimulant to appetite," Dumas later wrote, "I plunged the wooden spoon into each pot and made two pyramids of mustard in my plate." *Bon appétit*, indeed.

Located at the foot of the vine-covered slopes of the Côte d'Or hills, Dijon, former home of Philip the Bold and John the Fearless, passed in 1390 its first city ordinance prescribing how Dijon mustard should be made. And city fathers made sure it was enforced.

Dijon's purist approach to mustard making was reflected again in the ordinance of May 1634: producers had to swear before the aldermen to serve king and city well and faithfully, and perform a three-year apprenticeship under a master *moutardier* before mixing up their own batches. The strictly codified recipe for Dijon remains pretty much the same: black or brown seeds (more pungent than white) are ground and passed through a sieve. Then verjus or white wine is added to obtain a light yellow paste, then the mixture is packed into jars for shipment. No coloring, cereal flour or stabilizers are permitted.

Today France produces about 47 percent of all mustard from Europe, just ahead of Germany, and exports more than 4,000 tons of it, worth some $5 million, to the United States. Dijon mustard factories like Maille, Bornier and Reine de Dijon couldn't look less like those in 19th-century photographs, where a dozen gents in mustaches and flatcaps fiddle with stone grinding wheels and oaken casks of mustard paste. Now a batch takes only four hours, from pouring seed into the grinders to pumping consumer-ready paste into sterile jars. One or two technicians easily follow the whole mechanized process on computer screens.

The proliferation of varieties of mustard means that the major French makers are producing 50 or more kinds. Most are for the export market: straight, strong, sinus-opening mustard is by far the most popular in France. "We like the idea of a wide variety of mustards, and we brought out 15 new flavors last year," says Jean-Denis Bellon, marketing manager for the LMA condiment group that makes Maille, "but we can't go on at that rate. We think mustard should taste like mustard. If you get too fancy, you limit the kind of food it goes with. We make honey mustard, for instance, but only for the American market. The French won't touch it."

At the Reine de Dijon company, sales manager Luc Vandermaesen understands the trend. "The move to wider variety is here to stay," he says. "People have always mixed other things with mustard to get different flavors; now you can get something different straight off the shelf." He spends time in American supermarkets picking up mustards to bring back and analyze. "Look at this," he says indignantly as he reads the list of ingredients off a jar of American-made "Dijon" mustard. "Additives include citric acid, spices, coloring, cornstarch, sugar, liquid egg white, locust bean gum and flavoring, whatever that is. It has nothing to do with what we make here in Dijon."

Paradoxically, one thing they *don't* make in Dijon is mustard seed. "Lots of people think these are mustard plants," Jean-Denis Bellon tells me as we drive along fields of yellow-flowering plants near the Maille factory. "But Burgundy farmers stopped growing it years ago because they couldn't get as much subsidy for it from the Common Market as for rapeseed." At least they stay in the large and diverse mustard family, rapeseed also being a product of *cruciferae* plant. The family includes some 390 genera of plants with cruciform flowers and peppery leaves, such as radishes, broccoli, cauliflower, Brussels sprouts, turnips and watercress. Ornamental mustard family members include candytuft, honesty, rose of Jericho, basket-of-gold and, oddly in the case of mustard, wallflower.

Dijon mustard makers, like those elsewhere, import nearly all their seed from thousands of miles away: the endless plains of Western Canada. Unlike most other spices, mustard for export is grown mainly in the temperate zones, meaning the industrialized world. The 700,000 acres devoted to mustard in the country's Saskatchewan, Manitoba and

Alberta provinces produce some 250,000 tons of seed per year, enough to supply more than 90 percent of the world's export needs. To keep their competitive advantage, Canadian grain companies are constantly researching yellow (*sinapis alba*) and brown (*brassica juncea*) mustard plants at field stations to improve yield—now about 1,000 pounds per acre—and resistance to plant diseases like white rust fungus, and to achieve greater regularity in seed size for easier milling. And, of course, the plants must produce seed with a good, strong, mouth-freshening glow.

Its palate-cleansing quality is one thing Alain Passard loves about mustard. "It adds a perfect touch of acidity that offsets the cloying greasiness of meat," says Passard, who as chef and owner of Paris's three-star Arpège restaurant is one of France's greatest cooks today. He doesn't much take to all the aromatic mustards coming out now, preferring a natural flavor and color, and a silky texture on the tongue. "The slightly floral and fruity taste of real mustard lends an almost subversive elegance to many dishes like chicken or sweetbreads with mustard sauce, or a crayfish bisque," he says. "I like to add just a touch of it to many sauces for a subtle grace note. That usually surprises diners when they discover it's just mustard."

Update: *Mustard unexpectedly figured in the tensions between the French and American governments over the war in Iraq. The people at French's mustard were sufficiently concerned to issue a news release reassuring the American public. "The only thing French about French's mustard," they reminded anyone planning to pour the product down the drain along with French wine, "is the name!" And in India's Assam state, where marauding wild Asiatic elephants were wreaking havoc, killing people, flattening houses, and drinking local rice beer, authorities created buffer zones around villages with mustard plants, which repel elephants.*

4. Oh la-la!

Vacations with a Vengeance

Context: *The French used to be a hard-working people. When Catholic priests occasionally called on them to slow down and spend more time on religion, they would answer, "Father, to work is to pray." Whether the cause is an overdose of socialism can be debated, but, except for the likes of the Compagnons and a few small-business entrepreneurs, work today is a four-letter word in France, a necessary evil to be avoided. A recent poll reveals that only 15 percent of Frenchmen are interested in their work. In its place are* les vacances. *Vacations trump everything, from family relations to beloved household pets. France's heat wave of 2003 killed a large number of elderly family members who remained behind in suffocating apartments while their children and grandchildren headed for weeks at the beach. Every year thousands of dogs and cats, goldfish and parakeets are left behind to die in July and August, despite government poster campaigns saying, "Please don't forget them."*

During the summer, you often hear more English spoken than French along the Champs Élysées and at sidewalk cafes in Saint Germain-des-Prés. But that is only partly due to the peaceful invasion of American tourists.

Mainly, it is because the French have left.

Nationwide, some 30 million Frenchmen, or 57 percent of the population, leave on vacation in July and August. Paris itself, progressively emptier after July 1, reaches its nadir of activity the week of Ascension Day in August. Office and factory life comes to a standstill, most shops close, and stranded Parisians can walk the empty streets for blocks trying to find a croissant for breakfast.

The French are the world's champion vacationers. To start with, they have more time than anyone else: the legal minimum any employer can allow is five weeks with pay. Some professions, like journalists, get up to seven or eight weeks off annually.

Les vacances amount to a national obsession. As a conversational ice-breaker, you can't go wrong by asking a Frenchman about his vacation. He is always happy to talk about either the one he has just had or the one he is planning.

Besides the great summer exodus, it is customary to take some time off the week of All Saint's Day in November, at Christmas and Easter, plus a week of skiing in February or March. Vacations amount to about 10 percent of French family budgets. Nearly one-quarter of the population, according to polls, scrimps on other things to satisfy their craving for vacation.

It is difficult for an American to conceive of the intense passion the French bring to vacationing. They may be unemployed, as over 2 million are today; the price of gasoline may be sky-high—it's about four times as much as in the U.S.—and the Mediterranean beaches may be packed with Belgians and Germans, but none of this deters them.

Not even the horrendous traffic jams, the worst in Europe, discourage the lemming-like migration. On a recent July day, 9 million Frenchmen, nearly one out of five of the entire population, were on the road simultaneously, either returning from vacation or getting there. Despite the mobilization of about 60,000 gendarmes and some 2,000 motorcycle police, or maybe because of it, the traffic jams stretched in all directions.

One near the north-south choke point at Lyons was officially put at 30 miles long. In all, police calculate, vacationers lost close to 1 million man-hours waiting for the traffic to move.

Even family sentiment, usually so strong here, sometimes fades under the beckoning sun of vacation. In one family I know, the aging matriarch was found to have terminal cancer in the spring. As the illness dragged on, apprehension rose, both over her worsening condition and the possibility that the situation might continue all through the summer, ruining vacation plans. When she died in June, the tears were mixed with palpable relief. Within days the family was on its way to a vacation house in Provence.

The French caught vacation fever in 1936, when the socialist Popular Front government passed a law granting two weeks of paid vacation to all citizens as a birthright. Working-class couples hopped on bicycles for two and took off for their first taste of travel, while open trucks marked "Proletarian Tourism" loaded up groups for day trips to the country. Extending the legal minimum vacation became a popular vote-getter. The government accorded a third week in 1956, a fourth in 1969, and François Mitterrand's Socialists made it five weeks.

France pays dearly for its vacation mania. Most factories and shops close for a solid month, and the resulting drop in productivity costs the economy billions. Every administration of the past two decades has tried to convince businesses to stay open by spreading their employees' vacations over several months, but to no avail. The French remain convinced that the only "real" vacations are in July and August.

The government does manage to turn this to its advantage. It reserves the most unpopular new measures for August, when no one is paying attention. Thus embarrassing devaluations of the franc tend to be done in August if possible. And when Frenchmen return home at summer's end, they usually find that the officially regulated prices of things like gasoline, electricity and public transport have gone up, while the interest paid on their savings accounts at the government post office and state-owned banks will have decreased.

That will add to the usual end-of-summer surliness. But the French always have a consolation: If this vacation is over, can the next be far behind?

Update: *During the August exodus in 2004, gendarmes tallied up some 500 miles of bottlenecks on the country's roads during a single day. Since the socialists passed a law in the 1990s mandating a 35-hour work week, even the French hardly know what to do with all their paid time off. It now amounts to a three-day weekend every other week, besides the numerous weeks of vacation. Between 1980 and 2003, the number of hours worked in the U.S. rose by 39 percent, while in France it fell by 6 percent;*

on average, the French now work some 300 fewer hours a year than Americans. A recent best seller, Bonjour Paresse *("Hello Laziness"), gives tips on how to do the least possible during working hours.*

The Grand Sport of Driving in France

Context: *France has long had the worst record of fatal automobile accidents in Western Europe, with around 8,000 a year. Even that figure is half what it was a couple of decades ago. Partly this has been due to infrastructure problems—it was far behind Germany and even Italy, for instance, in constructing multi-lane superhighways, getting along with dangerous contrivances such as three-lane highways with vehicles darting in and out of the middle lane—and partly to the national* esprit. *The latter calls for driving with carefree verve oblivious of others that makes each driver consider himself king of the highway. Pedestrians are fair game: some 800 a year are killed, one-third of them attempting to cross a street in marked pedestrian crossings.*

French officials swear that the momentous change now taking place in the country's traffic rules has nothing whatever to do with the fact that France has a Socialist-Communist government. The Frenchman in the street, ever alert to political nuance, is skeptical about that.

However that may be, the unbending rule laid down in the Napoléonic Code—priority to traffic on your right—is gradually giving way to priority to the left. A paltry change, you may say. But then you may not have known the excitement, the exhilaration, the grand sport of driving on French roads.

You are, for example, cruising happily along a highway in your Peugeot or Renault at a fairly conventional speed, for France, like 85 miles per hour. Your attention has perhaps been momentarily distracted by a handsome hilltop château. When your eyes return to the road, you suddenly find you are bearing down on a beetling Citroën *deux chevaux* rattletrap that has exercised its inalienable right to charge onto the highway in front of you because it was coming from the right side.

Result: either excitement, exhilaration, etc., or another statistic making France's accident rate several times that of the United States.

Priority to vehicles on the right made sense in Napoléon's day, when horse-drawn conveyances set the pace. It has been dangerous nonsense for most of this century, accounting for innumerable dents in right front fenders, and worse. But although it contradicts common sense to give precedence to traffic from feeder roads, the idea appealed to the Frenchman's love of logic and order: one rule for all seasons.

Thus the new rule is being introduced in the most gingerly fashion. It will apply only to a few selected traffic circles in Paris, giving cars already in the circle priority over those arriving, as has always been done in many other countries.

Obviously the change is in everyone's interest, except the currently thriving automobile body shops. Traffic planners calculate that it will cut accidents appreciably. But will the devil-may-care French driver take to it?

Drive through Place de la Concorde and admire the precision and élan with which motorists wheel around it with screaming tires, keeping two inches off each others' fenders as if guided by radar. Here, truly, is cut and thrust worthy of latter-day D'Artagnans.

Or head for Place de l'Étoile, known officially as Place Charles de Gaulle, and savor the whirling scene as seven mighty boulevards pour traffic into it. Each incoming driver jockeys for his rightful priority until the whole mad carousel grinds to a halt. Paris police then charge in, blowing whistles and flailing arms until the jam breaks up—for a while.

Another indication that the new rule may not easily take hold is the difficulty the French government has had about headlights. After decades of driving in cities with only their parking lights on at night, French motorists were abruptly ordered to use their headlights. A sensible proposition, it seemed. French drivers disagreed. Headlights were blinding, they complained. Consequently, many still race through city streets with only their parking lights on, while others obediently use headlights.

The resulting visual confusion leaves many disoriented, unable to see parking lights for having been dazzled by headlights. That makes for still more excitement, exhilaration, etc.

Such difficulty in changing French driving habits notwithstanding, the government hopes that its coming campaign on television and billboards will foster support for the new rule. But if you plan to drive here, take the advice of an old Paris hand: Assume that you *never* have the priority on French roads, and you will get through without a scratch.

Update: *To the general surprise of the citizenry, France began an organized road safety campaign in 2003. It increased maximum penalties for driving offenses and installed automatic radar speed detectors on several major highways, with 1,000 of them planned by 2005. Mirabile dictu, driving habits have begun to change. French highways now bear perceptibly less resemblance to the Le Mans 24-hour race, and in cities, some drivers have even been spotted slowing or stopping for pedestrians in marked crossings. In the first year of the campaign, road accident fatalities dropped by 18 percent.*

The Outrageous Crazy Horse Saloon

Context: *Until the mid-1950s, French nightclub shows were seldom as risqué as most Americans seemed to think, the fond memories of war veterans returning home from gay Paree notwithstanding. The Moulin Rouge and Lido showed a few bare breasts, usually in a highly stylized way, and lots of feathers. But it was all pretty tame stuff compared with that American invention, the strip tease. Enter Alain Bernardin, who changed all that, for the better, by creating* l'art du nu, *treating the female form as a canvas on which to paint with light. An aesthete who followed art trends such as Pop Art and Op Art, Bernardin was an artist in a most unconventional medium. To me, he personified some of the best traits of the French: an artistic sensibility, intelligence, and an absence of hypocrisy. Although the show has changed since this article was done, the spirit of the place remains the same, at once* oh-la-la *and a parody of it.*

An evening at Le Crazy, as Parisians call it, is an outrage. Upwards of 250 innocent, eager customers of varying nationality are jammed into the bizarre, red-plush Victorian décor of a tiny basement. Their ears are assailed by elaborate polyglot absurdities, their pocketbooks blatantly attacked by piratical prices. And the show, especially for those out for heart-pumping kicks and an honest snigger, has little to do with strip tease as Americans know it.

It's an outrage that Alain Bernardin, owner-director of the Crazy Horse Saloon near the Champs Élysées, willfully and gleefully perpetrates seven nights a week on the naïve, the vulgar, the unimaginative, the dirty-minded. "The public is so stupid," he exclaims with mock despair. "How I love to annoy them."

What's outrageous and annoying about Le Crazy, and what delights those who love it, is that it resolutely refuses to take sex, itself, or its customers seriously. Everything about the place is parody except the prices.

The décor is that of a Gay Nineties San Francisco saloon, designed by a Frenchman with impeccable taste who had never visited either San Francisco or even the United States. Down a flight of red concrete steps at 12 Avenue George V, not far from the American Cathedral, are the swinging doors with orange and black illuminated signs on them: "Open every day at 10:30 p.m." and "Show every day at 11:15 p.m." In English. Over the small black bar at the left hangs a fine pair of long-handled steer horns. At right the spectator area is divided irregularly by red-plush balustrades. Tables, about one-foot square, are covered with dark red cloths, and small stools and wall benches are also covered in red velvet. Above them hang pink-shaded imitation oil lamps with brass fixtures. A carpet of billiard-table green covers the floor.

At the end of the room, no more than 50 feet from the bar, is the minuscule stage, measuring about 15 feet wide by five feet deep. When the green stage curtain is drawn, a painting of a pale, reclining nude in the best saloon tradition hangs in front of it. To the left are a postage-stamp dance floor and the bandstand where, this month, King Fan Fan and his Far Out Fantoms play. Here and there are dotted insolent signs, in English. Behind the bar: "Ask for credit and drop dead." Beside it: "It doesn't cost a red cent to enter the Crazy Horse Saloon. Ahem. The first drink will cost you 35 francs. No more? No more. The first drink at the bar is 20 francs. No more? Isn't that enough?" Beside the dance floor hangs a large yellowed photo of Chief Crazy Horse, dead since 1876.

The impassive chief gazes nightly on a three-hour show that in its deliberate mixture of the sublime and the ridiculous is typical of what Bernardin has offered (or, depending on your point of view, inflicted on) his audiences since 1954. It includes 14 numbers: eight strips, one specialty with five of the girls onstage, and five variety acts. At 11:15 sharp the house lights go down and the curtain opens on a movie screen. A raucous chorus of that American fall Saturday favorite, "Mister Touchdown U.S.A.," blasts out of the speakers and color slides of

each of the eight girls, in red-and-white Spalding football helmets, are
flashed on the screen, interspersed with shots of French, American,
German, British and Italian flags. Shown only from the neck up, the
girls variously mug determination, seduction, hilarity, and stupidity
under their helmets. Then the stage show begins. It includes:

Nadia Safari in "The Hammock." Before the curtain opens, a voice,
rough with wildly exaggerated suggestion, says, "A funny safari. All
night she had hit the bottle. You would think she had been at the
Crazy. Certainly a strange safari, Nadia." Nadia, dressed in a net
sarong that conceals nothing, is standing with her back to a taut hammock, marking time to "Didn' It Rain." She is detached, pensive.
Eventually she takes the sarong off, swings in the hammock a little.
The lighting, which has been streaked gold and black to suggest the
jungle, narrows at the end to a spot on her face, where finally there is
just a hint of a smile. That's all. No bump. No grind.

Bertha von Paraboum in "Anatomy: Eines Deutschen Kreatur."
Well-endowed Bertha, a turn-of-the-century cocotte with high black
boots, long black gloves, flowing red boa and garter, doesn't dance at
all. She assumes a heavily suggestive pose, utters something in German
like "Ach du liber" or "Why so many potatoes?" and the lights go out
to let a colored slide of her or patterns of black and white swastikas be
flashed on the screen. Then the lights are back on and she's in a different pose, uttering another banality in German or English. At last she
faces the audience and spreads her legs. There, serving as a G-string, is
a swastika.

Veronika Baum in "A Parisienne in Her Bath" is first seen in sharp
silhouette against an oval screen as she indolently undresses. Then a
quick shift and she is in a black marble tub lathering herself with fluffy
suds. She is caught by a square panel of orange light cut across with the
black stripes of venetian blinds. As she slowly caresses herself every
deliberate gesture becomes an art pose. Her face reflects only fixed
dreaminess. No leer.

Victoria Nankin in "The Ye-Ye Widow" is veiled throughout with marvelous light that covers her with black dots the size of silver dollars, as if a veil were actually held before a spotlight. The light caresses her as she lounges on a Victorian couch, first in a filmy gown, then without it. Graceful as a cat, she eventually straddles the couch, assumes a Sphinx pose with her forearms parallel before her. No bounce.

"And now come the touchdown girls," Bernardin announces in English with the gross overenthusiasm of stadium announcements at halftime. Five girls dressed in low-quarter football shoes, red tights up to the hips, shoulder pads and red and white helmets strut on and off stage several times, high-kicking steps in time to "Mister Touchdown U.S.A." It doesn't seem to matter that they don't bother to carry a football.

Bettina Uranium does "A Girl in Manhattan Dreams." She reclines on a couch, assuming different poses for each of the 10 or so color slides that are flashed over her and onto the screen behind. Photos which cover the whole stage are spectacular night shots of Manhattan, and shots of dollar bills and the American flag. She removes one pale green stocking, having started with not much more. The number ends with a slide of the well-known recruiting poster showing Uncle Sam pointing at the audience and saying, "I want you for the U.S. Army."

Natasha von Turmanov, "Die Preussiche Perle," starts with a pair of haute couture pajamas and removes them in the course of striding aggressively back and forth across the stage. Then a square panel of finely checkered light catches her squarely presented backside. When the footlights come back on, she carefully places a Prussian spike helmet atop her blonde head.

This is the tone of an evening at the Crazy. It moves from the highly refined beauty, grace, ambiguity and irony of the strip numbers to broad satire—the musical link between numbers is a loud, rollicking piano rendition of "Beer Barrel Polka." It is far more cerebral and aesthetic than the average nightclub carouser bargains for. He comes to see some skin and gets a subtle parody of a strip show. There are not many minutes when he can be absolutely sure he himself is not being mocked. He may decide that Alain Bernardin is a nut case.

He may well be, of course. But in any case, he is also an artist, an aesthete, an intellectual of sorts and a highly intense and impatient man. Tall, slim, balding at 48, Alain Bernardin receives visitors starting at 6 p.m. in his tiny office at the Crazy. Reflecting his taste, it has a small black fireplace with polished brass trimmings, compact antique desk, a red-plush Victorian settee, a couple of turn-of-the-century paintings with cyclists. Whisky, ice bucket and glasses are on a low table. The man himself is quiet and not readily approachable. Dressed in neat dark blue and sleek black loafers, he tends at first to inspect his interlocutor with a quizzical look and takes a long time to reply to the simplest question. He does not care to be thought affable. He would not suffer fools gladly.

"For several years now, France has had what are known as *son et lumière* spectacles at many châteaux," he says. "That's essentially what we have here, but instead of illuminating Chambord or Chenonceaux, we play lights on Veronika Baum and Victoria Nankin." As with everything he does, he is partly joking, partly serious. Every strip act at the Crazy is conceived by Bernardin from costumes and props through music and lighting, based to some extent on his reading of each dancer's personality. Her every move is done at his direction and rehearsed for weeks before he considers the number ready.

The essential element in the beauty he is trying to create is light. A one-time dabbler in painting, Bernardin sometimes refers to the 60-odd small spots that hang in two rows from the ceiling in front of the stage as his brush, the complex control board his palette. "There's really no tease in our strip," he says. "It's the nude treated as optical art. The papers and magazines are suddenly full of stories lately about Op Art. I've been doing that here for years. On the other hand, I suppress erotism almost completely by reducing it to its most simple, compact expression."

That's not bad for a man who, slightly over 10 years ago, didn't know quite what a strip show was. Bernardin was originally an antiques dealer and interior decorator by trade. After the war he opened a restaurant near the Ritz hotel. Because of its chic location and Bernardin's flair for publicity, it quickly became the in spot for visiting celebrities. The Aga Khan used to come to eat huge soufflés with his fingers, and Art Buchwald wrote an occasional column about the place. Bing Crosby frequented it and he and Bernardin became great pals.

Bernardin was itching to go into some sort of show business but didn't know what to do. Crosby suggested a Western-style saloon with barmaids, square dances and such. Bernardin liked the idea despite Buchwald's contention that Americans came to Paris to find typically French things, not an imitation of what they had back home. "Stick to your soufflés was Buchwald's advice," Bernardin now recalls with obvious pleasure.

When he found his cellar on Avenue George V, he had practically no capital to invest and couldn't get a loan ("In France the banks exist to make money, not loan it."), so he signed IOUs right and left with electricians, plumbers, decorators and furnishers. He had never visited the U.S. and wasn't too clear on what a saloon looked like. "So I went to see about 20 cowboy movies done by Universal Pictures," he recalls. "They always had saloons in those films, and since they always used the same set it was always the same saloon. I copied it for mine."

The swinging doors opened in 1951. The Crazy then offered square dances and a Gay Nineties revue. It managed to stay in the black, but it was far from an overwhelming success. Bernardin decided the thing to do was have a strip show, a rather far-out proposition at the time, considering there was not a single one in Europe in the early fifties. He found his dancer at the Folies Bergère, a girl who was half-Haitian and half-Polish. He dubbed her Miss Fortunia, the first of his many whimsical names for his dancers, and put her on as his show in 1952. "It was a little awkward, because I still didn't know exactly what a good strip show was," Bernardin says. "It wasn't quite right, but when I asked for criticism no one could tell me what was wrong. Then I saw a very bad American movie called 'Dancers of Desire' and I knew what a good show was. First of all, I needed more than one girl. And the dancers had to leave the stage a couple of times during their number so the audience would call them back to finish stripping."

With the principles of his new art form firmly in mind, Bernardin launched a new show in 1954 with six girls and a couple of top variety and singing numbers (the then unknown Charles Aznavour among them). It was an immediate success.

Since then Bernardin has honed his principles considerably. From introducing strip tease to Europe he has gone on to refine it almost to the vanishing point. In the process, he may have left his original mentors behind, in a less evolved state. "*Affreux*, awful, extremely primitive is the only word for it," he says now, speaking of American stripping with the distaste 20th-century man feels for his Neanderthal ancestors.

All he has done is keep up with artistic and intellectual trends, and assume his audience has too. Treating stripping as an art form, he has endowed it with some of the characteristics of modern art: the gratuitous absurdity of Pop Art, the visual shock and delight of Op Art, the emotional obliquity of the cool world. "There is nothing to understand in my show," he insists. "There is no reason why the numbers are what they are, and no deep significance to them. Some of them contain a mixture of parody and burlesque, of course. It's simply in the tradition of French cabarets that there be an element of parody. But other than that, it's just there."

Bernardin is constantly on the move in his Europe-wide search for new girls. He finds them mainly in ballet and dramatic classes, seldom picks one who is already stripping. "The thing I look for first is good eyes," he says. "A girl has to have a look in her eyes that holds an audience. Then of course her proportions must be right. She must have a long neck: the farther up a metronome the weight is, the slower it oscillates. The last year or so, the new girls have nearly all been dancers. They usually have good command of their bodies, and their leg muscles are well developed. But even then I often have to keep after them in rehearsal to pull their stomach in, stick their chest out, square their shoulders, and so on."

Crazy girls sign an exclusive contract with Bernardin and cannot dance elsewhere, though he gives them a couple of months off per year so they can do engagements in other night clubs if they want to. When they come back, he sometimes has to clean up their act: they become more exaggeratedly erotic, wiggling their hips all over the place. One of them complained to me when I was interviewing backstage that she had wanted to do a more sexy number, but Bernardin had held her back. I mentioned this to him. "Oh yes, they all wish they could be more daring," he replied. "If I let them do what they want, it would be incredibly vulgar. Girls," he says in a confidential tone, "are all such sluts at heart."

There is decidedly nothing sluttish behind the scenes at the Crazy. Dancers sign in when they arrive in the evening, and sign out when they leave, rather like the girls' dorm at a strict school. They are not allowed to mix with members of the audience or to stand in the back and watch the show. Some have not even seen all the other numbers.

Bernardin is convinced that racial mixing produces prettier girls. "That's why the Americans are such a big, handsome people," he says. Of 43 principal dancers at the Crazy over the last 10 years, only seven have been of parents of the same nationality. He has a definite leaning toward Polish girls: 15 of the 43 have had Polish blood. And he finds slightly cross-eyed girls irresistible. "Having one eye that's out of line gives a girl terrific charm," he says.

Once he has chosen them, he reserves to himself the delightful task of christening them with an outlandish stage name that's typically Crazy. Bertha von Paraboum is undoubtedly his greatest recent success, but she is in the line of Ann Burning, Miss Candida, Lili Lapudeur, Dodo d'Hamburg, Melody Bubbles, and Poupée La Rose. Bernardin figures a dancer's professional life to be between the ages of 18 and 28. "After that they can still be erotic enough, but it's vulgar."

He gets a kick out of the varied reactions of his audiences. The French: "They think they are the most intelligent audience in the world. All they come for is to see what they can find wrong with the show." The Germans: "They laugh. For them, a naked woman is something funny." The Italians: "They are aesthetes. They usually, along with women of all nationalities, appreciate the beauty of the show the most." The Americans? "So naïve, so open and receptive. They're my favorite."

Update: *Alain Bernardin was so taken with my line, "Everything about the place is parody except the prices," that he adopted it as his motto and printed it on the club's publicity material. Bernardin was found dead of a gunshot wound in his little office at the nightclub in September 1994, a pistol at his side. His children, Didier, Pascal, and Sophie, have carried on his aesthetic, light-painting approach, and expanded its commercial operations, opening an identical show in a Las Vegas hotel in 2001. They plan other Crazy Horse clones in Tokyo and Shanghai.*

PART TWO: *La Politique*

Political intrigue seems to be in the French blood. This, too, accurately reflects the national character. It was so under monarchy and empire, and continues through the five stabs at democracy the French have made with as many constitutions and republics, since 1789. Democracy, it seems, still has very shallow roots in France. Why else would French politicians keep repeating on every occasion, "France is a democracy!" "This is a republic!" They do protest too much, methinks. In nations where citizens are comfortable with government of the people, by the people, and for the people, such reminders—a bit as if the French woke up every morning, pinched themselves to see if they were still dreaming, and said, "I'm living in a democracy!"—are unnecessary because democracy is taken for granted.

The contrast between France and such nations is striking: in Britain, for instance, a monarchy fronts for a democracy, as Montesquieu observed. In France, one often has the impression, it is the other way around. Indeed, some French political scientists refer to their country as a republican monarchy. Partly this is due to the 1958 constitution, written to define France's fifth try at democracy since the Revolution. A custom fit for the imperious Charles de Gaulle, the constitution makes the French president one of the most powerful political leaders in the world, far more powerful than his American counterpart. Answerable to practically no one and immune from any sort of prosecution, he can dissolve the legislature at his pleasure and appoint a prime minister to head the government—and incidentally shield the president from criticism when things go wrong. But France's monarchical approach to government is also the natural outgrowth of the French mentality, which seems to mistrust, perhaps because the French mistrust their own volatility, genuine self-rule.

In keeping with the abstract, intellectual bent of the French mind, French politics is invariably, and rigidly, ideological. This may help account for its frequent excesses, whether the raging massacres of the post-Revolutionary Terror or today's vitiating right-left divide. The government itself is well aware of the risks of political volatility: fully five military or para-military organizations have as their primary duty to combat, not foreign invasion, but French citizens should they turn against their government. (Even the policeman on the beat can charge a citizen with "rebellion" if he talks back.) The dearth of basic consensus on the best form of government and the lack of political pragmatism make the country susceptible to demagoguery of all stripes, much of it based on spiteful, rancorous class hatred.

This leads to a penchant for all-inclusive ideological systems and tacit acceptance of state-imposed limits on personal freedom. Not for nothing is *raison d'état*, which can cover many forms of arbitrary authoritarianism, a French expression. The paradoxical result is that this land of The Enlightenment has often been inhospitable to its own thinkers. René Descartes, whose monumental studies ranging from metaphysics to mathematics and medicine formed much of the basis of modern science, wrote all his published works in Holland, where he spent 15 years to escape French Royalist oppression. And Voltaire admired the personal liberty and free thought in England and Switzerland, where he often found refuge from the French intolerance of the day. As he put it with his usual wit, he liked Switzerland because "The Swiss speak French, but they think in English."

The same ideological mind-set also means that totalitarian Marxism has always fallen on fertile ground in France. No less a contemporary French thinker than Jean-François Revel has warned his compatriots against "the totalitarian temptation." With Eastern Europe and China shedding their collectivist past as fast as they can, France often gives the impression of being the last country in the world whose people still believe that the government knows better than they do what is good for them. They pay heavily for that attitude, not only in socio-economic flexibility, but from their pocketbooks: their many forms of cradle-to-grave social security eat up nearly 30 percent of France's Gross Domestic Product. Direct deductions from their paychecks amount to a similar percentage.

This perennial bent to the left reached a culmination of sorts when the French woke up one spring morning in 1981 and learned, to their surprise, that they had elected a Socialist, François Mitterrand, president at the head of a Socialist-Communist coalition. The result was to make France officially the most leftist country in Western Europe. The government immediately went on a disastrous, two-year rampage of ideologically based nationalizations in industry and finance that came close to ruining the economy before the reality of the market place obliged it to change course.

In keeping with Raymond Aron's view that France's blockages—due largely to a corporatist attitude that incites every profession and trade to jealously guard the various, often ancient, privileges accorded it by governments past—prevent it from evolving normally, the last big political event in France was the May 1968 blow-up sparked by a half-baked student revolt. *Les évènements* of 1968, as the French obliquely call them, were the last time in modern French history that the citizenry actually challenged many aspects of the dead hand of the past that weighs on their society, and particularly on their young people. Aron himself termed the orgiastic, directionless turbulence a psychodrama, an epiphenomenon that allowed the French to vent their frustrations before going back to business as usual, including the same old blockages.

Apparently resigned to their endemic blockages, the French appear to have sunken into a slough of apathy, if we are to believe a report in 2004 by the country's elite corps of prefects, who are paid to keep their collective ear to the ground. "The French," it concluded gloomily, "no longer believe in anything."

1. The Dangerous National Pastime

The Great French Passion

Context: *By early 1983 it had become clear that the Socialist-Communist experiment with nationalizing whole swathes of French industry and most private banking was putting the country's economic stability in jeopardy. The franc plunged, exports declined, unemployment rose, and capital fled to safe havens abroad. Tensions were developing between the Socialists and their Communist partners. With municipal elections coming up, the French could again indulge their passion for the national pastime of politics.*

Bedroom farces and conventional wisdom about sexual prowess notwithstanding, the great French passion, the thing that really excites them, is not *that,* but politics.

When Francois Mitterrand and his Socialist Party unexpectedly won in May 1981, however, it left France in a state of shock. Most Frenchmen spent months in a political daze, trying to explain how it happened instead of participating in the national pastime.

Now things are getting back to normal. The two rounds of coming municipal voting constitute the first nationwide electoral contest since the Socialist-Communist coalition came to power. Inevitably, it is being treated as a national referendum, with all the attendant partisan fervor.

What is at stake are the town halls of some 36,400 municipalities, with the focus on 221 of the largest cities. The right hopes to turn the tables with wins across the country that would show national disapproval of Mitterrand's stewardship. With his popularity rating in February running at only 43 percent favorable—and that of Pierre Mauroy, his militant Socialist prime minister, even lower at 37 percent—that seems a distinct possibility. Even Socialist leaders talk publicly of losing 15 large towns; privately they say their losses could be much larger.

Certainly the French public is showing signs of having had enough doctrinaire socialism, at least in its more egregious aspects. After a year of nationalization of five major industrial groups and 23 of the largest private banks and financial institutions, a hefty majority of the public replied that they considered the nationalizations pointless, with an even larger proportion opposing any further state takeovers.

That did not prevent the government from injecting $2.9 billion more into the nationalized industries in hopes of making them something other than the loss leaders they currently are. But in true Socialist fashion, the government cannot quite decide whether the likes of Renault, Air France, Rhone-Poulenc and the Banque Nationale de Paris should be efficient and competitive or provide more jobs.

Criticism has come from within the Socialist ranks, notably from Jean-Pierre Cot, who was in Mitterrand's cabinet until a falling out over policy. "The Socialist program is running out of steam," Cot said recently. "If we Socialists don't get going, we will be as unsuccessful as almost all the European social democracies, in the wake of the failure of the welfare state. The truth is that the welfare state is living beyond its means."

The local election campaigns have brought the opposition back to life, though it remains fragmented. Former President Valery Giscard d'Estaing and two of the men who served his premiers, Jacques Chirac and Raymond Barre, are the three musketeers of the right.

But all they have in common is their enemy; each is promoting his own vision of what France needs. Giscard still dreams of liberal conservatism based on broad consensus, while Barre preaches hardheaded fiscal discipline. Chirac offers a Thatcheresque mix of social security cuts, lower taxes and denationalization.

Meanwhile, the Communists remain ambiguous partners in the coalition. It is widely expected that Mitterrand will have to impose unpopular new austerity measures after the elections. The Communists say they will have none of it. The stage is set for them to walk out of the cabinet and to go into open opposition, as they are almost certain to do at some point. The questions are what pretext they will seize, and when.

In that event, the country would likely become increasingly ungovernable, forcing Mitterrand to dissolve the parliament and call early national parliamentary elections. That in turn could produce a conservative National Assembly at odds with the government, possibly leading to early presidential elections.

This, at least, is the scenario many Frenchmen are weaving with relish, eying a virtual orgy of elections in the next few years. The alternative—no more voting for the next three years—would be as unthinkable here as a 3-year NFL strike in the U.S.

Update: *Alas for the scenario of early presidential elections, French voters had to wait three years. Mitterrand managed to retain control of the government until the parliamentary vote in March 1986, which the right won decisively. With two years still to run on his seven-year presidential term, the wily Mitterrand appointed his political opponent, the conservative Jacques Chirac, as prime minister, creating a bizarre, paradoxical form of government which the French promptly labeled "cohabitation." Chirac's popularity wilted as his government had to take the heat for unpopular austerity measures. Mitterrand handily won another seven-year term in 1988.*

Politicizing Culture

Context: *Culture is an important tool in France's* rayonnement, *or influence, in the world. This can be seen in the far-flung activities of the Alliance Française, a global network of some 1,000 centers with language courses, libraries of French publications, and screenings of French films. And since 1986 France has sponsored the International Francophonie Organization, with conferences attended by representatives of 50-odd countries where French is spoken, from Belgium to Burundi. In an effort to block "American cultural imperialism," France promotes, among other things, protectionist measures like high import duties on American films (except, perhaps, those with such French favorites as Jerry Lewis and Michael Moore) and television productions.*

It was the sort of pseudo-cultural flummery the French have long used to impress the world's would-be intellectuals and aesthetes. Held in the hallowed halls of the Sorbonne, the seminar entitled "Culture and Development" attracted an international galaxy of writers, artists and poseurs. For two days they discussed the role of culture in solving economic problems. President Francois Mitterrand called for nothing less than a new Renaissance uniting scientists and artists.

The premise was patent nonsense—true culture has nothing whatever to do with economic development—but the event gave the likes of John Kenneth Galbraith, Kate Millet and Gabriel Garcia Marquez the chance to strut their stuff on the Left Bank. It also promoted Mitterrand's international image as a man of ideas. And it was a feather in the cap of its organizer, Jack (sic) Lang, who considers culture a political tool.

Lang, who stage-managed Mitterrand's Socialist rallies during his long campaign for the presidency, was rewarded with the post of minister of culture. It was a controversial choice, but one thing is certain: With his long wavy hair and impish smile, he is definitely the cutest member of the French government.

French culture got along nicely without a cabinet minister—check out Montaigne, Molière and Monet if you have any doubts—until Charles de Gaulle created the job for a favorite conversation partner, André Malraux. The brooding, enigmatic Malraux personified French literary culture. No matter that his main achievement in the job was not cultural but aesthetic—the sandblasting of the monuments and buildings of Paris—he set the right tone by putting culture above politics.

Lang, on the other hand, seems uncertain whether he is the Socialist minister of culture, or the minister of Socialist Culture. When the Socialists took over in May 1981, he approached his task as a revolutionary. He would bring culture to the people.

Thus were bemused Parisians treated to the Comédie Française troupe playing Molière in the Metro. Another time, Lang exhorted them to descend into the streets with whatever instruments they possessed and tootle away on National Music Day. Plans were laid for a new "popular opera" house, appropriately at Place de la Bastille, cradle of the French Revolution.

Then there was Lang's crusade against "American cultural imperialism." That was the term he used in a diatribe at a UNESCO conference in Mexico. The American films that flood French TV—some 170 per year—the serials like "Dallas" or "Charlie's Angels," the popular music that pours from state-run French radio stations were all part of "an immense empire of profit." They were tools of America's "financial and intellectual imperialism that no longer colonizes territory but consciousness, ways of thinking, ways of living."

Lang's largely Third World audience at the UNESCO conference loved it. While in the Caribbean area, he stopped over in Cuba for a friendly chat with Fidel Castro, conveniently overlooking that Castro had imprisoned the great poet, Armando Valladares, for 21 years.

Not all Frenchmen approve of this cultural chauvinism. Actor Yves Montand, no stranger himself to leftist views, wryly counseled, "Let's bombard the Americans with great novels and films. Let's compete with them intelligently, without demagogy—if we can." A former French ambassador pointedly reminded his countrymen of how many French monuments, including Versailles, had been restored with American money.

Meanwhile, the French themselves seem to be voting with their feet on Lang's crusade against American popular culture. American films continue to set box-office records in Paris. American serials still are staple fare on TV. The average Frenchman's idea of a really socko evening with the tube is either an American serial or a western, preferably with John Wayne.

The television critic of the newspaper *Le Monde*, not usually a friend of the U.S., recently set out to make Lang happy by watching only French shows for an entire weekend. That meant channel-hopping furiously to avoid American serials in those two days. He never made it. Noting that French TV productions reached the height of "pretentious, soft-headed mediocrity," he succumbed to temptation Sunday afternoon and guiltily switched to "Starsky and Hutch."

French culture, though not as important to the world as the French like to believe, is dear to every civilized person. With luck, it will survive even the Great Socialist Culture Experiment.

Update: *France continues to use the culture ploy. The government's latest project to spread France's influence in the world is a French-speaking cable news network designed to fight "Anglo-Saxon hegemony" over global news. Due for 2006, its budget is $40 million, compared with the $1.2 billion CNN spends on international broadcasting. But despite the fact that the Francophonie movement now includes such unlikely countries as Bulgaria and Moldova, and that France is spending about $1 billion a year to promote its culture abroad, French still ranks only ninth among the world's languages. Worse, English as a working language is making inroads within France itself: some big French corporations now use English as an internal language, and French scientists know that, as they say, they must either "publish in English or perish in French."*

Testing the Myth of the Resistance

Context: *After World War II, France's underground Resistance movement was seized upon by Charles de Gaulle and others as a symbol of heroism to cover the shameful collaboration of many Frenchmen with their German occupiers. Though the Resistance was a reality, it was a very small one, involving only a relative handful of courageous men and women. When Klaus Barbie, the wartime Gestapo chief of Lyons who sent thousands of Jews and Resistance members to their deaths at Auschwitz and Buchenwald, was found in Bolivia in 1972 by the Nazi hunters Serge and Beate Klarsfeld, France demanded his extradition for trial for crimes against humanity. Many feared that the trial would reopen old wounds by revealing sordid details of collaboration and even treachery and informants within the Resistance itself.*

The odious Klaus Barbie, chief of the Gestapo in Lyons from 1942 to 1944, sits in France poised like a poisonous spider at the center of a web of suspicion, accusations and shame.

Barbie, an SS Obersturmfuhrer during the German occupation of France, has already been sentenced to death twice in absentia by French courts for 4,342 killings, deportation of 7,591 Jews to concentration camps, and arrest of 14,311 French citizens. His job, which he seemed to enjoy, was to hound Jews to death and break up the French Resistance.

But by the time of his conviction, Barbie, under the name Klaus Altmann, was living in Bolivia, courtesy of the U.S. Army's Counter Intelligence Corps. The "Butcher of Lyons," as he was known, was hired by the CIC in 1947 as a paid informant to monitor former SS officers and communists, and kept hidden in a safe house in occupied Germany.

Despite French requests for Barbie's extradition, the Army provided him a false Bolivian visa and a new identity and smuggled him to

South America in 1951, a deed for which the State Department later expressed its "deep regrets" to France when the truth became known.

Barbie lived prosperously under the protection of right-wing Bolivian military regimes. But the new civilian government of Hernan Siles Zuazo arrested him on the pretext of using false papers to obtain Bolivian nationality, and put him on a plane to Cayenne, French Guyana.

The French picked him up there and transported him straight to Lyons' Montluc prison, where many of his victims had been held. The statute of limitations having expired on his earlier convictions, he was charged with "crimes against humanity, assassinations, tortures, arrests, arbitrary detentions and kidnappings."

That was when the apprehension set in. For Barbie, now 70, made clear that his trial would also be the trial of France under Nazi occupation, a subject that many Frenchmen would much rather see gather the moss of time.

More French collaborated with the Nazis than opposed them. The Resistance, however brave its members, largely amounted to a fig leaf to save French honor. Its networks included a minuscule 75,000 in 1943, about two-tenths of 1 percent of the adult population. Even André Malraux, himself a fervent Gaullist and one of the brave few, called the Resistance "a myth."

Barbie threatened to show just how sordid and extensive was French collaboration with the Nazis, thus fulfilling Adolf Hitler's vow during a 1942 speech: "I will rot the countries that I occupy. I will make the people denounce each other and I will show them up as denouncers. I will cover them with mud." Acting through his aggressive French lawyer, Jacques Verges, Barbie began slinging mud.

He alleged that the venerated Resistance leader, Jean Moulin, who is buried in the Pantheon in Paris with other French greats like Victor Hugo, did not die in 1943 during interrogation by Barbie, but committed suicide. He killed himself in despair, Barbie claimed, over betrayal by fellow Resistance members who turned him in to the Nazis.

Unfortunately, the charge could not be dismissed out of hand. The Resistance was riven with political rivalry and jealousy. Moulin, Charles de Gaulle's personal representative in occupied France, wrote to the general in 1943, "What are we doing besides liberating France? It is your chance to take power against the Germans, against Vichy, against General Giraud, and perhaps against the Allies."

America was backing General Henri Giraud as leader of the Free French, finding him more malleable than De Gaulle, and distributing money to non-Gaullist Resistance networks, those that opposed Moulin. The noted French historian, Emmanuel Le Roy Ladurie, warned that the trial would be "an enormous national psychodrama."

Even many years later, the French Resistance is a closet concealing a great many skeletons. The gradual opening of it may revive a national nightmare.

Update: *During his eight-week trial beginning in May 1987, Barbie showed no remorse, only silent contempt, as he boycotted the courtroom except for two forced appearances to be identified by witnesses. The official myth was left to rest in peace, as his lawyers had little new to say about the Resistance. Forty-two years after the war, the French public, to its credit, followed the proceedings calmly and dispassionately, apparently seeing the trial as an opportunity to study the history of a painful period rarely discussed in public. The nine jurors and three judges found Barbie guilty on all 341 counts of crimes against humanity and gave him the maximum sentence, life imprisonment. He died in October 1991.*

Something Happened: May 1968

Context: *The year 1968 is remembered in the U.S. for things like the Tet offensive, the Prague spring, and the assassinations of Bobby Kennedy and Martin Luther King. By any measure it was an exceptional period in an exceptional time, the year, to quote the title of a recent book, "that rocked the world." In France, it was the year that something as trivial as spring-time student agitation nearly fissured from top to bottom the monolithic façade of one of the Western world's most integral, self-confident, and apparently rock-solid societies. Student demonstrations had long been such a traditional part of Left Bank folklore that "Sorbonne in State of Siege" was a familiar headline in Parisian newspapers. True, student protests against France's Algerian War and America's Vietnam War gave them a new level of political importance in the 1960s. But no one was particularly alarmed when students began marching down the Latin Quarter's Boule-vard Saint-Michel the first week in May 1968. It soon became clear, how-ever, that something unique in modern French history was happening. As a reporter for* Time, *I covered the confused events and tried to make sense of them on the spot. With the situation spiraling out of control, I was com-forted in my initial perplexity by the fact that President Charles de Gaulle could not understand it either, calling it "insaisissable," ("elusive" or "incomprehensible"). Only later did many observers, including myself, realize that we had witnessed a once-great civilization, now riddled with self-doubt, teetering on the brink of chaos.*

May 10—A week after the first demonstrations, the Sorbonne remains closed and the government is faced with what is beginning to look like a general student offensive on all fronts. The hope that the school could open and courses start again was dashed when student leaders threatened to take it over, and the education ministry decided to lock them out. Some 2,000 students who had turned up for courses and been turned back by busloads of helmeted police at Place de la

Sorbonne spent the day listening to fiery speeches by their leaders, including the ubiquitous Daniel Cohn-Bendit.

At one point, Cohn-Bendit sighted the old Communist poet Louis Aragon in the crowd and shouted through a bullhorn, "If you are with us, why didn't you come out in the streets with us?" The white-maned Aragon shouted back that he planned to devote an entire issue of the Communist literary weekly *Lettres Françaises* to the student movement. The pumped-up students booed him anyway. That evening they held a feverish mass meeting in a Left Bank hall and heard representatives of Italian, Belgian, Dutch, German and Spanish student movements pledge their support. That appeared to end the demonstrations for the day.

Meanwhile, representatives of the Communist and Socialist labor unions, hoping to jump on the anti-government bandwagon, met with student leaders to discuss joint action, including a mass march from Place de la République to Place de la Bastille, a route traditionally used by the unions for their demonstrations. And that pied piper of radical youth, Herbert Marcuse, paused long enough during a UNESCO-sponsored colloquium on the scientific thought of Karl Marx to comment that the student agitation constitutes "Not a revolution, as the students well know, but a vigorous protest that I understand well and that I sympathize with. Transformation of a society is a very long process."

The provinces, too, are catching fire, with student strikes and/or demonstrations reported at universities and lycées in Lyon, Lille, Clermont-Ferrand, Grenoble, Dijon, Rouen, Strasbourg, Aix, Nantes, Toulouse, and Rennes. Thus far, the government has taken no positive measures to deal with students' complaints and is hunkered down hoping the whole thing will blow over. At the moment, the situation is reminiscent of the dialogue between Louis XVI and the Duke of Liancourt in July 1789, the evening of the fall of the Bastille. "Is it a riot?" the king asked. "No, Sire," the duke replied simply, "it is a revolution." But if so, it is so far a remarkably non-violent one.

May 11—Like a banked fire that appears extinguished, the student demonstration that seemed over last night at 11 p.m. suddenly flared up into what Paris Police Prefect Maurice Grimaud called "one of the most lamentable nights Paris has ever known." When the incredible fighting on barricades formed of paving stones and burned-out automobiles was over at 6 a.m., there were 367 injured, including 102 students, 14 non-student civilians, and 251 police, gendarmes, and special Compagnie Républicaine de Sécurité (CRS) riot troops. Police arrested 468. This worst student riot in modern French history prompted President Charles de Gaulle to begin huddling with selected cabinet ministers at 6:30 a.m., the Archbishop of Paris to issue an urgent call for calm, and two of France's three national labor unions to order an illegal general strike for next week.

In the morning, fresh police reinforcements continued to cordon off streets in the heart of the Latin Quarter, and a triple line of them guarded the still-closed Sorbonne. On streets behind the school, barricades three to four feet high were being torn down by workers who were replacing the thousands of paving stones torn from the streets, which in many places show large scabs of sand where the stones are missing. Tear gas hanging in the air still smarts the eyes. Pedestrians permitted to enter the area because they live there pick their way through the rubble with eyes running. Students raised more than 50 barricades, most with paving stones but many improvised from the carcasses of some 200 automobiles which students had dragged into position, overturned and, frequently, set afire, blackening the streets and covering them in places with broken glass. The Latin Quarter is no longer only in a state of siege, it now resembles an urban battlefield.

The battle began about 2 a.m., after a calm of three hours during which it seemed that talks between student leaders and the rector of the Sorbonne might produce a compromise. But after the talks failed, the students, who numbered nearly 30,000, began tearing up the streets and piling the square gray cobblestones into barricades. Billboards were torn down and added, along with traffic lights and felled sycamore trees lining the streets. With Prime Minister Georges Pompidou on an official trip to Afghanistan, the interior minister, Christian Fouchet, gave the order to clear the area around the Sorbonne.

Moving in on the barricades around Boulevard Saint-Michel and Rue Gay Lussac, the police fired volleys of tear gas grenades and red flares, holding blue metal shields on their left arms before them like gladiators against the flying paving stones. Students also made Molotov cocktails and threw them from rooftops. Between repeated but ineffectual police charges, the students sang the Marseillaise and the Socialist Internationale, and threw up a banner saying "Long live the commune of May 10." To ward off police charges, students began setting fire to some 60 autos; the sharp explosions of their gas tanks mixed with the muffled pop of gas grenades. For the first time, De Gaulle's name was chanted: "*De Gaulle assassin*" ("De Gaulle murderer").

After three hours of combating what Paris Prefect Maurice Grimaud called "a veritable guerilla action," the police took the barricades. The students had almost a square mile of Paris in their grip. Eyes streaming from tear gas and many bearing injuries from vigorous beatings by police batons, the remaining students dispersed and left the smoldering streets to the exhausted police. With over 500 students and some 600 police injured, it was the end of the most violent night Paris has known since the Second World War. Its consequences only began to appear the next day.

One of the most serious of those consequences was the announcement that the Communist and Socialist labor unions ordered a 24-hour, nation-wide general strike for next week, the first time since the serious events of the Algerian War that the Communist union, with its close ties to the Moscow-lining French Communist Party, has called one to try to destabilize the government. The strike could paralyze France, leaving it without railroads, buses, subways, electricity and other public services. Besides that, the unions plan to couple the strike with joint demonstrations with the students. In this unprecedented situation in France, the possible political results of that remain incalculable.

May 16—Like all successful revolutionaries, the students of France are now confronted with the toughest problem of all: what they are going to do with their initial victory won last week on the barricades of the Left Bank. That the revolution has begun is no longer in doubt in their minds. Visit the Sorbonne, and the first thing you see is the school's familiar gray slate dome festooned with red flags, with another red banner fluttering from the peak of the neo-classical façade fronting on Place de la Sorbonne. In the tree-lined square itself, the bust of the 19th-century mathematician and philosopher Auguste Comte is draped in red. Knots of students are gathered in feverish discussion, often with grizzled Communist Party veterans.

On the venerable institution's walls are plastered posters reflecting the frustration of French young people in a rigid society that changes only at a glacial pace: "For the first time since 1848, this place is getting a dusting;" "The barricade closes the street but opens the way;" "Imagination takes over;" "Smoking obligatory" (instead of the usual no smoking signs); "It is strictly forbidden to forbid;" "Permanent dialogue." And in red manuscript on bright yellow paper, a copy of the New China News Agency version of what happened in the May 10 street battles: "…the clique of French revisionists, contemptible accomplices of the establishment, went so far as to act in close cooperation with the fascist police in their bloody suppression of the students."

The Sorbonne opened Monday morning, true to Georges Pompidou's televised promise, and was promptly occupied by the students, who have been there day and night since. They have turned it into a student's dream and a teacher's nightmare: one interminable, mad, multifarious bull session with no courses to interrupt it. The subject is what is wrong with the French university system and French society.

During one session, a heavy-lidded extremist leader with wild black hair and an old red scarf around his neck harangued a classroom packed to bursting with attentive students on their new-found power. "We have proved what we can do when we march together," he cried. "We can change the university and the society that produced it. And there will be no exams until we get satisfaction." When he finished, a serious, concerned girl in a neat blue suit raised her hand to speak (the sessions are remarkably orderly, and the groups of "revolutionaries" are damned well dressed, too) and expressed doubt over what good it would all do since even if there were no exams this year, the government would have things in hand again by the following school year. "Listen," the leader retorted, "if the government goes back on its promises, we will fill this place with *merde* and start again from scratch."

In the cobblestoned courtyard of the Sorbonne, hundreds of students mill around between sessions in the amphitheaters. One I overheard commenting to a classmate, "I've never seen so many here before. There are never this many when there's class." Sometimes an improvised jazz band plays, or a pianist. There are sandwiches, fruit juice and beer at a buffet. At two or three stands they sell selected works of Lenin and Mao in addition to the inevitable little red book of Chairman Mao's thoughts. Illustrated propaganda magazines straight from Peking are there too, along with color portraits of Mao and pictures of Mao and Ho Chi Minh shaking hands.

The students of France, themselves the first to be astonished at seemingly accomplishing what many of the world's other students have been talking about for so long, looked a bit lost at mid-week. The fact was that only a tiny minority had any interest in the goal enunciated by the extremist leader Daniel Cohn-Bendit, of "the total suppression of capitalist society."

No one knows at this point what France's revolution-minded students will finally obtain, largely because the government is holding its fire, letting the movement talk itself out in the knowledge that it is when the establishment makes a move to oppose that the students get up their best steam. So far the only official government statement has been Georges Pompidou's masterful declaration at the National

Assembly in which he held out something for everyone without compromising the government's basic position.

Premier Pompidou's speech followed a week not only of unprecedented student clashes with police, but also a mass march of students, professors, and labor union members through Paris, a general strike, and a censure motion tabled by the Communists and other leftist parties.

The march, the largest seen in Paris since the war, surpassed the hopes of its organizers. The crowd filled the huge Place de la République and overflowed into surrounding streets as far as the Gare de l'Est train station. Students climbed all over the gigantic allegorical statue of the draped lady representing the Republic, and when they left she was waving a red flag in one hand. The march stepped off at 4 p.m. under a sunny sky, banners proclaiming "Solidarity of students, teachers and workers" flying. Oddly for revolutionaries, most marchers were smiling and having a good time. Just as oddly, they were cheered by "bourgeois" spectators leaning from windows and by crowds lining the sidewalks four deep.

(This almost masochistic support by the middle class for people attacking everything they stand for is one of the strangest aspects of this situation and could indicate a tectonic shift in values in French society seemingly riven with self-doubt. During some pitched battles between stone-throwing students and police, men in suits and ties, carrying briefcases, are seen egging the students on, shouting, "Hit 'em again, kids.")

When not singing the Socialist Internationale, which has become the students' theme song, they chanted "De Gaulle to the museum," "De Gaulle resign," "Ten years are enough," and other slogans against the government and the bourgeoisie at large. The march of around half-a-million persons took fully five hours.

The strike on the same day, called illegally without the five days' advance notice required by law, was not as severe as it might have been. The government did nothing to try to stop it, despite its patent illegality. In Paris the Metro and buses were cut by only half, and across the country 40 to 60 percent of the trains kept running. Air traffic was hit hard when controllers walked off the job, however, and mail and telegraph service was practically nil. Gas and electricity were cut in Paris at 7 a.m., but were back to normal by early afternoon. The strike's severity was lessened due to its being called on such short notice, and also because many workers refused to go along with a purely political strike that had little to do with gut issues like better pay.

Over at the National Assembly, the Communist-Socialist opposition presented its censure motion against the government, but not before two members of parliament nearly came to blows. After a suspension of 20 minutes to restore order, the motion was read. It charged that the students were denouncing a sick society while the government answered only by closing the Sorbonne and "police repression of unheard-of brutality." Farmers and workers were hard hit by a poor economic policies, the motion claimed, and young people were doomed to joblessness before even beginning their working lives.

Thus the stage was set for a packed National Assembly to hear Premier Georges Pompidou's important speech. First he launched into the "small, very active group of students who believe in the doctrine of direct action and violence. They believe they are innovators, but there is nothing new about that." He admitted that they had the right to criticize society, but not to try to make the law in the society they reject. He also referred darkly to well-financed persons, equipped with special street-fighting weapons and apparently belonging to an international organization which was trying to create disturbances in Paris during the American-Vietnamese peace talks.

Before ending, Pompidou, a former professor of literature and a genuinely thoughtful man, took a profound look at the underlying causes of student unrest that sounded like the symptoms signaling the end of Western civilization. Discipline had largely disappeared, the family as such was in disorder, radio and television put young people in direct contact with life, all the values and beliefs that had supported humanity for centuries had been shaken, he said. God was dead for many, and even the Church was questioning itself. Youth was naturally turning against society, and not only capitalist society, judging by what students were doing in Warsaw, Prague and Moscow, because to them it had become materialist and soulless. "The only precedent I see in our history was that period of despair that was the 15th century when the structures of the Middle Ages collapsed, and when, already, the students of the Sorbonne revolted." When he closed with an appeal for the cooperation of all and observed that the basic problems were more philosophical than political, it did not even sound like demagoguery.

May 17—Though France's revolutionary students may not know quite where they are going, they are still going there energetically. Wednesday night they spent their third evening occupying the Sorbonne. So great was the crowd, including curious Parisians come to see the cultural revolution for themselves, that the student police had to direct traffic at the door, allowing inflow for one minute and then a minute's outflow. New posters are up: "Don't look now, God, but the world's collapsing;" "Let's dechristianize the Sorbonne;" "The more I make revolution, the more I want to make love." A general assembly voted to auction off the academic frescoes that decorate the main amphitheater, but no one has solved the admittedly ticklish problem of how to get them off the walls.

The effects on French cultural life are beginning to be understood by the public. As the audience was exiting from the state-subsidized Théâtre de France, also known as the Odéon, one of the monuments of French culture, they saw a column of students advancing with banners saying "The Odéon for the workers." About a thousand of them stormed in, to the astonishment of the ushers and stagehands, and took over the theater, which is only a short walk from the Sorbonne. Soon it was filled from orchestra to the last balcony with madly chattering students, and provisions were being brought in and stacked for the long stay. Across the building's façade was stretched a banner: "Students and workers! The Odéon is open!" The attack on the age-old elitist French approach to culture could not have been clearer.

The theater's director, Jean-Louis Barrault, a cultural institution himself, was alerted and returned. "I understand your aspirations," he shouted through a megaphone. Barrault's actress wife also chimed in. "We play Ionesco, Genet and Beckett here. We are not a bourgeois theater. You should take over other theaters." The answer was brief: "Our revolutionary action is beginning. We are going to hold a permanent convention here, a meeting place for workers, a permanent creative revolution." Another poster went up on the building's front: "Imagination takes over the former Odéon Theater. Free entry."

When a group of actors showed up at midnight, a student leader exhorted them to search for "new forms of theater as a means of action against the bourgeoisie." He charged Jean-Louis Barrault, long a favorite of the theater's Latin Quarter audience, with being "in the vanguard of the bourgeoisie." Barrault, by then clearly discouraged and shaken, replied weakly that he was there "as a simple actor, to listen." The theater, he said, was dead.

May 20—Paris woke up to the revolution today. Until now, the student demonstrations, the barricades, the takeover of the Sorbonne and the Théâtre de France by slogan-chanting, Marxist-mouthing youngsters all had entertainment value that outweighed the alarm in most Parisians' minds. Indeed, dropping by the Sorbonne after work or on weekends to check the latest posters and see the red flags has already become part of the Paris scene for even the squarest bourgeois. But this morning there was real worry, and it keeps growing.

The difference was due to the country's creeping paralysis. Paris Metro and bus systems started grinding to a halt Saturday. By this morning the only way to get around was on foot, by personal car, or taxi. The boulevards swarmed with footsore office workers hoofing it to their jobs, the thoroughfares impossibly clogged with twice the normal traffic. At least they did not face the problem of gasoline, which has become scarce overnight as a result of panic buying. Pumps all over France carry "No more gas" signs, and there are long lines at stations that still have some.

Panicked housewives lined up at food shops, where they stocked up on canned goods, sugar, cooking oil, potatoes, and candles. Also assaulted by crowds were banks and savings associations, the main fear being that a strike could close tellers' windows, effectively leaving the French without enough francs to buy an aperitif, much less a meal.

Once they have solved the basic problems, Parisians face an even graver one: how to get away from them. The Opéra is closed, with crude banners across its classical façade. No joy at the Comédie Française or the Opéra Comique either, and most non-subsidized theaters will remain dark tonight due to a 24-hour actors' strike. The movie houses are closed by a projectionists' walkout, and there are few newspapers at the kiosques due to a distributors' strike. You can't get out of town—air service at Orly and Le Bourget is minimal, the trains haven't run since Saturday—except by car, and gas is short for that.

Perhaps the only comic relief in the whole mess, including the overflowing garbage cans lining the streets beneath the chestnut blossoms, was the announcement early today that Metro and bus administrative personnel were dispensed from going to their offices "due to transportation difficulties."

May 23—Glancing at the ornate skylight above the speakers' rostrum in the French National Assembly later yesterday afternoon, Valéry Giscard d'Estaing, former finance minister and now leader of the pro-Gaullist Independent Republican party, said, "Never has the light falling from that skylight seemed to me to illuminate such an unreal world." Millions of workers were on strike, he noted, French universities were boiling over, public services interrupted—and the Assembly was indulging in "an academic controversy.... Faced with this withdrawal from reality, from life, I experience a feeling of sadness, of solitude."

The National Assembly has been irrelevant to France's crisis ever since it began—witness the massive indifference of students and workers toward it—and this week's debate on the opposition's censure motion could have been taking place on the moon for all the bearing it had on the situation.

The Opposition attack was led by the Communists and François Mitterrand, leader of the Federation of the Left. "Outside the doors of this Assembly, censure is already voted," the eager, ambitious Mitterrand charged, sensing a chance to take power. "We propose an alternative. We are ready to assume the responsibilities of government." And Giscard d'Estaing, while not supporting the censure motion, put an intelligent finger on France's problem with her young people: "Youth is searching for the definition of a new civilization which rejects two mediocre leitmotivs, the pursuit of material goods and the stultifying disguises of conformity."

When Pompidou rose to counter the motion, he spoke slowly and hesitantly at first, apparently not having had time to prepare a written speech. He was in fine form nonetheless, snapping confidently at one Opposition member who heckled him, "Things will go better than you think, and certainly better than you hope." He went on, "It goes without saying that events of this importance must have profound causes. After this, nothing in France can be quite the same as before." He was ready to negotiate on specific demands, but not on the basis of political strikes: "It is not up to the unions to substitute for the sovereign people."

He admitted there were "profound reforms" to be thought out, particularly in the university system. But changes could not be immediate, and it was indispensable that exams take place. Finally, he dropped the veiled threat that if censure were voted, it would end not only his administration, but the current membership of the National Assembly, a reference to De Gaulle's intention to dissolve the Assembly and call new elections if the motion passed.

At 8:10 p.m. Assembly President Jacques Chaban-Delmas announced the result of the vote: 233 votes had been cast for the censure motion, 11 short of the majority required. The French government will stand a while longer, but as Georges Pompidou noted, things in France will never be the same.

Update: *Charles de Gaulle, who appeared disoriented, suddenly left Paris by helicopter on May 29, amid rumors that he might resign as president. He visited top French Army commanders based with French occupation troops in Germany and returned with their vocal support—and menacing rumors of tanks approaching Paris. The government ended the strikes by buying off the unions with a 14 percent wage increase across the board that cost the economy dearly. De Gaulle dissolved the National Assembly and called elections for the end of June. Thanks to a nervous citizenry that saw France's institutions disintegrating before their eyes, the vote produced a landslide victory for the Gaullists. The whole episode ended in early July, when the government cleverly released supplies of gasoline it had been holding back, threatening the usual summer exodus. The French went on vacation with a sigh of relief. De Gaulle, whose confident hold on French affairs was shaken, abruptly left office the following April. Georges Pompidou was elected president in June 1969. It had not been a revolution—today the French ironically call the nostalgic would-be revolutionaries of the time* les soixante-huitards*—but the dumbing down of French education under the guise of reform and the loss of authority of French institutions had begun.*

Where are the Stones of Yesteryear?

Context: *"Beneath the cobblestones, there's a beach" was one of the more popular of the students' 1968 posters, referring to the sand they found under the Paris paving stones they dug up to build barricades and hurl at police. The French government was not amused. It resolved that never again would it be so easy to find projectiles in Paris. The 15th century poet François Villon, whose rowdy career entitled him to be condemned to hanging before receiving a pardon, asked wistfully in one poem, "But where are the snows of yesteryear?" Those of us who loved the city's cobblestones feel the same way.*

Paris's trademark cobblestones have been a fixture in the city since 1185, when King Philippe-Auguste decided that the stench of its malodorous, garbage-filled mud streets was really too much, and had the first cobblestones laid. It was an expensive operation, and he could afford only to pave the city's main north-south and east-west axes. King Charles the Wise had nostrils as sensitive but a more shrewd approach, and made the citizens of Paris pay taxes to support his paving program in 1388. But it was really only under Sun King Louis XIV that Paris got the streets it deserved. Despite his preference for the good life at Versailles, he made sure Paris thoroughfares were solidly covered with the gray granite stones that today cover a good part of the 1,153 kilometers, or 700 miles, of the city's streets.

But those stones have been put to other uses over the years, notably by insurgents against the French government itself. That began in earnest in 1830, when the leaders of the July Revolution threw up barricades to protest the Restoration by Charles X of the privileges of the aristocracy. (They won: Charles went into exile and the liberal Louis-Philippe took over.)

The next time the City of Light saw barricades rising from its streets was during the Revolution of 1848, when Louis-Philippe was in turn overthrown by revolutionaries fired up on the new Socialist ideology that had begun circulating. Three days of barricades in February of that year were enough to send Louis-Philippe packing and bring in the Second Republic. Finally there was the great street battle of the Paris Commune, when an insurrectional government was established behind barricades on the Right Bank in March 1871, and lasted until May before being crushed.

From May 1871 until May 1968, there were no barricades in the streets of Paris, unless you count a few built during the liberation of the city in 1944. Thus the student revolutionaries in the spring of 1968 were acting on an instinct that must be in the French blood, because they could have had no experience of them during their lifetimes. And if the government has its way, they will have no more in the future, at least in the vicinity of the Sorbonne.

Apparently deciding that the way to hell can be paved with cobblestones as well as good intentions, the Paris city fathers are covering up patches of the ever-handy paving. Parisians returning from summer vacation will find that Rue des Écoles, which runs in front of the Sorbonne's main entrance, has now been blacktopped with a heavy covering of asphalt making the cobblestones inaccessible. Ditto for Rue Saint-Jacques, which runs along the sprawling building's east side, and Boulevard Saint-Michel, main artery of the Left Bank student quarter.

Aesthetically, it's a pity, since the neatly cut square stones are laid with great art in rilling fan patterns, a visual delight for connoisseurs of the back platform of Paris buses. Practically speaking it is a loss as well, since the *pavés* make a perfectly smooth street surface which requires almost no maintenance and never has potholes. And for the students who return in October hell-bent on revolution, it's a disaster. They have been deprived at a stroke of their best offensive weapon and defensive barrier.

The Sorbonne, which a mere two months ago was foundering dangerously in the waves of barricades rising from the cobblestone streets around her, today sails serenely on a flawless lake of thick black asphalt.

Update: *Successive Paris mayors have continued to lay asphalt over the city's cobblestones, so that a trip down a street of* pavés *is becoming a rare treat. And Parisians need no longer dig the stones up to find a beach: after taking over the Hôtel de Ville in the municipal elections of March 2001, the Socialists, the first leftists to run the city since 1871, created* Paris Plage *on a strip of the Right Bank riverfront. Complete with tons of sand trucked in and potted palm trees, the beach exists only in the month of August.*

3. L'Amérique

How They See Us

Context: *It often seems that there are few peoples more temperamentally incompatible than the Americans and the French: we have fun, they are amused; we are pragmatic and results-oriented, they theoretical and given to Jesuitical casuistry to win arguments; we have a self-deprecating sense of humor, they a tradition of wit, not humor, and with their implacable self-satisfaction, are incapable of anything like self-deprecation; we believe bigger is better, they seek quality; we are boisterous, they fastidious to the point of stifling a sneeze. The writer Paul Claudel, while serving as French ambassador to Washington, noted "not only such divergences, but such contradictions" between us. Franco-American relations sometimes remind me of the old French film—was it* Quai des Brumes?*—where Jean Gabin and Michèle Morgan meet in a Paris bar, and Gabin says in exasperation, "Anyway, men and women can never understand each other." "No," Morgan replies softly, "but they can love each other." If that is so of America and France, then verily, the course of true love never did run smooth.*

If it is true, as Paul Johnson argues in his masterful study of the 20th century, *Modern Times,* that anti-Americanism was "the most ubiquitous form of racism," then anti-Americanism joins that long list of things that ain't what they used to be.

For America-haters worldwide, the 1970s were great days. They marched in the streets of every European capital to protest the war in Vietnam. Third World leaders thundered against American "neo-colonial imperialism." American multinational companies on the six continents were denounced as bloodsuckers. American troops in Europe were often treated as a nuisance at best.

The whole venomous decade came to a climax at the American Embassy in Tehran, with American diplomats held hostage and humiliated for months as a contemptuous world looked on with barely concealed schadenfreude.

Today that sort of vicious anti-Americanism has receded to some extent, due partly to the dawning realization in the rest of the world that Marxism has failed wherever it has been tried, most spectacularly in the Soviet Union. But resentment of the United States still smolders just beneath the surface in many countries.

The fact that the American economy still leads the world, for example, rankles many in France, who see their own economy mired in high unemployment and low productivity. Particularly in leftist circles, it is the conventional wisdom that U.S. prosperity can only be the result of hot money fleeing Western Europe. And, of course, American exploitation of the Third World.

Besides, those grapes of prosperity must be sour. "There are still some idealists among American youth," a French author writes bitterly, "but most young people only think about their bank accounts. During the Reagan years the American Dream has assumed the form of a safe deposit box."

French attitudes toward America are always a revealing litmus of how we are seen by others. As the writer Paul Claudel noted when he was French ambassador to Washington from 1927 to 1933, "There are no other two nations in the world whose temperaments, characters, ways of seeing and feeling present not only such divergences, but such contradictions."

One main contradiction concerns attitudes toward money. This has long been a taboo subject in France, despite, or perhaps because of, the fact that the French are probably the most implacably avaricious people in Europe. As a thoughtful French observer put it recently, "We would like to be able both to despise money and to have it at the same time." That conflicted, neurotic mentality contrasted, he said, with the American outlook, where "The poor really do hope to become rich, or at least see their children rich."

But such candor is rare. More typical of a certain jaundiced French view of American wealth is the remark by Jack (sic) Lang, French minister of culture: "Is it our destiny to become the vassals of this immense empire of profit? We call for a veritable cultural resistance movement, a crusade against this financial and intellectual imperialism."

The idea that it is necessary to actively resist American values and "domination" is a frequent one in France. Whereas it would never occur to most Americans to ponder whether they were pro-French or anti-French, many French citizens seem compelled to define their attitude toward the United States. Indeed, some French observers have suggested that this need to react one way or the other to America is a symptom of a national identity crisis.

Perhaps one of the most judicious views of France's love-hate relationship with America comes from Georges Suffert, a Parisian journalist who knows the United States well. Writing in *Le Figaro*, he regretted that it is still fashionable to be critical of "those awful Americans." In his analysis he traces such anti-Americanism to French frustration over their decline from world power status.

"We have trouble getting used to being a second-rate power, and we secretly dislike the United States for becoming a major power," he writes. "Thus our attitude is based to some extent on hidden bitterness and jealousy."

Suffert calls for a healthier, more realistic view: "Despite America's thousand-and-one faults, the essential thing is that, for the first time in history, it has created a multiracial, multireligious planetary civilization. Over there the next century has already begun, and when we cross the ocean we change centuries. Why not admit it?"

Anti-Americanism waxes and wanes. Not the least of the French paradoxes is that they will be psychologically mature only when they can at last accept the success of the American experiment.

Update: *French officials, egged on by the media, still feel compelled to stick their thumb in Uncle Sam's eye whenever possible as a form of grandstanding. The United Nations in particular makes a splendid international grandstand, thus the perennial French support for it. It is not that French citizens individually are anti-American; on the contrary, I personally have* *never encountered any hostility living in France, and occasionally a French acquaintance will apologize for the official line. I always reassure them that the only places to find anti-Americanism in France are in the hallways of the media, the Élysée Palace, and the foreign ministry on the Quai d'Orsay. Still, the old French stereotypes about America as a nation of Indian killers, slave drivers, and capitalist fat cats die hard. To satisfy a certain small segment of the French public, books criticizing the United States are a minor cottage industry, with titles ranging from* After the Empire: The Decomposition of the American System, *and* The 21st Century Will Not Be American, *to* America the Whore.

Kerry Loses, Bonjour Tristesse

Context: *Sensitive souls that they are, the French are not known for steady nerves and grace under pressure. Thus the collective* dépression nerveuse *(freely translated as a hissy fit) they went through after George W. Bush won a second term in the White House. The deep trauma they suffered was directly proportional to the high hopes the French had for John Kerry.*

As one man, the French media, that good and faithful servant of the Élysée Palace and Quai d'Orsay, painted an adoring portrait of Kerry as Someone Like Us. He spoke French, it was repeatedly pointed out, spent his childhood summers in France, had a French cousin, and, *mon dieu!*, a wife who could say hello in five languages. He understood Us. So unlike that boorish, cretinous, bellicose religious fanatic (a Texan, of course) who had been elected by accident, or probably fraud. In Germany the best-selling newspaper, *Bild,* might have good words for Bush, but *Le Monde,* the thinking Frenchman's newspaper, couldn't resist prominently publishing an editorial calling for Kerry's victory.

Although French government officials from President Jacques Chirac on down avoided expressing a preference publicly—calculating that their well-known penchant for Kerry could be counterproductive with the American electorate—opinion leaders across the political spectrum joined in the chorus of Bush bashing. "Bush and Bin Laden: two of a kind," said Jack (sic) Lang, a former Socialist minister of culture. "Bush the imperialist is worse than Hitler," claimed the right-wing politician Jean-Marie Le Pen.

Despite their well-earned reputation for cynicism, the French usually tend to believe whatever line their government/media Establishment feeds them. So after months of this drumbeat, accompanied by riffs of visceral anti-Americanism, including spitefully acclaiming Michael Moore's *Fahrenheit 9/11* best film of the year at Cannes, it's small wonder that up to 90 percent of all Gauls prayed for a Kerry victory. Citing poll figures, *Le Figaro* gleefully headlined a week before the election, "Kerry Wins French Plebicite."

Hélas, it was not to be. Some early TV and radio reports, misled by the infamous early exit polls, gave brief hope that Kerry had practically won. But as the actual results started coming across the Atlantic in the early hours of November 3, the disbelief and dismay on the faces of French television reporters and commentators was poignant to behold. One lady reporter for a French channel actually burst into tears on camera as she announced the dreadful news. A quick poll showed that Bush's win was "a catastrophe" for 43 percent of the French, "bad news" for another 26 percent.

Sadly, I witness French post-election *tristesse* daily. When my upstairs neighbor, a cosmopolitan lady who worked with an international company and whose daughter has lived in the U.S., asked me how I felt about the election, her eyes grew large and her lips pursed in suppressed shock when I replied with insensitive candor that it reflected the choice of the American electorate. The conversation ended there. And my friend Georges, a usually savvy businessman, didn't even wait to ask me my opinion when we met the day after the election. "I'm devastated," he told me glumly, launching into a tirade. "How could you people have voted for a blatant liar like Bush? A man who starts a war for no valid reason. In hock to Christian evangelicals. What a disaster!"

The French puzzled particularly over this thing called "moral values." Many concluded that it might just have something to do with a turn to—*quelle horreur*—conservatism. Politically, they might have understood if Bush had won because of his leadership style, or because his gauche manners appealed to the coarse American heartland. But *values?* In a country where the great cathedrals now echo emptily to the footsteps of a few visiting tourists, where only one person in 10 says religion is of any importance, indeed, a nation that has entered an enlightened, post-Christian millennium, the very idea of moral values is quaint, if not risible. As *Le Monde* summed up grimly, "Whether we like it or not, America has become more conservative, more religious and more unilateralist." *Libération* sounded the alarm: "America at the start of the 21st century is reactionary. It might become ultra-conservative and aggressive…The rest of the world deplores it, but we'd better get used to it."

The French chattering class and media gnashed their teeth and braced for the worst. Typical was the former foreign minister, Hubert Védrine, who likes to call America a unilateralist hyperpower, implying immense danger for all. Bush's re-election, he said darkly, revealed "a large and lasting incomprehension between the American people and the rest of the world," with little likelihood of improved transatlantic relations. Headlined the newsweekly *L'Express*, "Bush: Uncontrollable Master of the World."

Among European leaders, both Tony Blair and Gerhard Schröder made congratulatory telephone calls to Bush, while Italy's Silvio Berlusconi and Russia's Vladimir Putin openly applauded. But Jacques Chirac, who still sees political capital to be garnered both at home and abroad, particularly in the Middle East, with anti-American gesticulation, condescended only to dash off a perfunctory written note. His "Cher George" message had the usual reference to historic Franco-American ties before doing some serious finger wagging about the need for "mutual respect" (read "Pay more attention to France"). He closed with a self-serving exhortation to "a close transatlantic partnership" (read ditto) and the assertion that "France and the United States have an essential role to play" (read "We're just as important as you") in solving the world's problems. It would be a week before Chirac got around to actually calling the White House.

Chirac then ostentatiously hustled over to Yasser Arafat's bedside at a French military hospital, thereby currying favor with France's volatile 5 million Muslims and doubtless counting on a TV feed to the al-Jazeera satellite channel. (Their publicized half-hour talk must have been one-sided, Arafat at the time being in a coma.) Chirac's next stop was an EU summit in Brussels specially attended by Iyad Allawi, Iraq's interim prime minister, there to appeal for European help. Chirac used that to make a double carom shot at Bush. After first loudly promoting his vision of the need, "now more than ever," to strengthen Europe in opposition to America, he then deliberately snubbed Allawi by leaving the conference early to avoid a scheduled meeting. Ever the Friend of the Arab World, he was in a hurry, he explained, to attend the funeral of Sheikh Zayed in Abu Dhabi.

Update: *Actually, Jacques Chirac was probably one of the few Gallic citizens secretly happy about the election. After hearing Kerry lauded to the skies, the French would have had trouble understanding their government's rebuff if he had won the White House and then asked for European cooperation in Iraq. But they expect Chirac to say* merde *to Bush.*

Parlez-Vous Franglais?

Context : *The Académie Française is fighting a losing battle with Franglais, that incessant adoption by the French of American expressions, often transformed almost beyond recognition. It is as if the French feel, obscurely, that their culture, and particularly their language, are rigidly old-fashioned, a tight corset preventing them from joining the modern world. True, American English is today the de facto lingua franca of the world of commerce and technology. Some nations, the practical Dutch and Scandinavians, for instance, adapt to this with relatively little travail while retaining their cultural identity. In France, however, it is controversial and fraught with self-consciousness. Even pilots of Air France airliners sometimes bridle at air-traffic instructions given in English, the official language, for safety reasons, of international aviation. If imitation is the sincerest form of flattery, Americans should feel very flattered indeed by the French inclination to adopt our popular culture wholesale and, unfortunately, indiscriminately.*

"I learned Italian to speak to the Pope, Spanish to speak to my mother, English to speak to my aunt, German to speak to my friends, and French to speak to myself," said Charles V, the son of Philip the Handsome and Joan the Mad, who grew up to be Holy Roman emperor, king of Spain, and archduke of Austria. It may be some consolation to today's Parisian that even in the 16th century, French was essentially a language one spoke to oneself. For as he sits in his cafes, reads his newspapers, walks the streets of his city and chats with his friends, he must have the impression that no one is speaking French.

The lingua franca of France has become American English, or a pidgin version of it. Witness the recent magazine advertisement for an Alpine ski resort in which a contented vacationer recounts his pleasures: *"Je slalome, je skie, je rocke, je scotch, je bridge, je poke* (i.e., play poker), *je girl, je shopping…"* And for shopkeepers who want to be *up-to-date*, to use the current French expression replacing *au courant*, a trade journal recently published a guide to Franglais terms they must be ready to use daily: "The retailer of today is a *businessman* who has his *job* in his shop. *Self-made man* or not, owner of a *discount*, of a *self-service*, of a *drugstore* or a *building*, the retailer uses *brainstorming* to analyze the *tests* guiding his *marketing*.

The important thing, the journal went on, is to use *merchandising* to turn *teenagers* into buyers of *blue-jeans, polos, twin-sets, sweaters, spencers, raglans, trench-coats,* and *blazers*, and to incite their elders to wear *le smoking*. It is not enough to transform his shop into a *supermarket*. He needs to install *gadgets* while a *juke-box* plays *twists, surfs, rocks, be-bop* which are on the *hit,* cutting in with publicity *flashes* by a *speaker* with an *in* style. This formula is sure to produce a *boom* and a *rush* for *pulls, fully-fashioned, slacks, tweeds* and *Shetlands*. He must encourage the passer-by to transform his *footing* into *shopping,* using if necessary a bit of *forcing*.

In itself, this aping of Americanisms on the part of the French is nothing new. It was already disturbing enough to language purists some years ago to prompt books and campaigns against it. The shrewd French satirist Pierre Daninos, for instance, wrote a newspaper column condemning French touchiness on the subject, saying "All this strikes me at first glance as being extremely healthy. At second glance (often the one that counts), as extremely unhealthy. This whole subject, and in particular the crusade led by [some purists], has a wicked whiff of anti-Americanism."

But the crusaders were not about to let the whole subject drop, and French efforts to "defend" their language continue apace. In 1966 the government set up the High Commission for the Defense and Expansion of the French Language under the direct patronage of the prime minister, then Georges Pompidou. At the commission's inaugural session Pompidou exhorted it to "think big and act quickly." Among the threats to French, as he saw it, were "a relaxing of syntax, a bastardizing of vocabulary, less intellectual rigor, a decadence of taste, and finally, an insensibility to ridicule."

The premier further warned against "linguistic barbarism…verbal profligacy…the very negation of culture and good sense." Citing a letter from the Académie Française to Cardinal Richelieu in 1634, he urged the commission to work at "cleaning [the language] of the filth it has picked up." There was no doubt in anyone's mind that the "filth" in question was American terminology.

It was about then that the Académie Française decided it would issue lists of neologisms, inevitably dominated by English words and expressions, which it proscribed, together with suggested equivalents. A glacier moves like lightning compared to the Academy, and when the list was published it was a modest one. Still, it marked The Immortals' entry into the fray.

They said that the frequently used English term "check-up," in the sense of medical exam, should be replaced by *bilan de santé*. Likewise, "open," whether an airline ticket reservation or a tennis tournament, should be *ouvert* or *libre*. It waffled on two sticky terms for which French simply has no replacement, "management" and "mass media." The former could be used in a pinch, the Academy said, as long as it was pronounced *à la française*, while the latter should become the awkward *masses-media*. An administrative official of the Academy, not an academician himself, observed that "There is a greater sense of urgency now" to defend French. The Academy planned to issue its lists several times a year. Unfortunately, the Frenchman in the street has manifested no interest whatever in the exercise.

Publishing lists of French equivalents to Franglais is becoming the preferred way to combat the nefarious, and ubiquitous, infiltration of Americanisms. Indeed, if the number of organizations determined to defend French is any sign of concern, then Francophones appear to be in a state of near panic. Doctors set up a study commission and then issued a list of French substitutes for English terms, proposing *noeud sinusal* for the often-used "pace maker," and, so help us, *pied d'athlète* for "athlete's foot."

Besides the physicians, other organizations include—take a deep breath—the Study Commission for French Technical Terms, the Treasury of the French Language, the French Association of Normalization, the Young Francophones Association, the Association of Partially or Entirely French Language Universities, the Research and Study Center for French, the Consultative Commission on Scientific Languages, the French radio system's Committee for Defense of the Language, the Federation of Universal French, the General Inventory of the French Language, the Office of Good Language, and the International Council of the French Language.

The International Council is probably the most active of these hardy little bands flying the linguistic tricolor. Its main project is a glossary of universal French, which divided French words into four categories. Those on red pages are unequivocally and forever condemned without recourse as unacceptable at any time. Green pages are reserved for marginal words, possibly of doubtful American parentage but usable all the same. Blue pages hold words and expressions current and acceptable in francophone countries but not in France itself. The absolutely okay words are on white pages.

Another Council project is a "word bank." When a conscientious Frenchman is at a loss for a good French word and is tempted to use an Americanism, he can call the Council and request a substitute from the bank. Though far from finished, the bank now contains some 2,500 words and equivalents. Examples include the predictable *communiqué* for "press release," as well as the more creative *technocrate* or *chef de service* for "manager," and *phono mécanique* instead of "juke box." There is just no word in French for the English "climax," so the Council accepts it with the French pronunciation, *kleemax*. Even so, it warns solemnly that "one should not use it without justification. Abuse would be reprehensible."

Another problem being taken up by the Council is the feminine form of job titles. This is no mean problem when you consider that some French positions entitle the holder to be called *mon maître*. This leads to considerable embarrassment among many of the world's 200 million Francophones, who understandably feel uneasy calling their female boss *ma maîtresse*.

The latest and most visible example of how badly the anti-Franglais campaign has failed is popping up all over Paris streets. Indeed, Council members are hard-pressed to find a shop or store with truly Gallic nomenclature. What they see instead are shops on both Right and Left banks called Dream Store, Bus Stop, Broadway, Fashionable, 5ᵗʰ Avenue, Western House, Modern House, Please, and To Day (yes, two words).

Blasé Parisians are no longer surprised by *un drugstore* on the corner, but a haberdasher went further and called his shop Drugsold, further evidence that the French never hesitate to invent English words. (Other inventions: *le footing* for jogging and *tennisman* for tennis player.) Cheek by jowl on the Champs Élysées are the New Store, the Grill Shop, and the Drug West, with its restaurant, the Snob Snack, where a hamburger is named The Classic.

The fad for American-sounding shop names is of course an attempt to jump on the Franglais bandwagon. At Bus Stop they explain that there is indeed an *arrêt d'autobus* across the street, and an English name is very *à la mode*. Clients even ask if they have branches in America, a mark of ultimate success in picking a name. At Ranch, a young saleslady admitted that "When we opened seven years ago, the ranch thing was fashionable. That's not so any more, so we're looking for another American name." At Mod'In they explain patiently that Mod has something to do with contemporary clothes, and In, well, that means *dans* in French. At least that explanation is slightly more coherent than that of the blonde salesgirl in Murphy's clothing store. Pressed for the etymology of the name, she furrowed her pretty brow, then replied brightly, "Why, that's from Greek mythology, isn't it?"

Update: *The Academy doggedly carries on its losing battle. The word* fun, *like the concept, does not exist in French, so* le fun *has been cheerfully* *adopted, along with* cool. *And when having* le fun, *the French often now exclaim, "waaoou," two syllables, which is how the English word* "wow" *is pronounced in this diphthong-challenged nation. Though French has no lack of naughty words and expressions, a number of pungent four-letter Anglo-Saxon expletives are now in use, along with a gesture involving a finger instead of the traditional Latin forearm. A recent lexicon has 620 pages of English words now current in French. The unkindest cut for the Academy: a new study for the ministry of education recommends compulsory English instruction in elementary school. But maybe the seemingly parlous condition of French is not really all that serious. As my talented journalistic colleague in Paris, Mary Blume, has written, "French is not a language but a state of mind."*

Napoléon Sells Louisiana for a Song

Context: *In April 1803 Thomas Jefferson purchased the Louisiana Territory from France, changing the shape of a nation and the course of history. At a stroke, the United States almost doubled in area and was put on track to becoming a world power, while France gave up its 120-year-old territorial ambitions in North America. What was Napoléon Bonaparte thinking of?*

Understandably, Pierre Clément de Laussat was saddened by this unexpected turn of events. Having recently arrived in New Orleans in March 1803 from Paris with his wife and three daughters, the cultivated, worldly French functionary had expected to reign for six or eight years as colonial prefect over the Louisiana Territory, which was to be France's vast North American empire. The prospect was all the more pleasing because the territory's capital, New Orleans, was, he noted with approval, a city with "a great deal of social life, elegance and good breeding." He also liked the fact that the city had "all sorts of masters—dancing, music, art, and fencing," and that even though there were "no book shops or libraries," books were ordered from France.

But almost before Laussat had learned to appreciate a good gumbo and the relaxed Creole pace of life, Napoléon Bonaparte had abruptly decided to sell the territory to the United States. This left Laussat with little to do but officiate when, on a sunny December 20, 1803, the French tricolor was slowly lowered in New Orleans's main square, the Place d'Armes, and the American flag raised. After William C.C. Claiborne, the territory's new governor, officially took possession of it in the name of the United States, assuring all residents that their property, rights and religion would be respected, celebratory salvos boomed out from the forts and batteries around the city. Americans cried "Huzza" and waved their hats, while French and Spanish residents sulked in glum silence. Laussat, standing on the balcony of the town hall, burst into tears.

The Louisiana Purchase nearly doubled the area of the United States. By any measure, it was one of the most colossal land transactions in history, nearly 830,000 square miles stretching from the Gulf of Mexico to Canada, and from the Mississippi River to the Rocky Mountains, an area larger than today's France, Spain, Portugal, Italy, Germany, Holland, Switzerland and Great Britain combined. And the price, $15 million, or about four cents an acre, was a breathtaking bargain. "Let the Land rejoice," exulted General Horatio Gates, a prominent New York State legislator, to President Thomas Jefferson when details of the deal reached Washington. "For you have bought Louisiana for a song."

To be sure, it was still a land where wildlife like deer, raccoons, bears and alligators far outnumbered humans. But, rich in gold, silver, and other ores, enormous forests, and endless grazing and farmlands, the new acquisition would make America immensely wealthy. Or, as Jefferson put it in his usual understated way, "The fertility of the country, its climate and extent, promise in due season important aids to our treasury, an ample provision for our posterity, and a wide-spread field for the blessings of freedom."

American historians today are more outspoken in their enthusiasm for the acquisition. "With the Declaration of Independence and the Constitution, this is one of the three things that created the modern United States," says Douglas Brinkley, director of the Eisenhower Center for American Studies in New Orleans and coauthor with the late Stephen E. Ambrose of *The Mississippi and the Making of a Nation*. Charles A. Cerami, author of *Jefferson's Great Gamble*, agrees. "If we had not made this purchase, it would have pinched off the possibility of our becoming a continental power," he says. "That, in turn, would have meant our ideas on freedom and democracy would have carried less weight with the rest of the world. This was the key to our international influence."

Despite his orchestrated pomp, his strategic cunning, and France's long engagement in the Louisiana Territory, it appears that Bonaparte got the short end of the deal in 1803, abandoning forever France's enormously rich foothold on the North American continent.

The Louisiana Territory was in fact born on April 9, 1682, when the French explorer Robert Cavelier, Sieur de La Salle, erected a cross and column at the mouth of the Mississippi and solemnly read a declaration to a handful of bemused Indians. He took possession of the whole Mississippi River basin, he avowed, in the name of "the most high, mighty, invincible and victorious Prince, Louis the Great, by Grace of God king of France and Navarre, 14th of that name." It was in honor of Louis XIV that he named the land Louisiana.

The large Louisiana Territory settlement at the mouth of the Mississippi was named la Nouvelle Orléans for Philippe, Duke of Orleans and Regent of France. Founded by the French explorer Jean-Baptiste le Moyne, Sieur de Bienville, in 1718, it was ceded by France to Spain in 1762 and remained Spanish until it reverted to France briefly just before being sold to the United States as part of the Louisiana Purchase. Its population at the time is estimated at 8,000, about evenly divided between whites, slaves of African origin, and "free persons of color." A picturesque assemblage of French and Spanish colonial architecture and Creole cottages, New Orleans boasted the handsome cathedral of Saint Louis and a thriving economy based largely on exports, worth some $2 million in 1803.

For more than a century after La Salle took possession of it, the trackless Louisiana Territory, with its scattered French, Spanish, Acadian and German settlements, along with those of Native Americans and American-born frontiersmen, was traded among European royalty at their whim. Though fascinated by America—which they often symbolized in paintings and drawings as a befeathered Noble Savage standing beside an alligator—the French could not decide whether it was a new Eden or, as the naturalist Georges-Louis Leclerc de Buffon declared, a primitive place fit only for degenerate life forms.

But the official view was summed up by Antoine de La Mothe Cadillac, whom Louis XIV named governor of Louisiana in 1710:

"The people are a heap of the dregs of Canada," he sniffed in a 42-page report to the king. The soldiers there were untrained and undisciplined, he lamented, and the whole colony itself was "not worth a straw at the present time." Considering the area worthless, Louis XV secretly gave Louisiana to his Bourbon cousin Charles III of Spain in 1763. The territory changed hands again in 1800, when Napoléon negotiated the clandestine Treaty of San Ildefonso with Spain's Charles IV, returning the territory to France in exchange for the small kingdom of Etruria in Tuscany in northern Italy for Charles's daughter Louisetta.

When Jefferson learned of Bonaparte's secret deal, he immediately saw the threat to America's westward expansion and its vital outlet to the Gulf of Mexico. If the deal was allowed to stand, he declared, "it would be impossible that France and the United States can continue long as friends." This must have been a wrenching moment for Jefferson, who had long been an ardent Francophile. Years before, he had shipped to his Virginia home, Monticello, 86 packing cases of furnishings and books he had picked up during his five-year stay in Paris as American representative. Some of Jefferson's French possessions provide insight into the sort of world he lived in, a world he furnished with tasteful comforts such as an elegant footed silver goblet made in Paris to his design, a Sèvres porcelain vessel for cooling wine glasses, and a mahogany chair by the renowned Parisian cabinetmaker Georges Jacob.

The crunch came for Jefferson in October 1802. Spain's King Charles IV finally got around to signing the royal decree officially transferring the territory to France, and on October 16, the Spanish administrator in New Orleans, Juan Ventura Morales, the highest civilian official, arbitrarily ended the American right of duty-free deposit of cargo in the city. He argued that the three-year term of the 1795 Treaty of San Lorenzo, which had authorized that right of deposit, had passed. This meant that American merchandise could no longer be stored in New Orleans warehouses. American products, from trappers' pelts to agricultural produce and finished goods, sent down the Mississippi from fur-trading posts and towns like Prairie du Chien and Saint Louis for forwarding to markets on the East Coast and on across the Atlantic, thus risked exposure and theft on open wharfs in New Orleans while awaiting transshipment. With no road system from the Mississippi Valley across the Appalachians, there was no alternative shipping route for western settlers. Thus the entire economy of America's western territories was in jeopardy. "The difficulties and risks…are incalculable," warned U.S. Vice-Consul in New Orleans William E. Hulings in a dispatch to Secretary of State James Madison.

As Jefferson wrote in April 1802 to his friend and U.S. minister at Paris, Robert Livingston, who had helped him draft the Declaration of Independence, it was absolutely crucial that the port of New Orleans remain open and free for American commerce, particularly that coming down the Mississippi. "There is on the globe one single spot," he wrote, "the possessor of which is our natural and habitual enemy. It is New Orleans, through which the produce of three-eighths of our territory must pass to market."

Jefferson's concern was more than merely commercial. "He had a vision of America as an empire of liberty," says Douglas Brinkley. "And he saw the Mississippi River not as the western edge of the country, but as the great spine that would hold the continent together."

As it was, frontiersmen, infuriated by the abrogation of the right of deposit of their goods, threatened to seize New Orleans by force. The idea was taken up by Washington lawmakers such as Senator James Ross of Pennsylvania, who drafted a resolution calling on Jefferson to form a 50,000-man army to take New Orleans; the resolution appropriated $50 million to finance the attack. The press joined the fray. The United States had the right, thundered the *New York Evening Post*, "to regulate the future destiny of North America," while the *Charleston Courier* advocated "taking possession of the port in question…by force of arms." As Secretary of State James Madison explained, "The Mississippi is to them everything. It is the Hudson, the Delaware, the Potomac, and all the navigable rivers of the Atlantic States, formed into one stream."

With the Congress and a vociferous press calling for action, Jefferson faced the nation's most serious crisis since the American Revolution. "Peace is our passion," he declared, and expressed the concern that hotheaded members of the opposition Federalist Party might "force us into war." Determined to seek a solution short of war, he had already instructed Livingston in early 1802 to approach Bonaparte's foreign minister, Charles Maurice de Talleyrand, to try to prevent the cession of Louisiana to France, if this had not already occurred, or, if the deal was done, to try to purchase New Orleans. (In fact, the secret deal between the Spanish and French had already been struck.) In his initial meeting with Bonaparte after taking up his Paris post in 1801, Livingston had been warned about Old World ways. "You have come to a very corrupt world," Bonaparte told him frankly, adding roguishly that Talleyrand was the right man to explain what he meant by corruption.

A wily, slippery, political survivor who held high office with no compunction under regimes as various as the French Revolution, Napoléon's Empire and the restored Bourbon monarchy, Talleyrand had spent two years in exile in America following the French Revolution, traveling from Maine to Virginia. While there he conceived a virulent, typically French contempt for Americans and what he considered their materialistic, uncouth ways. "Refinement," he declared, "does not exist" in the United States. Talleyrand's own conception of refinement included furnishings and accouterments like an elegant swan bed and nightstand that had belonged to one of the most famous French beauties of Bonaparte's era, Madame Récamier.

As Napoléon's foreign minister, Talleyrand customarily demanded outrageous bribes for diplomatic results. Despite a clubfoot and what contemporaries called his "dead eyes," he could be charming and witty when he wanted, which helped camouflage his basic negotiating tactic of delay. "The lack of instructions and the necessity of consulting one's government are always legitimate excuses in order to obtain delays in political affairs," he once wrote. When Livingston tried to discuss Louisiana, Talleyrand simply denied that there was any treaty between France and Spain. "The Minister will give no answer to any inquiries I make on the subject," a frustrated Livingston wrote to Secretary of State Madison on September 1, 1802. "He will not say what their boundaries are, what are their intentions, and when they are to take possession."

But Livingston, like all good diplomats, kept himself well informed about the country to which he was ambassador. His informants had told him of France's intentions with regard to Louisiana. He warned Madison in March 1802 that France planned to occupy New Orleans with up to 7,000 troops with a view to eventually having "a leading interest in the politics of our western country." Indeed, in November 1802 Napoléon had ordered General Claude Victor to set out for New Orleans with an expeditionary force from the Dutch port of Helvoë Sluys in the French-controlled Netherlands. But, due to a disastrous French campaign in the summer and fall of 1802 in the Caribbean colony of Saint Domingue (now Haiti), where slaves led by Toussaint L'Ouverture had revolted and were slaughtering French residents and the thousands of French troops sent to save them, Victor was too short of soldiers, ships and provisions to sail immediately. By the time he had assembled a sufficient force in January 1803, ice blocked the Dutch port, making it impossible for him to set sail.

Meanwhile, that same month Jefferson asked James Monroe, former member of Congress and governor of Virginia, to join Livingston in Paris as minister extraordinary with discretionary powers to spend $9,375,000 for New Orleans and East and West Florida, to consolidate the U.S. position in the southeastern part of the continent, or $2,000,000 for the city alone. In financial straits at the time, Monroe sold his household china and furniture to raise funds, asked a neighbor to manage his properties in Virginia and Kentucky, and sailed for France on March 8, 1803, with Jefferson's parting admonition ringing in his ears: "The future destinies of this republic" depended on his success.

By the time Monroe arrived in Paris on April 12, the situation had, unknown to him, radically altered: Napoléon had suddenly changed strategies. He had always seen Saint Domingue as France's most important holding in the Western Hemisphere, with a population of more than 500,000 producing enough sugar, coffee, indigo, cotton and cocoa to fill some 700 ships a year. The Louisiana Territory, in Napoléon's view, was useful mainly as a granary for Saint Domingue. But with the colony clearly in danger of being lost, Louisiana was less useful. Then too, Napoléon was gearing up for another campaign against Great Britain and needed funds for that.

When Napoléon's brothers Joseph and Lucien had gone to see him at the Tuileries Palace on April 7, they were determined to convince him not to sell Louisiana. For one thing, they considered it foolish to voluntarily give up an important French holding on the American continent. For another, Britain had unofficially offered Joseph a bribe of £100,000 to persuade Napoléon not to let the Americans have Louisiana, hoping to prevent the U.S. from becoming a world power. But Napoléon's mind was made up. The First Consul happened to be sitting in his bath when his brothers arrived, and that is where he announced his decision: "Gentlemen, think what you please about it. I have decided to sell Louisiana to the Americans." To make his point to his astonished brothers, Napoléon abruptly stood up, then dropped back into the tub, drenching Joseph. A manservant slumped to the floor in a faint.

French historians point out that Napoléon had several reasons for his decision. "He probably concluded that, following American independence, France couldn't hope to maintain a colony on the American continent," says Jean Tulard, one of France's foremost Napoléon scholars. "French policy makers had felt for some time that France's possessions in the Antilles would inevitably be 'contaminated' by America's idea of freedom and would eventually take their own independence. By the sale, Napoléon hoped to create a huge country in the Western Hemisphere to serve as a counterweight to Britain, and maybe make trouble for it."

Four days later, when Livingston called on Talleyrand for what he thought would be yet another futile attempt to deal, the foreign minister, after the de rigueur small talk, suddenly asked whether the United States would perchance wish to have the whole of the Louisiana Territory. Talleyrand concluded by telling Livingston that he should deal in the future with the French finance minister, François de Barbé-Marbois. The latter knew America well, having spent some years in Philadelphia in the late 1700s as French ambassador to the United States, where he got acquainted with Washington, Jefferson, Livingston and Monroe. Barbé-Marbois received his orders on April 11, 1803, when Napoléon summoned him. "I renounce Louisiana," Napoléon told him. "It is not only New Orleans that I will cede, it is the whole colony without reservation. I require a great deal of money for this war [with Britain]."

Thierry Lentz, a Napoléon historian and director of the Fondation Napoléon in Paris, contends that, for Napoléon, "It was basically just a big real estate deal. He was in a hurry to get some money for the depleted French treasury, although the relatively modest price shows that he was had in that deal. But he did manage to sell something that he didn't really have any control over—there were few French settlers and no French administration over the territory—except on paper." As for Jefferson, notes Charles A. Cerami, "he actually wasn't out to make this big a purchase. The whole thing came as a total surprise to him and his negotiating team in Paris, because it was, after all, Napoléon's idea, not his."

Showing up unexpectedly at the dinner party Livingston gave on April 12 for Monroe's arrival in Paris, Barbé-Marbois discreetly asked Livingston to meet him later that night at the treasury office. There he confirmed Napoléon's desire to sell Louisiana for $22,500,000. Livingston replied diplomatically that he "would be ready to purchase provided the sum was reduced to reasonable limits." Then he rushed home and worked until 3 a.m. writing a memorandum to Secretary of State Madison, concluding: "We shall do all we can to cheapen the purchase; but my present sentiment is that we shall buy."

The serious haggling began in the absence of Monroe, who, ironically in view of the financial effort he made to take up his post in Paris, fell ill and was confined to bed for the next two weeks. On April 15 Livingston proposed $8 million. At this, Napoléon pretended to lose interest in the deal unless America upped the ante. By April 27 Barbé-Marbois announced that Napoléon had lowered his asking price to $16 million. Livingston countered with $12 million. The deal was struck for $15 million on April 29, the treaty signed by Barbé-Marbois, Livingston and a recovered Monroe on May 2 and antedated to April 30.

Although this was undeniably a bargain, the price was still more than the young United States treasury could afford. But the resourceful Barbé-Marbois had an answer for that, too. He had contacts at Britain's Baring & Co. bank, which agreed, along with several other banks, to make the actual purchase and pay Napoléon cash. The bank then turned over ownership of Louisiana to the United States in return for bonds, which were repaid over 15 years at 6 percent interest, making the final total purchase price around $27 million.

Undaunted by the fact that neither he nor Monroe had been authorized to buy all of Louisiana, or to spend $15 million (transatlantic mail took weeks each way, so they had no time to request and receive approval of the deal from Washington) an elated Livingston, aware that nearly doubling the size of the United States would inevitably make it a major player on the world scene one day, permitted himself some verbal euphoria: "We have lived long, but this is the noblest work of our whole lives," he said. "From this day the United States take their place among the powers of the first rank."

It wasn't until July 3 that news of the purchase reached U.S. shores, just in time for Americans to celebrate it on Independence Day. A Washington newspaper, the *National Intelligencer*, reflecting how most citizens felt, referred to the "widespread joy of millions at an event which history will record among the most splendid in our annals." Not all Americans agreed, however. The Boston *Columbian Centinel* editorialized, "We are to give money of which we have too little for land of which we already have too much." And Congressman Joseph Quincy of Massachusetts so opposed the deal that he favored secession by the northeastern states over it, "amicably if they can; violently if they must."

The favorable majority, however, easily prevailed and New England remained in the Union. As for the ever-succinct Thomas Jefferson, he wasted little time on rhetoric. "The enlightened government of France saw, with just discernment," he told Congress on October 17, 1803, with typical tact, "the importance to both nations of such liberal arrangements as might best and permanently promote the peace, friendship, and interests of both." But, excited by his vision of the West as America's future, Jefferson, even before official notice of the treaty reached Washington in July, had already dispatched Meriwether Lewis to lead an expedition to explore the new acquisition and the lands beyond. All the way to the Pacific.

Update: *All or parts of 15 western states eventually would be carved from the former Louisiana Territory. America's role in the world today owes much to Napoléon's unwitting, impulsive move. The 2003 bicentennial of the Louisiana Purchase was virtually ignored in France.*

PART THREE:
Le Bon Dieu

The idea of God has always been important in France, although not always for the right reasons. Since Charlemagne, king of the Franks, united practically all the Christian lands of western Europe in the 8th century, and was duly anointed Christian king and emperor by Pope Leo III at Christmas Mass in Rome in the year 800, religion and politics have been intimately intertwined in France. Later, in the 16th century, the Protestant Henri de Bourbon-Navarre became King Henri IV but faced resistance from staunch Catholics. He solved this by converting to Roman Catholicism and, to make his point, attended mass at Paris's Notre Dame Cathedral, commenting privately, "Paris is well worth a mass." But the flagrant use of religion to reinforce political power created a vicious backlash during the French Revolution, when clerics were murdered and churches desecrated. Since then, France's relations with God have been marked by Enlightenment skepticism and the bludgeoning of Marxism. To counter the latter, the French Catholic Church tried the risky experiment of worker-priests, who infiltrated working class milieux to preach Christianity but sometimes ended up adopting Communism themselves. Nor have the French been immune to the appeal of dangerous cults that prey on those disillusioned with formal religion but still looking for meaning in their lives.

On Familiar Terms with the Deity

Context: *Since the days of Voltaire's biting satire,* Candide, *which mocked the idea that God had created the best of all possible worlds, the French have not seemed particularly awed by the Creator. As a nominally Catholic nation—despite the fact that less than 10 percent of those baptized actually practice their religion except for marriages and funerals—they have cultivated an easy familiarity with the Deity, known colloquially as* le Bon Dieu, *as befits the self-styled Eldest Daughter of the Church. Modern French thinkers have frequently held Him responsible for the evil and stupidity and in the world. They often seem to take mischievous pleasure in bearding Him in ways that more literal-minded believers would find blasphemous. Simone de Beauvoir, writer, intellectual, feminist and, incidentally, Jean-Paul Sartre's official if unmarried companion, summed up the viewpoint of many French skeptics when she wrote, "It is easier for me to think of a world without a creator than of a creator loaded with all the contradictions of the world."*

A case in point is a book recently written by Robert Escarpit, a respected *homme de lettres* who writes a daily satirical column on the front page of *Le Monde* and teaches literature at the University of Bordeaux. His "Lettre Ouverte à Dieu ("Open Letter to God") in the form of a long letter written while, *naturellement,* on vacation, is a highly civilized form of wrestling with metaphysical anguish. "You, monsieur, whom they call all-powerful, how is it that you have never been able to interest me seriously in the problem of your existence?" he begins.

What follows are 155 pages of various unsolemn descriptions of the agnostic situation, such as, "I know of 20 drugs which could easily make you disappear the way an aspirin tablet makes the little pink elephants disappear from the drunk with a hangover." Referring to the Communist opposition to the idea of God, he counsels, "If you are going to resist it, if you are able to, you had better change your habits and make a serious effort to adapt." After a good deal of such advice and no little tweaking of the divine nose, he concludes, "It doesn't matter whether you are the more or less morbid product of my angst, or a reality that plays on appearances. The fact is that the dialogue I have begun with you will only finish when I die."

In a world placed "under the double sign of growing rationality and growing absurdity," as the French philosopher Paul Ricoeur has it, doubt is something many are learning to live with. The Romanian-born playwright Eugene Ionesco, who took French nationality and settled in Paris years ago, told me during our conversation in his Montparnasse apartment that he was once asked by a newsman, "What is your conception of life and death?" His answer: "I told him, 'That is what I ask myself, and I write to find out.'"

Ionesco describes this spiritual malaise with typical tough-mindedness. "First of all, I must admit personally that theology and philosophy have not helped me understand why I exist. They have not convinced me, either, that something must be done with this existence, and that one should or can give it significance. I don't quite feel that I belong in the world. But if I feel a little that I belong here, it is simply because, by existing, I have gotten into the habit." The idea of God means nothing to him.

Edgar Morin, head of the sociology department of France's National Center for Scientific Research, speaks easily of "what I might call either my indifference or my resistance to the notion of God."

When he reconsiders all the traditional arguments against the existence of God formulated since the Renaissance, he finds they are still valid for him. He ticks them off as the relativistic, anti-ethnocentric argument (why would the religion of my village be better than others?), historical criticism both of the New Testament and Christianity considered as an amalgam of known religious movements in the Mediterranean area in the first century B.C., the modern scientific arguments explaining the universe, and the modern socio-economic and psychological arguments of Marx and Freud. "All these arguments remain valid for me," he says. "That's why I don't worry about the question."

Since he accepts the contradiction and mystery of the universe, he does not need to oppose a humanist or positivist view to the religious view. He rejects equally God and the man-God of the humanists. Noting man's tendency to deify things that have nothing to do with formal religion, such as national feelings, political parties, even love relationships, he opts for neo-atheism. Philosophers, poor things, need God as the keystone of their ideological schemes, he says. "The God of philosophers is a rational construct of the world. But that supreme rationality may at the same time be the supreme rationalization in the clinical sense of the word, rationalization meaning justification, camouflage of an obscure emotion. In this sense, it becomes the mask of irrationality."

The prestigious holder of the chair of social anthropology at the Collège de France is another French intellectual who believes he has every reason not to believe. "Personally, I have never been confronted with the question of God," says Claude Lévi-Strauss, the 57-year-old leader of France's currently fashionable structuralist philosophers.

He was raised by agnostic parents, and when he went to live with his maternal grandfather, a rabbi, at the age of six, the good man was unable to influence him in the least. Today he says with a relaxed, tolerant smile, "I experience no difficulty at all in living with the relativity of truth. I find it's perfectly possible to spend my life knowing we will never explain the universe, that we will continue to know more and more about it, but not everything."

The question of God is not something he has ever bothered to argue with believers. "Of course I am aware of the arguments for the existence of God, but they have never touched me because no argument can prove something that is non-existent. To argue a question I must be able to feel something about it. If someone said this table in front of us had eight legs instead of four, I wouldn't bother to argue." It's that simple.

There is no such thing for Lévi-Strauss as an absolute—"All absolutes are relative"—and consequently no ultimate sanction on which to found a system of values. Neither does he take refuge in humanism. "I don't believe in God, but I don't believe in man, either. I can see that one day the earth will no longer exist and neither will man. All his struggles and efforts will ultimately mean nothing."

As to what may replace God in man's future religious thought, Lévi-Strauss is confident that the sacred will always have its institutions. Indeed, he believes, modern man is already worshipping new gods. "To many today, what is sacred is often signs of our own development, including even things like old locomotives and automobiles and other human creations irrevocably behind us." This can include the highly institutionalized form of worship of art. Because they represent our past development, art collections are holy in our culture and museums are their cathedrals. Families set up their little household art altars, and art historians are their theologians.

One of the main problems of the Catholic Church in France today is living down the 19th century. If most French intellectuals can't take the idea of God seriously, it is in large measure due to religion's identification with power. That has been true all through the Church's history, of course, but in France it was most glaring when poor and wealthy were sharply confronted. God became, for many French, "*la chose de la bourgeoisie*," closely identified with the Establishment, and Marxist philosophy was born in part to combat that.

François Châtelet, 41-year-old professor of philosophy at the prestigious Lycée Louis le Grand in Paris, is a thoroughgoing Marxist thinker and writer. Predictably, he holds that, "The dechristianization of France began when France started to confront the social problems of the industrial age. At the time when the interests of the working class were most sharply opposed to the bourgeoisie, the Church was on the side of the government, the vested interests. The clergy ignored the poor, was content to preach the Gospel to people who were desperate for something to eat. It's not surprising that today you find maybe two percent of the working class are practicing Catholics."

His Marxist explanation of man's need today of God and religious ideas is that they derive from the false foundations of society. "In a false world, it's only natural to find religious ideas as a spiritual compensation. With constant social tension the rule, the individual becomes suspicious even of rationality. So people turn to religion, where they find comforting explanations of why things are so bad." So where does the professor find meaning in life? "In itself, life has no value, man's existence no object, his life no meaning. But it does have value in an epicurean way. Pleasure is what makes life worth living, pleasure in the largest sense including knowledge. The play of ideas as well as more basic pleasures. You might put it this way: there are two things that really interest me in life, *faire la philosophie et faire l'amour.*" The young blonde woman apparently sharing his apartment smiled knowingly.

As for French clergy and theologians, they are changing their approaches to the question of God. For one thing, they are much less self-assured about it, more aware that faith is a gift. When asked directly, "Can the existence of God be proven?" most acknowledge that it cannot except within a certain context. There are no new proofs, but a few new ways of getting at the problem.

At the Institute of Advanced Pastoral Catechistics of Paris, Father Joseph Bournique, the director, notes three stages in man's search for God. First came the traditional, authoritative approach stressing law, obedience, submission, a brutal Providence. "That was all right as long as man lived in an agrarian society," he says, "but when man begins to control nature itself it is no longer valid." Then in the 18th century there was "a particularly French approach" stressing lucidity and self-awareness: it was through what was most noble and conscious in the believer that God operated. The relationship with God was strictly personalist. Bournique calls this "extremely bourgeois and intellectual, good only for the leisure class."

The approach favored today at the Institute, which gives intensive three-year courses in catechistics to clergy and religious from all over the world, emphasizes the solidarity of mankind, the work that must be accomplished with others and the responsibility of the individual to them. "God works through the total of humanity, and we discover him through our experience in the collectivity," Bournique says. "At the same time, we identify with Christ, who came to earth to accomplish a task." Thus the center of gravity of man's rapport with God has shifted from above, to within the individual, to the collectivity.

The basic idea of Bournique, a dynamic, middle-aged man who, in the fashion of France's *nouveaux prêtres*, wears no Roman collar, is to make an absolute of the human community and hope man will find God through analogy. In any case, "You cannot define God or put Him in any formula. Nowadays even in catechisms for children we avoid giving definitions of God. And we shun illustrations of him as an old man with a beard sitting up on the clouds."

France's young people first have to outgrow their education if they are to believe in God, notes Father Jean-Marie Lustiger, director of the Centre Richelieu, an organization for Catholic college students near the Sorbonne. Around 5,000 students from the Sorbonne and other parts of the University of Paris participate annually in its retreats, discussions and debates, and the annual spring pilgrimage to Chartres Cathedral. "Most are still suffering from 19th century Rationalism," Lustiger says. "When they first get here after graduating from the lycée, they are full of Positivist atheistic ideas inculcated by their teachers. To answer their fundamental question of whether a modern man can believe in God, we first have to overcome their cultural heritage. We have to explain not only what God is, but what science is."

Lustiger has no pat formula for getting God across. "There's not really any single main difficulty to believing in God. It depends on the individual's own preoccupations. Students in history and literature usually worry about the historical validity and interpretation of Scripture. Those in psychology wonder if the need of God isn't a result of the death of their father. Philosophy and math majors have their own problems. But in general I think it is actually easier to believe in God today than it was 30 or 40 years ago. The 19th century is finally being demystified. We can't explain everything by science, and the humanistic visions of the perfectibility of man have been discredited. Man has become less pretentious and has fewer illusions about what he can accomplish. The 19th century was like adolescence. We're more mature today. The first thing is to be honest with ourselves. I don't pretend to have all the answers."

For another grassroots view of how the French see God, I went to see Father François Dupire, assistant pastor at the church of Saint-Germain-des-Prés in the heart of the Left Bank literary-intellectual quarter. He works every day with parishioners in a neighborhood known for a high degree of education and skepticism. His method of dealing with questions about God is simple: he speaks with such sincere, uncompromising conviction that he's not even unctuous.

"Most French people today believe in a watchmaker God, the one that's necessary because the universe is there," he says scornfully. "That doesn't have anything to do with being Christian. Christ is the hinge of our faith in God, and Christ doesn't lie. Faith comes through him, it can't be proven. If God could be demonstrated, only the intelligent would believe. And you can't lose the faith because it's not a possession. You simply act like a believer or you don't."

He finds that many of the staunchly anti-clericals who abound in his parish are actually more devout than confirmed believers, who are often disillusioned in an idea they had of what God ought to be. "Actually they're believing in an absolute despite themselves. God is a question that is on everyone's mind today. Even the chic young people that run around thinking only about where they'll go dancing tonight have a craving for God. I try to show them that you can't believe in God without grace, and you can't have grace without God. But grace is not something, it is somebody. God gives Himself. Believe it or not, He needs to be needed, because He is love. I'm sorry if this sounds silly." The way he said it, it didn't.

Update: *With most of the French now believing they have entered, along with the rest of Western Europe, the Postchristian Era, it is hard today to stir up such lively conversations about God. (Allah, on the other hand, is something else. Islam is now the most actively practiced religion in the country, accounting for nearly 10 percent of the population. Far more mosques are being built than churches.) France fought tooth and nail against including a phrase in the new "constitution" of the European Union referring to Europe's Christian origins, much to the dismay of still-religious nations like Poland. Thus French commentators view the frequent references to God in the United States with curiosity and irony, when it is not with derision or alarm. "In God We Trust" as a national motto? How very quaint. The very idea of anyone, especially a president, calling himself a born-again Christian, seems as strange to them as Montesquieu's Persian. French writers regularly foray into the American hinterland and return, as if from some heart of darkness, to publish books such as "Bible Militants in the United States," "Religion in the White House," and "The Last Crusade: God's Madmen in America."*

Worker Priests: Infiltrating the Masses for God

Context: *It could only happen in France, where one of the West's strongest currents of Marxism ran into a rapacious middle class backed by a Catholic Church long identified with the Establishment. When French bishops realized in the early 1940s the extent to which the French working class had fallen away from the Church since the Industrial Revolution, they began a perilous experiment to deal with what they considered a desperate situation. The drastic move was unique in Christendom. It allowed priests, dressed in mufti, to take full-time jobs in industry, agriculture, construction and fisheries, to join labor unions, and otherwise to live the life of ordinary workers. It was an attempt, as one French bishop put it, to do nothing less than break down "the wall which separates the Church from the masses."*

The worker-priest movement, always perilous, was an experiment that the Catholic hierarchy in Rome watched with increasing trepidation. When two French worker priests were arrested for taking part in communist riots protesting against the arrival in Paris of American General Matthew Ridgeway as commander of Supreme Headquarters Allied Powers Europe in 1952, the Holy See became convinced that the worker priest idea had failed: not only were *prêtres ouvriers* proving ineffectual in bringing workers back to the Church, many were themselves converting to Marxism.

The extent to which the theology of worker-priests was tinged by militant Marxism was clear in the interview I had with one in a drab Paris suburb. For him (he insisted on anonymity), one of the most encouraging signs of religious renewal in France was the Church's willingness to listen to the laity, especially militant workers: "It's beginning to speak to men as they are and as they live, not as it would like them to be. The militants have a right to say what they and their comrades expect of the Church."

Furiously anti-bourgeois and anti-capitalist, he remembered that when he settled in his massively working-class area 20 years ago the parish priests were literally scared to death of the workers. They depended entirely on the bourgeoisie for moral and financial support. "Here and all over France, the Church had become the servant of those people," the priest said. "Today it is liberating itself from that class and, believe me, it is costing it dearly, in both senses."

What this ultimately meant for the Church, he thought, was "humbly searching for ways to present God. It will finally present Him as he presented Himself. In the Old Testament the prophets presented Him as the liberator and savior of the people. Christ had the same role, coming to save man from what was dehumanizing him. He is evidence that God takes part in the life of the people, knows war and peace and sickness and health, the whole tissue of their condition."

How did this translate into everyday action? He cited the example of a bishop in the South of France who, just the week before, had led shipyard workers in a protest. In the same week there were priests participating in a seminar on Marxist thought. "And I know of priests who work every day to find jobs for the unemployed, cheap housing for the poor. This is the new way of presenting God."

But it was just such ideas and activities that prompted the apostolic nuncio in France to summon several French cardinals in 1953 and tell them that the experiment must end. The three prelates countered with a trip to Rome to talk with the pope, and returned to France with papal authorization to continue the worker-priests after adopting measures to tighten up the program.

Pressure from Rome continued, however, and shortly thereafter the French episcopate issued orders forbidding worker priests any "temporal engagements" such as union activities, ordering them to adhere strictly to their sacerdotal duties, and changing their designation to "priests in the worker mission." It also limited to three the number of hours they could work daily, effectively removing them from jobs in industry.

The hundred-odd worker-priests in the field felt betrayed. Torn between their commitment to evangelizing the working class and their vow of obedience, some declared they would defy the bishops and continue their work, outside the Church if necessary. Seventy-three of them published an open letter charging that the bishops had let themselves be influenced by "circles accustomed to placing religion at the service of their own interests and of their class prejudices."

In phrases with a similar Marxist ring, they declared that, "At a time when millions of workers in France and abroad are on the march toward unity in order to defend their bread, their liberties, and peace, the employers and the government increase their exploitation and their repression to stop at all costs the progress of the working class. To safeguard their privileges, the religious authorities impose on worker priests conditions that constitute an abandonment of their worker's life and a denial of the struggle that they lead together with all their comrades."

A few did break with the Church, some continued their work under the new conditions, and others, particularly those belonging to religious orders such as Jesuits, Benedictines and Dominicans, left the movement for other assignments. For all practical purposes, it was the end of France's worker-priest experiment.

Update: *French bishops, loath to give up the worker-priest idea in the face of a French Communist Party that had more practicing members than the Catholic Church, kept trying to get the Vatican to change its mind. To their surprise, even the liberal Pope John XXIII totally refused to reconsider the experiment. But eldest daughters can be stubborn indeed, and the program sputtered on, more or less officially, through the 1960s. Declining in parallel with the Communist Party, the worker-priest movement was an exceptional episode in the modern history of the Catholic Church.*

Victims of a Killer Cult

Context: *As in many countries, the erosion of traditional morality and strong family ties has left many in France vulnerable to the dangers of pseudo-religious cults. Parliamentary surveys have found nearly 200 cults in the country. "Millenarist and apocalyptic cults are proliferating in France, and acts like those of the Solar Temple may well be repeated in Europe and the rest of the world," a French Interior Ministry official has said. The vicious acts he referred to were in France and French-speaking areas of Switzerland and Canada.*

The muscular, athletic man who landed at Montreal's Mirabel airport on Swissair flight 138 from Zurich had little time to admire the glorious fall foliage in Canada's Laurentian hills. Joel Egger, a fanatical 34-year-old Swiss member of the secret Order of the Solar Temple, headed straight for a green chalet in nearby Morin Heights to rendezvous with Dominique Bellaton, mother of the Cosmic Child. Together they would lure the Antichrist to his death.

The next day, September 30, 1994, Nicky and Tony Dutoit arrived at the chalet with their infant son, Christopher Emmanuel. Nicky, a cheerful, dark-haired British woman who used to make ceremonial capes for the Order, and Tony, a Swiss craftsman who served it as general handyman, had left the cult four years before. But they liked to see their friend Dominique, who was still an active member. First, though, Joel had something to show Tony in the basement, he said. When Tony reached the dark bottom of the stairs, Egger grabbed a baseball bat and swung it viciously at Tony's head, crushing his skull. Then he took a kitchen knife and jerked it through Tony's throat from ear to ear. Like some killing machine gone berserk, Egger plunged the knife again and again into Tony, 50 times in all. Then he went upstairs.

Petrified with terror, Nicky put up no resistance as Egger raised the bloodied knife and ritualistically stabbed her eight times in the back, four times in the throat, and once in each breast. Turning to the crib of the three-month-old Antichrist, he dug the knife into the baby's chest 20 times. Before leaving to return to Zurich, Egger and Bellaton placed a symbolic wooden stake on the infant's mutilated body. Canadian cult members Jerry and Colette Genoud connected timers to an ignition system; they died when the chalet burned completely on October 4.

On that same day 3,000 miles across the Atlantic from Morin Heights, villagers in the Swiss hamlet of Cheiry were celebrating the re-opening of La Lembaz, a popular local restaurant. At 11:55 p.m. they saw flames shooting from the stables of a hillside farm. Arriving firemen found a man's body lying on a bed, a plastic bag over his head. Groping through the smoke, they located a secret door leading to an underground room with mirrored walls and 22 corpses laid out in a ceremonial circle, dressed in white, gold or black capes with plastic garbage bags over their heads. All had been given hypnotic drugs and tranquilizers; 20 had been shot repeatedly point blank in the head and face with hollow dumdum bullets designed to spread and scatter as they tear through flesh.

At 2:50 a.m. the same night, two chalets in the village of Granges-sur-Salvan, 60 miles east of Geneva, burst into flame simultaneously. After breaking in—openings had been nailed shut from the out-side—firemen discovered 15 bodies on three floors in one, 10 in another. All were dressed in ceremonial capes except four children aged four to 15. Most, including Joel Egger, were charred beyond recognition, some reduced to cinders only three feet long. As at Cheiry, all were members of the Order of the Solar Temple.

Just another bunch of wackos who had wiped themselves out, most people thought. But the reality is different: most of these people were coldly, methodically murdered, with more deaths to come. And no one so far has been able to explain satisfactorily why they were killed or by whom. Compounding the mysteries of the Solar Temple are its many layers: behind the pseudo-religious facade and mystical flimflam lay a sophisticated operation for managing far-flung financial interests. When he had had a look at the Solar Temple's financial books following the massacres, one awed examining magistrate called its money movements "colossal and intriguing."

Handling most of the money was Joseph Di Mambro, who had an unerring eye for spotting people's weaknesses and playing on them. Aged 70 when he died in the flames at Granges-sur-Salvan, Di Mambro was an unlikely-looking Knight: pudgy, dumpy, with weak brown eyes behind thick glasses, a toupee hiding his balding pate. The psychological portrait by police says he had an inferiority complex and was spiteful and self-pitying, but a superb liar.

Born in the South of France the son of an immigrant Italian glass worker, Di Mambro picked up the trade of watch repairman and worked in a local jewelry shop, going nowhere and making so little he was dispensed from French income tax. Already he was tempted to take the money and run. He was convicted in 1972 of fraud, breach of confidence and bouncing checks, and sentenced to six months in jail. Later he created a series of his own small occult outfits, including the Center for Preparation for the New Age in France and the Golden Way Foundation in Geneva.

Led by a world-class liar and manipulator, the Solar Temple used people mercilessly. Usually recruited by stages, beginning with innocuous lectures on subjects like homeopathy, yoga, body/mind harmony and stress management, prospective new members were screened for attitude and income. If they had the right profile, interested parties would be invited to join a secret order claiming to be heir to the medieval Knights Templars, the wealthy, swashbuckling Christian warriors who guarded the Holy Land and protected pilgrims. Initiation rites included swearing absolute secrecy, loyalty and fidelity. Article 5 of its secret regulations states, "The names of its officers, its internal organization and its activities must in no case be divulged by members to outsiders or even to other members."

Di Mambro preferred to stay behind the scenes and pull the strings. His front man was a French-speaking Belgian homeopath named Luc Jouret. The darkly handsome 33-year-old Belgian, who had dabbled in

Hindu mysticism in India and believed in Filipino healers, had the charisma and mesmerizing manner Di Mambro lacked. Jouret quickly became the Order's top drawing card. His lectures on subjects from nutrition (organic only), to sex (the more the better), the meaning of life (merely a passage to death) and the apocalypse (imminent) were a heady cocktail of New Age, Christianity, Buddhism and the occult.

Members were persuaded they were an elite. "They played on your ego," one former member says. "They made you feel special." One of Di Mambro's favorite techniques was to solemnly inform new members they were the reincarnation of persons from ancient times. Thus he explained to one woman that she was unhappy because she reincarnated the Roman soldier who had lanced the crucified Christ in the side. Another had been the Egyptian queen Hatchepsout, and still another was Anthea, queen of the fabled submerged island of Atlantis. Di Mambro himself baldly claimed to be Moses reincarnate.

Solar Temple ceremonies were in darkened inner sanctums decorated with symbols inspired by a mishmash of Catholicism, astrology, spiritualism, Templarism and Rosicrucianism, usually including a chalice and a painting of a bearded Christ-like figure with a rose above the head. "During ceremonies we would hear sounds from the star Sirius and vibrations, followed by apparitions of chandeliers, swords and so on, leading up to a crescendo of the appearance of the Masters," recounts a former member. Often appeared the death-mask face of a Master who sometimes held a sword and tapped the floor in a coded message. Or it could be King Arthur's sword, Excalibur, that materialized before the members' ecstatic eyes. Or the slow, hovering appearance of the Holy Grail, the chalice Christ used at the Last Supper.

"Di Mambro would tell us, 'Do you realize that we are the only people on the planet to see these things?'" says Thierry Huguenin, a former member who barely escaped being the 54th victim in October 1994. "'Even great saints never saw such signs.' We fell on our knees when the Holy Grail appeared before us." What Huguenin and others later learned was that the Masters were usually Di Mambro's wife,

Jocelyne, perched on a tall stool wearing a mask and a black floor-length cape; the apparitions were cleverly designed holograms.

In the basement of a police headquarters, I examined some of the stage props confiscated from Solar Temple sanctums. King Arthur's Excalibur was a large, tinny broadsword crudely painted fluorescent green and red; at secret ceremonies in a dark room, black light made it appear suspended in mid-air with blood running down its tip. Another sword had a small 9-volt battery taped to its hilt. Electrical wires, masked with black tape, ran down the blade to a tiny red light at the tip. If the Master pointed the sword at a female member and the mystical light flashed, it meant she would conceive via theogamy, impregnated by cosmic spirits without sexual contact.

Di Mambro used that trick to achieve one of his most blatant deceptions of Solar Temple members. One evening in the inner sanctum a Master's face appeared in the dark and the sword emerged from beneath his black cape. The Master directed it toward Dominique Bellaton, who happened to be Di Mambro's mistress, producing a flash of light when the tip touched her. Di Mambro announced grandly that she had conceived of the Cosmic Child and would give birth to a new Christ. The Cosmic Child died in the flames of a Swiss chalet at the age of 12.

In his manipulation of Solar Temple members for power and profit, Di Mambro toyed with married couples like playthings. Recalls Huguenin in his book, *The 54th*, "He would say to a couple, 'You've been together quite a while, you're at the end of your karmic cycle and it's time to change partners.'" He made Huguenin divorce his 32-year-old wife, Nathalie, and ordered her to live with Di Mambro's 15-year-old son, Elie, to introduce him to sex; meanwhile Huguenin had to marry Di Mambro's French secretary so she could obtain a Swiss passport.

Completely in thrall to the cult, many members sacrificed not only their personal lives and self-respect, but everything they owned. "Before joining the Solar Temple my brother had a nice big apartment with elegant furniture," says Rosemarie Jaton, who became secretary of the International Association for Defense of Victims of the Solar Temple. "At the end, when he was killed with seven bullets in his head, he lived in one room with a few pieces of cheap furniture. Everything he had earned during his career was gone."

Besides paying dues of up to $300 a month, members often sold homes and other assets and possessions and turned over the proceeds to the Order. Thierry Huguenin sold his share of a small business and gave the $32,000 to Di Mambro, receiving $107 a month pocket money in return. One wealthy member gave nearly $1 million to the Temple, while another spent over $2 million on it, and still another several million dollars in the space of only five years. Why? Explains Huguenin: "Because leaving the Solar Temple would have meant our perdition, leaving the Masters, returning to the status of the ordinary people we used to be and that we hated."

Members' contributions allowed Di Mambro to live like a king. He traveled around the world, staying at the best hotels, buying real estate in Europe, Canada and Australia, driving Jaguar and Mercedes automobiles. An opera lover, he would jet over to New York for a performance at the Metropolitan Opera when he liked, accompanied by his current Templar mistress. And he always paid cash.

Besides contributions, money poured into the Solar Temple's coffers from creative real estate deals, using a classic technique known to criminal money launderers as "land flipping." Its portfolio of expensive properties included some from Australia to the South of France to posh areas around Montreal.

Eventually watchdogs in several countries began sniffing at the Temple. Di Mambro imprudently had an account at the Ottawa branch of the Bank of Credit and Commerce International (BCCI), the same bank used by big international drug traffickers until authorities closed it in July 1991 for widespread fraud and money laundering. He closed his account just before the scandal broke. But shortly after he moved to the Royal Bank of Canada, it alerted the Royal Canadian Mounted Police to suspicious transfers of funds.

France's consulate in Montreal also got curious about the guru. "According to data provided by the police, it appears that Mr. Di Mambro has been involved in currency trafficking (notably the transfer of $93 million to an Australian account from Switzerland)," it cabled Paris in the spring of 1994. "This would explain why the person in question possesses a set of passports he uses to avoid drawing attention to his frequent trips." Meanwhile, the Australian Federal Police had noticed that Di Mambro had been transferring large sums of money into his Australian accounts. When he arrived there in the fall of 1993, they put him under house arrest for four months for questioning about money laundering, but were unable to pin anything on him.

But now the heat was on. Wiretaps on Solar Temple phones reveal increasing doubts and unrest among members. There were whispered questions about finances, the Masters of Zurich, even the special effects at ceremonies. Recordings by police show Jouret increasingly pessimistic and apocalyptic. He told a mistress to start taking target practice with a pistol. "Death is an illusion," he told her in a sleepy, languishing voice that seems deeply depressed or drugged. "We're living a crazy ending. You can't imagine what I have to do to keep the machine running. Thank goodness we're reaching the end."

There was growing panic. "We don't know when they'll close the trap on us," says a document found in one of the Order's word processors. "We're followed and spied on in everything we do." But it remains unclear who or what they thought had laid the trap. It may have been the police. Or the Masters of Zurich, whoever they are, who decided to liquidate a Solar Temple no longer useful. After all, a secret organization is worthless once it makes the front pages.

The trap began closing on September 29, 1994, when Joel Egger took his flight from Zurich. It would keep on closing, and killing, for the next two and a half years. As Di Mambro told a meeting of members just before that, "Don't try to disengage from the Order, because you'll have to deal with the occult. With the occult you don't fool around."

The satanic stage settings and the "testament" left behind saying the cultists had died "in joy and plenitude" were designed to give the impression of a mass suicide pact. To be sure, some 25 fanatical members gathered with Di Mambro and Jouret at the two chalets in Granges-sur-Salvan may have been ready for "the transit to Sirius" preached for years by the two gurus. The circumstances—intravenous injections of a lethal mix of opiates, curare and tranquilizers, followed by a carefully organized fire—seem to indicate voluntary death. But then why would the chalets' openings have been nailed shut from the *outside*?

Authorities were still trying to understand what happened when the Solar Temple reached out 14 months later to again kill its members. Thirteen Temple members and three children aged two, four and six, were shot in the head and burned in a remote area of southeastern France called the Vercors. They were killed in the middle of the night on December 16, 1995. An examining magistrate, impressed with the professionalism of the murders, said, "We are faced with a veritable criminal organization."

Does the Solar Temple still exist? "It does, and someone is pulling the strings behind it," says Janine Tavernier, head of France's anti-cult Union for the Defense of Families and the Individual. "I can tell you there will be more Solar Temple tragedies. Former members still talk as if they are programmed."

Meanwhile, victims' families mourn and wonder where the truth lies. "I begin to despair of getting the real story of what happened," says Jean Vuarnet, a well-known former French Olympic ski champion who lost his wife and a son in the Vercors slaughter. "None of us believes what the authorities are telling us, they treat us like idiots. We're convinced there's something behind the Solar Temple."

As of now, the official view is that all the persons guilty of the Solar Temple massacres, one of the biggest murder cases in modern European history, are themselves dead. No one is being charged. Case closed.

Update: *Ten years after the Solar Temple massacres, no one has been convicted of any crime. One former member now is vaguely charged with belonging to a criminal organization, but his trial has dragged on for years inconclusively. Like Jean Vuarnet, the families of the victims doubt that, for whatever reasons, the truth will ever be known. "The police have never come up with the right evidence or found the guilty parties," says Rosemarie Jaton, secretary of the International Association in Defense of the Solar Temple Victims. "And I doubt they ever will. Those murderers are still running free."*

PART FOUR:
Mère des Arts

One of the many French paradoxes, besides eating foie gras and fat-filled *charcuterie* and apparently getting away with it, is that, compared with several other European countries, this land now known as a center of the art world actually came late to great art. There is little in France comparable to the glories of 15th century Italian painting, or the 17th century Dutch/Flemish masters, or 18th century German classical music, or 19th century Italian opera. To be sure, French monks produced splendid illuminated manuscripts, and the Compagnons and other French artisans, from stonemasons to cabinetmakers and workers in medieval stained glass, did superb work for their royal and ecclesiastical patrons. But this remained at the level of careful craftsmanship, not creative high art.

It was only in the 19th century, after the Revolution had broken the monarchy/church hold on creativity, that French fine arts burst on the international scene with music by the likes of Berlioz, Ravel and Debussy, writing by Balzac, Flaubert and Zola, and, especially, painting by Cézanne, Monet, Pissarro and the others who created Impressionism. But besides its own artistic heritage, one of France's main contributions to the art world has been its hospitality to and nurturing of foreign artists. In some cases, such as the most widely published novelist in the world, the Belgian Georges Simenon, it is a question of borrowing France's language and using it better than most Frenchmen. And when the world comes to France to see its art treasures, many of them are foreign—such as those pilfered by Napoléon in Vienna, Venice and Egypt to fill French museums—including those produced by non-French artists like Picasso, van Gogh and Chagall. Not to mention Leonardo da Vinci, who spent his last three years in France at the invitation of King François I, and left behind what would become the Louvre Museum's proudest and most popular possession, the Mona Lisa.

The Prolific, Prodigious Georges Simenon

Context: *As everyone knows, Georges Simenon wrote crime novels. And he wrote a lot of them. His famous hero, the pipe-smoking, taciturn French detective Inspector Maigret, often played by Jean Gabin in films, figured in nearly 100 novels. The grimy police offices on Quai des Orfèvres, dank Parisian streets and smoky bistrots he described so minutely give the impression of a Paris-based writer, and most readers assume he was French. In fact, he was Belgian and lived in many places, including years in New York, Arizona and Connecticut, but seldom in France.*

Georges Simenon's crime novels are so well known that, like Frigidaire and Kodak, Maigret has become a generic term. In bookstores and airport magazine stands all over the world, "a Maigret" is synonymous with mystery thriller. Less well known is that Maigret's creator is as serious a writer, as careful a craftsman, as modern literature has known. His books are constructed with all the care of a skilled cabinetmaker, his characters are complex creations of a compassionate imagination that readers can identify with in a flash of recognition and understanding. His literary purpose reflects high seriousness.

Simenon achieved this literary quality despite a prodigious production of nearly 500 novels, 200 under his own name and the rest under 19 pseudonyms. He has written as Georges Sim, Aramis, Christian Brulls, Germain d'Antibes, and Jean Sandor, as well as the more improbable Poum et Zette and Gom Gut. Since he wrote his first novel, *Au Pont des Arches*, at 17, he has cranked them out at a pace that ranges from the fantastic—he did 40 under six pen names in 1928—to the merely astounding overall average of four per year. Translated into some 50 languages, his oeuvre is outsold only by the Bible and the works of Lenin.

Maybe it wouldn't be so surprising if the stuff was all pulp. But Simenon's power of characterization and setting long ago won him the praise from the likes of the French writer André Gide. "Simenon is now our greatest novelist," Gide said, "but he has the dangerous reputation as a writer of detective novels, a suspect genre that relegates him to the outskirts of literature. Never mind that he has written, one after the other, 10, 15, 20 novels of an entirely different nature." The works of a different nature are his psychological novels, which he prefers to call *romans durs*, or "hard novels." Just as his detective novels are called Maigrets, his other works are called, generically, Simenons.

His literary seriousness in both genres is reflected in his statement to the *The Paris Review* that "writing is not a profession, but a vocation of unhappiness." In the same interview he recalls the only piece of literary advice he ever followed. It was from the French writer Colette, whose critique of his early work was, "It's too literary, always too literary." Ever since, his prose has been cut to the bone: "Adjectives, adverbs, and every word there just to make an effect gets cut," he says. "Every sentence there just for the sentence. You know, you have just written what you consider a beautiful sentence—cut it."

Simenon uses an artisan's methods when writing. He constructs his books solidly around a few characters. From a few initial traits, he builds them up, giving each a complete family, often down to an address and phone number—he keeps a stock of telephone books as a source of names—even if these details are never used in the book itself. Then he draws a diagram of the apartment, office or house where the action takes place, carefully noting which way doors open, which windows admit the sun in morning or evening.

That done, he becomes the main character himself and enters what he calls "a state of grace" in which he thinks as little as possible, letting his subconscious have its head. He sustains this for up to two weeks, writing a chapter a day and reserving three or four days at the end for revisions. His concentration is so intense that if he misses a couple of days of writing due to illness or other interruption, he usually is unable to continue the book and gives up on it. He seldom has the whole plot in mind when beginning. He puts his characters in a situation and watches, a spectator, as the action develops.

For a man who never finished high school (he had to take a job when he was 15 to support his family after the death of his father, a clerk in an insurance firm in Liège, in eastern Belgium), Simenon is widely read in medicine, law and psychology; the psychologist Carl Jung, a neighbor in Switzerland, was an admirer of his novels. During his early knockabout life he worked to shore himself up against insecurity and disorder, marrying at 17 "to protect myself from myself," possibly an indirect reference to his gargantuan appetite for sex—he claims to have had sex with more than 10,000 women, including many prostitutes. He admits that he was tempted to be a *clochard*, or tramp. "I am not far from thinking that the tramp state is ideal. Obviously a real tramp is a more complete man than we are. He lives without any concessions."

Now Simenon lives a disciplined life. As a form of psychological protection he has always liked big, well-built houses. The house where he received me at Epalinges, a village set amid the rolling hills and vineyards of Switzerland's Vaud canton five miles from Lausanne, is an example. A modern, spanking white, two-story affair on a large plot of land delineated by a neat white rail fence, the house was tailored to Simenon's order. It has rooms for Simenon and his second wife, Denise, their three children and his servants, with plenty of office space and sitting rooms, 26 rooms in all, with 21 telephones. A large enclosed swimming pool is a few yards away, and a dark green 3.8-liter Jaguar sedan sits in the carport.

A lover of art, though not really a collector, Simenon has covered his walls with original drawings and paintings by Maillol, Matisse, Braque, Picasso, Derain, Signac, and one, signed "Merry Xmas," by Henry Miller. There are pencil or ink portraits of the author by his close friend Bernard Buffet, as well as by Vlaminck and Jean Cocteau.

Simenon's day habitually begins at 6 a.m., when he rises, has a leisurely breakfast, and checks the newspapers. At 8:15 he goes downstairs to his office and works with his secretary at answering a voluminous correspondence from admirers, publishers—he deals with publishers in seven or eight countries nearly daily—and friends. When he is turning out a book, he writes mornings using a light-gray IBM electric typewriter rather than the frequently changed (every three lines) pencils he used to favor. He usually gives himself eight days for a novel, crossing off the days on a Trans World Airlines calendar. When the first draft is done he lets it sit for three weeks, then takes it up again for revisions, which are limited to word editing. He doesn't touch the plot.

Simenon received me in his upstairs sitting room in a yellow-and-black plaid dressing gown over white pajamas, wearing black patent leather slippers, and without the mustache he affected for so long. Under the weather due to a viral infection, he was sipping Pommery champagne.

"Personally, I prefer my straight novels, what the critics call my psychological novels, to the Maigrets," he says. "When I started writing I wrote a lot of pulp, and I liked the detective novel form because it follows a nice neat story line. I haven't needed that for a long time, but I don't want to just drop Maigret. So now I do the Maigrets for fun, when I'm tired but want to write something." The score is now 74 Maigrets and 126 psychological novels or *romans durs*, and he expects the former to continue to decline in proportion.

Which of all his works is the most satisfied with? "The last one, as usual." As to what Maigret means to him, he says, "Maigret tries to put together the little things that make people fail in life. He wants to see what it is they lack to be 'normal.' In this sense, I identify with Maigret, since that's what I'm trying to do in my novels."

Simenon is a ferocious individualist and loner. One of the things he liked best about his life in the United States was the lack of clubbiness among writers. "How lucky you are not to have literary cafes," he says. "In France, they think I'm a barbarian because I don't mix with other writers." He never reads fiction, mainly to avoid being influenced. Agatha Christie? "I read one about 15 years ago."

He is uncertain about his own place in literature. What is certain is that he rejects being thought of as just a writer of thrillers. "All I want to do is scratch the surface of the truth about man," he says, "and I don't mean some kind of literary truth, but the real truth." He has known personally many great contemporary writers, including Gide, Faulkner, Thornton Wilder and James Thurber, who was a neighbor when Simenon lived in Lakeville, Connecticut, and they shared the same barber.

"The great drama of writers is that we always die without knowing whether we're a success or not," he says. "After death, there's always a period of purgatory for a writer's reputation, when it's uncertain what the final judgment will be. Maybe I'm a writer who counts, maybe not." How would he like, finally, to be classed? "Among those writers who helped understand man a little better, like Chekhov." Faulkner, in fact, once told Simenon that he reminded him of Chekhov.

However that may be, Simenon will surely keep his reputation as a teller of detective stories. I get the impression that he doesn't really mind that so much. Before I leave, he proudly breaks out a heavy, silver-plated medallion, a police commissioner's badge issued by the Paris Prefecture of Police. Given him years ago by the prefect as a token of esteem, the badge bears the name Maigret.

Update: *Simenon died in 1989 at the age of 86. He would have been pleased to know that his literary success was confirmed in 2003, the centenary of his birth, when he took his place alongside writers such as Hemingway, Montaigne, Dostoyevski, and Proust with the publication of 21 of his novels in the French publisher Gallimard's prestigious Bibliothèque de la Pléiade collection. Over the years, more than 150 of his books have been turned into movies. The creator of Inspector Maigret surely would have savored the irony in the situation of his great-niece Geneviève Simenon: a Brussels court sentenced her in 2002 to a five-year suspended prison sentence for murdering her lover with 18 hammer blows.*

Picasso Superstar

Context: *Pablo Picasso of Malaga, Spain, discovered Paris as a young man of 18 in the autumn of 1899. He moved there permanently in the spring of 1904. Dividing his time between Paris and the Riviera, he became the very model of a modern expatriate artist. France claimed him as her own and in 1966, when he was a still-robust 85, mounted the largest retrospective show of his work ever given a living artist. Perhaps only Rubens could have properly recorded this apotheosis, with a monumental painting showing Picasso rising to the heavens from the glass roof of the Grand Palais, buoyed by fleecy clouds of critical effusion and public adulation.*

On the other hand, perhaps the whole phenomenon should have been treated by Andy Warhol. For the lesson of the massive retrospective, reverently entitled "Homage to Pablo Picasso," was that Picasso had become Pop. "He now has the status of a movie star," commented one critic, referring to the human waves that assaulted the steps of the cavernous Grand Palais daily for weeks. "I'm not sure all these visitors to the show understand anything about it, but they do know he's a celebrity."

The public had to wait until the exhibit had gone through three openings before they finally got a look at it. First was the press opening, at which we harried reporters dashed around trying to ingurgitate enough of the largest retrospective ever given a living artist to write something about it. We surveyed 284 paintings at the Grand Palais, then shuttled across Avenue Alexandre III to the Petit Palais—both buildings are stylish remnants of the 1900 Paris World's Fair—to view 205 drawings, pastels and watercolors, 186 sculptures, and 115 ceramics. The rest of the exhibit, 157 etchings and lithos, was halfway across Paris at the Bibliothèque Nationale.

The next morning the minister of culture, André Malraux, mounted the steps of the Grand Palais between two rows of chrome-helmeted

Gardes Républicains and moved through the show quickly, pausing occasionally for a second take on a work. Stopping before *Jacqueline aux Mains Croisées* and *Jacqueline en Costume Turc*, the old revolutionary made one of his typically cryptic remarks, declaring Picasso's oeuvre "The greatest enterprise of destruction and creation of forms of our time, and perhaps of all time."

That evening an invitation-only crowd showed up for another opening. Seven thousand invitations had been issued, each good for two persons. The resulting crowd included students, artists, art collectors, gallery owners, and a goodly representation of every trade and profession, class and quarter of Paris. They began arriving at 5:30 p.m., and almost immediately there was a line 10-abreast and 20 yards long outside the entrance. The crowd could not have been more avid if it had been Brigitte Bardot nude on a pedestal inside instead of *Les Demoiselles d'Avignon*. Most kept their good humor in the crush, though the critic from the New York Times came away from it to write a petulant story describing "The scholar and the genuine art lover" being "pushed and buffeted by the mere gapers and, worse, the curiosity seekers," regretting that the rest of the press would not treat the exhibit "only in terms of serious criticism directed toward knowledgeable readers." Pity, that.

Meanwhile, the real public poured through the show at an average 6,000 persons a day. Lots of students—lycée girls in white fishnet stockings, boys in suede jackets and long hair—but also people of every age and status. "It's not just the bourgeoisie," an attendant told me, unconscious of any irony in mentioning the bourgeoisie in connection with Picasso, "you also see a lot of workers from the Renault plant here with their families. They want to go out somewhere on weekends, and this is cheaper than a lot of other outings."

Working class or not, most visitors to the show displayed more genuine interest in what was on the walls than the critics and press. They look intensely at the paintings and sculptures, often pointing things out to one another, sometimes simply contemplating with head cocked to one side. Occasionally one will chuckle at one of Picasso's visual jokes, the kind of thing "the scholar and genuine art lover" would never do. One dowdy, middle-aged lady looked up at a painting entitled *Pierrot au Masque* and sighed beatifically: "*Qu'il est beau!*"

Among the crowd was Waldeck Rochet, secretary general of the big French Communist Party, dutifully accompanied by his politburo and central committee, all come to see the work of their famous member—even if Picasso was never very big on either politics or painting Socialist Realism. Earlier, Rochet had sent Picasso a birthday greeting, noting that "You are one of the most prestigious members of our party, and we are very proud of that." It's just possible that Pablo's Party membership did serve some useful purpose: the number of paintings from the Soviet Union's Hermitage and Pushkin museums were far more than the exhibit's organizers had dared hope for.

If, as the French writer Paul Valéry once said, fame is "the sum of the misunderstandings that form around a name," then Picasso is very famous indeed. That was obvious during this exhibit as public and critics tried, without notable success, to decide whether it was Picasso's draftsmanship or his originality, his use of color or his sense for the revealing trait and gesture, his manipulation of forms or his sheer protean productivity that made him great. What came through most clearly was his vitality, his inventiveness.

The works on view in Paris, including sculptures that often are reduced to a few sticks of wood or pieces of cardboard, create an overall mental picture of Picasso at work: There he is in his atelier, eyes dancing mischievously, grabbing materials, holding and shaping them this way and that, seeing what effects he can get. Brisk, sure-footed, goaty, having the time of his life. No metaphysical intention whatever. Just keeping on keeping on. Surviving all the nonsense written about him.

Update: *Before his death, Picasso had another big exhibit in Paris. The one in 1969 at the Right Bank Galerie Louise Leiris (coupled with one at the Art Institute of Chicago) showed the old Minotaur in fine form. So* *fine, in fact, that many visitors to the show, which consisted of 347 engravings turned out in a creative spurt of nearly two works a day, wondered at such an obsessive interest in sex at his venerable age. The staid Paris daily* Le Monde *gushed that "the nude triumphs everywhere, in more unbridled contortions than ever, and in a chronic glorification of sex." Since its creation in the historic Marais quarter of Paris in 1985, the National Picasso Museum, formed from a large collection of works that Picasso's heirs gave to the government in lieu of paying estate taxes following his death in 1973, attracts some 500,000 visitors a year. Its library, archives and documentation center make it a world center for students of Picasso.*

Saul Steinberg: New Yorker in Paris

Context: *Another example of a foreign artist who was appreciated by the French, at least briefly, was Saul Steinberg. The Rumanian-born son of a box manufacturer, Steinberg studied psychology at the University of Bucharest and architecture in Milan before moving to New York and becoming one of the most original and cerebral cartoonists at* The New Yorker. *Thus it was surprising that he should show work in Paris that might be puzzling to any but an American public, and mainly New Yorkers at that. But after a 13 year, self-imposed ban on exhibitions, he chose Paris to display his work because, as he explained, it "has a tradition of intellectual painters, and I think of myself really as a writer who paints."*

The dumpy figure in a white raincoat and soft checkered cap walking down Avenue de Messine on a brisk, sunny spring day glanced up at a large poster filled with portentous, illegible script. "That's the most beautiful poster I've ever seen," he said of the poster advertising his new exhibit in Paris, with just a trace of irony. "It's pure invention, but there's a message there."

Saul Steinberg had just left behind a roomful of messages, most of them as difficult to decipher as a page of the flamboyant nonsense script that has become his signature. That the messages had real content there was no doubt. But whether the French visitors to Steinberg's new exhibit at Paris's Galerie Maeght were grasping it was another question.

Among the 67 new drawings and collages in the show, entitled Le Masque, there were few of the direct satirical lampoons that Steinberg used to be identified with. Instead of the baroque, outrageously chromed automobiles, burlesqued cowboys and drum majorettes, and steel-faced, monumental businessmen, there are allegorical landscapes, metaphysical dreams, ominous sphinxes and fantastic masks. The visual pun was still in evidence—lines doing unexpected things to people, media suited to subject, false perspective, and outright optical illusion—but on the whole this exhibit is more cerebral and more work for the spectator than usual.

Dominating the show, for example, is a four-panel, 10 by 23-foot mural covering the end of the gallery. *Exhibition* is made of cloth: a brown cloth base with cloth images, also basically brown but with a few colors painted on, stapled and nailed to it. It shows eight women spectators wearing absurd high heels and mini-skirts squinting at paintings. They are done in styles ranging from stiff primitive African to rounded, curly romantic, to cubistic, and finally grotesque Steinbergian. The paintings they are looking at are in side-view perspective, as if hung on walls almost perpendicular to the live spectator. They are parodies of landscapes, with only conventional blue tops and green bottoms visible, hinting at sky and fields. The women are making remarks, represented by comic strip-like balloons filled with illegible script. Also included is an artist's easel with a false landscape, script-filled balloon, and phonograph record on it. The whole mural is full of abrupt changes of perspective and illusions, like the steps beneath the easel on which the spectator stubs his optical toe.

"It makes a statement, a declaration about art exhibits," Steinberg says. He doesn't like to do much explaining, believing that, first, the viewer should make his own interpretation, and, second, if he could explain it in words, he would not have done it visually. But this work, he says, "hints at the prejudices about painting, like the blue-top, green-bottom landscapes, and through the various styles and subjects alludes to the history of painting. It's also mimicry of an exhibit and the people who attend it, but it's not cruel mimicry, it's done with charity. I did it for myself and I identify with it. For example, there are drawings hidden behind the easel that you can't see. But I know they are there, and that's what's important."

The five masks in the show that give it its title are drawn on brown wrapping paper. They are entitled *Beauty Mask, Provincial Mask, Business Mask, Bikini Mask, and Hostess Mask.* To my mind, the bikini, business and hostess masks are as cruel caricatures as Steinberg has done, and I tell him so. He doesn't agree. "These are not caricatures, they are real portraits," he says earnestly. "They are real people that you have known. They are the faces, the masks of the middle class, a synthesis of middle-class expressions. They have the middle class's instant smile, they represent its official optimism, its bureaucratic happiness."

Grave, rarely smiling, with a large, regular mouth and nose and elliptical eyes, looking like a creation by his painter compatriot Victor Brauner, whom he knew, Steinberg says this without a trace of sarcasm, almost with indulgent understanding. He explains further: "What people do, especially in America, is to manufacture a mask of happiness for themselves. They put a perpetual, reassuring smile on their faces. It makes them look nice, friendly and healthy, and we don't have to worry about them." But while Steinberg wants to avoid, or at least play down the satirist label, the masks reveal more explicitly than ever his contempt for convention for its own sake.

Other examples of his satire dotted through the show:

- *The Treaty of Sagaponak*, a pompous official document including a map which clearly indicates that gentlemen sitting around a conference table have once again coldly and precisely settled the borders of a small country.

- *Sam's Dream* shows Uncle Sam sleeping, with an Indian-head-dressed Statue of Liberty holding the torch at the foot of the bed while he dreams a maze of overlapping circles, some precise and some awkwardly childish, and one colorful rainbow. He perhaps does not know what his dream means, but it is big and grandiose.

- *New York Cops* is a garish picture of an aggressive New York of colorful cabs, steaming manhole covers, glowing Chrysler Building, and apartment buildings going in all directions. The city's finest strut on horseback or roar around in cruisers with brightly colored lights flashing. A yellow moon in a black gouache sky broods over all.

• *East Hampton* is a jumble of wooden houses on the shore with two aggressive bird-women (Long Island hostesses?) and a grim male bird (their successful husbands?) under a moon and dark sky.

Though the imagery of these satirical pieces is often complex enough, it's nothing compared to the ambiguity of the more metaphysical drawings. *Masked Landscape* has the artist dutifully at his easel, manfully trying to capture a zooming, exploding, jet-speed reality. His canvas is blank. *Artist and Invented Landscape* also shows the artist at work, clearly placed between conventional and abstract reality. Seated before his blank canvas in a romantic setting including flowers, a comfortably green tree and friendly dog, he looks out on an incomprehensible maze of lines and colors producing an interconnecting order that promises meaning if it can be broken down into its elements. *Passage to Fiction* shows a man climbing a ladder from a small island to a map in the sky listing places where Steinberg has lived: Milan, Bucharest, Santo Domingo, New York. Which is the fiction, the island or the places on the map?

Among the most frequent motifs are comic strip balloons, phonograph records, and waves of illegible script. They reflect Steinberg's concern with objectifying language, words, ideas. In his world, it is drawings that are legible while writing is not. "Words are like vitamin pills," he says wryly. "We swallow them and think we have got something valuable inside us. But we don't. Reading anything but poetry or studying a drawing is mediocre because it is ready-made to be poured into us. When we look at a drawing, we must hunt and invent our own meaning."

"There is actually less satire in this show than I used to do," he continues. "I've become bored with satire, even find it rather childish now. I have become more understanding, more forgiving." And what about that old target, the American businessman? "I leave him alone now. It's like this: At first one protests against specific types of human beings, kings, generals, police and so on, and then against general classes of people like the bourgeoisie. Now I'm attacking new monsters. Not the people or classes themselves, but the things that make them the way they are. Satirizing people is like making fun of invalids: they can't help being the way they are."

But what *are* the new monsters? "It's hard to say, really. They are things like the seven cardinal sins, hate, vanity, and so on, and ideas, conventions that formalize or freeze people. It's difficult to say just what form these monsters take, even in my drawings. In *Exhibition*, for example, the optical illusion steps represent conventions and bureaucracies that block life. But it's impossible to talk about it. You have to see it in the pictures."

This show at Paris's prestigious Galerie Maeght marks the first time in 13 years that Steinberg has exhibited his work. The show he had in the same gallery in April 1953 was the last of many over a seven-year period in the U.S. and Europe. After that he found he did not have to exhibit any more. As he tells it, "No artist wants to exhibit, he does it because he has to. It's humiliating to put yourself on display, in the market, open to criticism. Also, I hate to separate from my work by selling it."

His contract with *The New Yorker* pays "very civilized" wages, and the magazine is most undemanding: a messenger comes by once a week to bring a copy of the latest issue and ask him if he has anything to send in, with no questions asked if he does not. So for the last 13 years he has lived the good life, traveling when he wanted to, notably to the Soviet Union, and puts out books including both published drawings and new material. "Essentially, magazines and books are the most satisfying way of showing my work," he says. "Things published in *The New Yorker* are seen by, say, a million people. At an exhibit maybe a few thousand will see it, and eventually the pictures get hung on people's bedroom walls. What good is that?"

The gallery owner Aimée Maeght made repeated proposals for a show, but Steinberg always turned them down. Then when the two talked about it again last year, the quirkiness of Steinberg's own character dictated that he exhibit. "I like to contradict myself, to reevaluate, to start again," he explains. "It's a way of renewing myself."

French critics had a field day intellectualizing about this very American view of things. One such is Michel Butor, an avant-garde writer who declares that Steinberg's work "is a reflection of drawing on itself and on everything in our world related to drawing. To see this is to become aware of the immense role of drawing, almost as large as language, to which it is closely related. Steinberg analyzes its aspects, excerpts its alphabet, isolates certain kinds of lines for study." He sees Steinberg's landscapes as "philosophical landscapes in which there is nevertheless a remarkable feeling for nature, in which we have the pleasant surprise of discovering a rainbow, the moon, even a sunset. This primordial landscape, this desert, this wilderness that the alphabet of painters permits us to reconstitute, is discovered deep in our imagination already populated with inhabitants. This is the first time that Steinberg touches on the theme of the Indians and their combat against the American Sphinx next to its unfinished pyramid which adorns the back of each dollar, Sphinx or female Sphinx which quickly becomes a harpy." Well, sure.

Steinberg's own view of himself and his talent is more straightforward. "What I have is an eye for seeing things that most people don't, and expressing what I see—it's a talking eye," he tells me over lunch at his favorite Paris restaurant, the Grand Vefour. "I'm an artist in the most general sense of the word, not a cartoonist. I express myself, and a cartoon is the form it takes. It could be through writing, but I can't write, it's too hard. I tried poetry but it was no good. If I were a writer, I would be a sort of James Joyce, the Joyce who observed so well in "Dubliners," but also the Joyce of "Ulysses" who experimented with new forms of expressing what he saw. But I hit this jackpot of expressing myself in pictures. Art historians always want to classify, to put artists in categories. I don't fit into any pigeonhole, unless it's my own."

Steinberg is still searching for new ways of expression, of getting at those monsters. "There's often the temptation to repeat yourself. But if you do, you don't feel good about it because you know you have missed a chance to invent." As long as that eye keeps on talking, he feels obliged to give it new voices. "What counts is innovation."

Update: *When Saul Steinberg died in May 1999 at 84, the critics had a hard time finding the right pigeonhole for him, just as he had said during our talks. Everybody admired his work, but was he a sharp-eyed cartoonist, draftsman extraordinaire, or some kind of Renaissance genius? There were comparisons to Picasso and Miro. The obituary in* The New Yorker, *for which he had done 85 covers and 642 other drawings over 50 years—including the famous and much-copied* View of the World from 9th Avenue—*said he was nothing less than "the greatest artist to be associated with this magazine, and the most original man of his time." I myself like to remember our lunch in Paris, and how he happily eyed his dessert of crêpes flambées that the waiter had just set aflame. "Artists should eat fire," he told me with a wink.*

The Free Spirit of Marc Chagall

Context: *Marc Chagall was only 24 when he first arrived in Paris from his native Russia in 1911, seven years after Pablo Picasso. By then the city was becoming a magnet for foreign artists, who appreciated the chance to be near repositories of great art like the Louvre, to which Chagall ran straight from the train station. They also liked to live and work in mutually stimulating artists' communes like La Ruche in Montparnasse. Chagall took advantage of those features of Paris, but he remained very much his own man, bucking the fashionable trends of 20th-century art. Like Saul Steinberg, he was unique and shunned pigeonholes.*

Looking back, David McNeil fondly remembers the time in the early 1960s when his father the painter took him to lunch at a nondescript little bistro on Paris's Ile Saint Louis in the middle of the Seine. It was the kind of place where they scrawl the menu du jour in white letters on the mirror behind the bar. That day, McNeil recalls, the specialty was a blanquette of veal with white sauce. Wearing a battered jacket and beret and a coarse checkered shirt, his father fitted in perfectly with the masons, house painters, plumbers and other workingmen downing a hearty lunch along with unlabeled bottles of *vin ordinaire*. With conversation flowing easily among the close-set tables, one of the coveralled patrons looked over at the man in his mid-70s whose muscular hands were covered with splotches of paint. "Working on a place around here?" he asked companionably. "Yeah," McNeil's father Marc Chagall replied nonchalantly as he tucked into his appetizer of hard-boiled egg and mayonnaise. "I'm redoing a ceiling over at the Opera."

Chagall, the Russian-born artist who literally turned 20th century painting on its head with his magical, variegated images of blue cows, flying lovers, bird-headed women, Biblical prophets and green-faced fiddlers on roofs, had a firm idea of who he was and what he wanted to accomplish. But when it came to guarding his privacy, this basically shy man was a master of deflection. Sometimes, when people came up and asked him if he wasn't that famous painter, Marc Chagall, he would answer "No," or, even more improbably, "I don't know," or point to someone else and say slyly, "Maybe that's him." With his slanting, pale-blue eyes, unruly hair, and the mobile face of a mischievous faun, he gave one biographer the impression of being "always slightly hallucinating." One of those who knew him best, Virginia McNeil, David's mother and Chagall's companion for seven years, characterized him as "full of contradictions—generous and guarded, naïve and shrewd, explosive and secret, humorous and sad, vulnerable and strong."

He himself said he was a dreamer who never woke up. This painter-poet covered his canvases with views of his interior world, his personal visions. "Some art historians have sought to decrypt his symbols," says Jean-Michel Foray, curator at the Marc Chagall Biblical Message Museum in Nice, "but there's no consensus on what they mean. We cannot interpret them because they are simply part of his world, like figures from a dream." Pablo Picasso, sometime friend and rival ("What a genius, that Picasso," Chagall once joked, "it's a pity he doesn't paint."), marvelled at Chagall's feeling for light and the originality of his imagery. "I don't know where he gets those images," said the naughty Minotaur of modern art. "He must have an angel in his head."

Movcha (Moses) Chagall was, as he put it, "born dead" on July 7, 1887, in the Belorussian town of Vitebsk, near the Polish border. His distraught family pricked the apparently lifeless body of their firstborn with needles to try to stimulate a response. Then, in desperation, they took the small body outside and put it in a stone trough of cold water, where the baby boy began to whimper. With that rude introduction to life, it's small wonder that Marc Chagall, as he later chose to be known in Paris, grew up sensitive, emotional, and subject to fainting.

Shy and stuttering as a boy, he was not really interested in growing up. Early, the painter whose metamorphosed beings would puzzle many began to perceive things differently: a hand towel seemed to the child to morph into a ram or an old man. When he glanced down at his father's reflection in a river, he was struck by the fact that the head was upside down. His only discernable talent was for drawing. That was too bad for the finances of a poor and numerous family, to which Marc, as the eldest of nine children, was normally expected to contribute.

His father worked in a herring warehouse, his mother ran a small grocery. Both nominally adhered to Hasidic Jewish religious beliefs, which forbade graphic representation of anything created by God. Thus Chagall grew up in a world devoid of images, without a single painting or engraving on the walls of his house. Still, he pestered his mother until she took him to an art school run by a local portraitist. Marc was the only student who used the color violet. A pious uncle refused to shake his hand after he began painting.

For all his pictorial reminiscing about Vitebsk, Chagall found it stifling, provincial, "a strange town, an unhappy town, a boring town." In 1907, when he was 20, he wangled the small sum of 27 rubles from his father and left for Saint Petersburg to attend the undistinguished Society for the Protection of the Arts. He hated it. "I, poor country lad, was obliged to acquaint myself thoroughly with the wretched nostrils of Alex of Macedonia or some other plaster imbecile," he recalled. The meagre money soon ran out and, though he made a few kopecks retouching photos and painting signs, he sometimes collapsed from hunger.

His break came in 1908 when he entered the art school of Leon Bakst, a theatrical designer for Diaghilev's Ballets Russes. Having been to Paris, Bakst carried an aura of worldly sophistication. He indulged Chagall's unconventional approach to painting and dropped names, so exotic to the young man's ears, like Manet, Cezanne, and Matisse. He spoke of painting cubes and squares, of an artist who cut his ear off.

"Paris!" Chagall wrote of that period in his autobiography. "No word sounded sweeter to me!" In 1911, at age 24, he was there, thanks to a stipend of 40 rubles a month from a supportive deputy in the Duma, Russia's first elective assembly, who took a liking to the young artist. The day he arrived he went directly to the Louvre museum from the train station, suitcase in hand, to look at the famous works he had heard about. He found a closet-sized room at an artists' commune in a circular, three-storey building in Montparnasse called La Ruche (The Beehive). He lived frugally. Often he cut a herring in half, the head for one day, the tail for the next. Friends who knocked at his door had to wait while he put his clothes on; he painted in the nude to avoid getting paint stains on his only clothes.

La Ruche swarmed with the sort of talent that made Paris's reputation for the rest of the 20th century as a center of avant-garde creativity. Chagall rubbed shoulders with painters like Fernand Leger, Chaim Soutine, Amedeo Modigliani and Robert Delaunay. True to his nature as a storyteller, he seemed to have more in common with the writers like Blaise Cendrars, Max Jacob and Guillaume Apollinaire, who coined the expression *surréel* (surreal), when he saw Chagall's work in his studio in 1913. Cendrars, a restless, knockabout poet, wrote a little descriptive poem about his friend that seemed to capture his fluid imagery: "Suddenly he paints/He grabs a church and paints with a church/He grabs a cow and paints with a cow."

But life at La Ruche was not all intellectual speculation on the future of art. One night Soutine, who had the room directly above Chagall's, splashed fresh blood on a cow carcass he was painting, in order to get the color right. The blood ran through the cracks in the floor and dripped into Chagall's studio. Chagall ran into the street shouting, "Help! Soutine's being murdered!" Arriving gendarmes found Soutine in good shape—and an embarrassed Chagall pretending not to speak French.

Returning to Vitebsk in 1914, intending to stay only briefly, Chagall was trapped there by the outbreak of WW I. But that gave him the chance to spend time with his fiancée, Bella Rosenfeld, the beautiful, cultivated daughter of one of the town's wealthiest families. She had won a gold medal as one of the best students in Russia, had studied in Moscow, and had ambitions to be an actress.

But Bella fell for Chagall's strange, almond-shaped faun's eyes and soon was knocking on his window to bring him cakes and milk, and boards for easels. "I had only to open the window of my room and blue air, love and flowers entered with her," Chagall remembered. Shocked villagers gossiped: "She even climbs through the window to get into his room. It's gone that far!" Despite her family's worries that she would starve as the wife of an artist, they married in 1915. How Chagall felt about it can be seen in the first of many paintings of flying lovers such as *Above the Town*, with he and Bella blissfully soaring above Vitebsk.

Came the revolution in 1917 and Chagall embraced it enthusiastically. He liked the new Communist regime that gave Jews full citizenship, no longer requiring them to carry passports to leave their designated region. And he liked being appointed commissar for art in Vitebsk, where he started an art school and brought in avant-garde teachers. But it soon became clear that the revolutionaries preferred abstract art and Socialist Realism—and how, they wondered, did the comrade's blue cows and floating lovers support Marxism-Leninism? Giving up his job as commissar in 1920, he moved to Moscow, where he decorated the interior of the Jewish Theater. But, unable to sell his work or even get an exhibition, left for the West, settling in Paris with Bella and their daughter Ida in 1923.

Ironically, France, which now likes to present Chagall as one of its cultural stars, initially rejected his request for naturalization on the grounds that he had been a Communist in Vitebsk. While that was being worked out, he kept on painting, but with a pronounced stylistic break. "Chagall's work changed upon his arrival in France," notes Jean-Michel Foray. "It seems to become softer, to lose its wild side." In any case, he changed direction after meeting the Paris art dealer Ambroise Vollard, who commissioned him to illustrate the *Fables* of La Fontaine. Chauvinists in the National Assembly cried scandal over this choice of a Russian Jew, a mere "Vitebsk sign painter," to illustrate a classic of

French letters. That blew over and afterwards Chagall went on to do resonant illustrations of the Bible for Vollard.

Increasingly alarmed by Nazi persecution of the Jews, he made one of his strongest political statements on canvas in 1938 with his *White Crucifixion*. Now 51 and in his artistic prime, Chagall here shows the crucified Christ, more human than divine, symbolizing the suffering of all Jews, his loins covered with a prayer shawl. A synagogue and houses are in flames, a fleeing Jew clutches a Torah to his breast while another one burns, elders lament in the sky, emigrants try to escape in a rudimentary boat. Not long after, in May 1941, Chagall and his family took a ship for the United States, settling in New York.

The seven years Chagall spent in America were not among his happiest. He never got used to the pace of New York life, never learned English. "It took me thirty years to learn bad French," he said, "why should I try to learn English?" The one thing he seems to have enjoyed was strolling through Jewish neighbourhoods in lower Manhattan, haggling in Yiddish for good prices for strudel and gefilte fish, buying Yiddish newspapers. He was largely unknown in American art circles, considered a Surrealist with a Russian Jewish imagery. His palette often darkened to a tragic tone, with Christ as sacrificed Jew and symbol of suffering humanity a frequent theme. When Bella, his muse, confidante and best critic, died suddenly in 1944 of a viral infection at the age of 52, "everything turned black," Chagall wrote.

After weeks of sitting in his apartment on Riverside Drive immersed in grief, tended by his daughter Ida, then 28, he began to work again. Ida found an English woman, Virginia McNeil, who had fallen on hard times, to mend his socks, then to be his housekeeper. A bright, rebellious, cosmopolitan diplomat's daughter who had been born in Paris and raised in places like Bolivia and Cuba, England and Canada, Virginia was 30 and Chagall 57 when they met. She was married to John McNeil, a Scottish painter who suffered from serious depression, and had a four-year-old daughter, Jean. Soon she and Chagall were talking painting, then dining together. She left McNeil and went with

Chagall to live in a village near the Catskills, High Falls, where they bought a simple wooden house with a cottage next door he used as a studio. The area's heavy winter snowfall reminded him of his childhood in Vitebsk.

But while he did several important public works in the United States over the years—backdrops and costumes for a 1945 New York production of Stravinsky's *Firebird*, large murals for Lincoln Center, stained glass windows for the United Nations headquarters and the Art Institute of Chicago—he never felt at home in America. "I know I must live in France, but I don't want to cut myself off from America," he once said. "France is a picture already painted. America still has to be painted. Maybe that's why I feel freer there. But when I work in America, it's like shouting in a forest. There's no echo."

In 1948 he returned to France with Virginia, Jean, and their son, David, born in 1946. They settled in Provence, in the fragrant hilltop towns of Vence and later Saint Paul. Virginia chafed in her role, as she saw it, of "the wife of the Famous Artist, the charming hostess to Important People," and abruptly left Chagall in 1952. Once again the resourceful Ida found him a housekeeper in the person of Valentina Brodsky, a 40-year-old Russian living in London. They quickly married—Chagall was 65—and Vava, as she was known, proceeded to manage Chagall's affairs with an iron hand.

"She tended to cut him off from the world," says David McNeil, a successful French singer and songwriter who lives in Paris. "But he didn't really mind because what he needed most was a manager to give him peace and quiet so he could get on with his work. I never saw him answer a telephone himself. After Vava took over, I don't think he ever saw his bank statements and didn't realize how wealthy he was. He taught me how to blow my nose by holding a finger on one nostril to save on handkerchiefs, and to visit the Louvre on Sunday, when it was free. He always picked up all the sugar cubes on the table before leaving a restaurant." McNeil and his half-sister Ida, who died in 1994, gradually found themselves barred from seeing their father, except for occasional escapades like McNeil's bistro lunch with him. But the marriage apparently suited Chagall, and images of Vava figure in many of his paintings.

Chagall continued to create. Besides his regular painting in his Provençal studio, he undertook demanding projects such as designing stained glass windows for the synagogue of Hadassah Hebrew Medical Center in Jerusalem. His ceiling for the Paris Opera, peopled by Chagallesque angels, lovers, animals and Parisian monuments, took eight months. In a book of reminiscences published in France, McNeil describes Chagall at work: "He prepared his charcoal pencils, holding them in his hand like a little bouquet. Then he would sit in a large straw chair and look at the blank canvas or cardboard or sheet of paper, waiting for the idea to come. Suddenly he would break the charcoal with his thumb and, very fast, start tracing straight lines, ovals, lozenges, finding an aesthetic structure in the incoherence. A clown would appear, a juggler, a horse, a violinist, spectators, as if by magic. When the outline was in place, he would back off and sit down, exhausted like a boxer at the end of a round."

Remaining both childlike and sophisticated, Chagall, whose prodigious output of more than 10,000 works spanned nearly 75 years of painting, stubbornly stuck to his conception of the artist as storyteller. His warm, human pictorial universe, full of allegory and narrative, set him apart from most 20th century art, with its intellectual deconstruction of objects and arid abstraction. As a result, the public has generally loved his work, while the critics were often dismissive, complaining of sentimentality, repetition, and the use of stock figures. Some critics said he drew badly. "Of course I draw badly," he retorted. "I *like* drawing badly."

Perhaps worse, for the critics, he did not fit easily into the accepted canon of modernity. Not only did he not fit, he resolutely rejected a rational approach to art. In this he was very Russian. Tolstoy had called reason "the greatest moral evil," Gorky referred to "Russian distrust of the power of the intellect." Against the followers of 20th century art fads, Chagall thundered, "Impressionism and Cubism are strangers to me. Art seems to me to be above all a state of soul…Let them eat their fill of their square pears on their triangular tables!" Notes the veteran Paris art critic Pierre Schneider, "He absorbed Cubism, Fauvism, Surrealism, Expressionism and other modern art trends incredibly fast when he was starting out. But he used them only to suit his own aesthetic purposes. He was sui generis, with no predecessors and no followers. That makes it hard for art critics and historians to place him. He can't be pigeonholed."

When he died in Saint Paul de Vence on March 28, 1985, at 97, Chagall was still working on drawings and watercolors, still the avant-garde artist who refused to be modern. That was the way this free spirit had always said he wanted it: "To stay wild, untamed…to shout, weep, pray."

Update: *Marc Chagall remains a ubiquitous, inescapable icon of modern art, a situation he would no doubt have despised. Google him and you get over 300,000 responses. Rare is the major gallery or museum in the world that doesn't possess at least some sample of his work. Art speculators are still betting on those old Paris neighbors, Picasso and Chagall: when New York's Museum of Modern Art sold Chagall's mystical* Le Temps n'a point de rives *in 2004, the price reached $1,239,500.*

Van Gogh and Gauguin: Creative Tension in the South of France

Context: *The sparks that flew when Vincent van Gogh and Paul Gauguin briefly lived, experimented, argued and dreamed together in the South of France mark one of the most dramatic episodes in the history of painting. Their tense friendship and unspoken rivalry in late 1888, in the Provençal town of Arles, lasted only briefly. But it produced works that set the stage for Postimpressionism, Symbolism, Cubism, Expressionism, and much of what we know today as modern art. It has also inspired writers and filmmakers to the point where most of the Western World knows what happened to van Gogh's ear.*

"My dear Gauguin," said a contrite, sober Vincent van Gogh, "I have a vague recollection that I offended you last evening." The offense having been merely a glassful of absinthe thrown at his head, Paul Gauguin readily forgave his high-strung friend. But his doubts about their two-month experiment in communal living in the South of France were confirmed the next night, when van Gogh, distraught over Gauguin's impending departure, ran after him in the street hurling wild accusations and waving a razor. Gauguin turned and stared him down, whereupon van Gogh returned to the house they shared. There he used the razor to cut off part of his left ear, carefully wrapped it, and presented it to an inmate at the local brothel. Van Gogh was hospitalized, and Gauguin left for Paris the next day. But after his discharge from the hospital, Vincent wrote him a letter begging him not to speak ill of "our poor little yellow house." Some dreams die hard.

When van Gogh met the 39-year-old Gauguin at a Paris art gallery in November 1887, the Dutch painter was at a pivotal point in his life. Then 34, he had finally emerged from many years of false starts and failure, having worked for an art dealer in London and Paris before turning to language teaching and lay preaching, then moving on to theology studies and missionary work among impoverished Belgian coal-miners. He was 27 before he discovered his vocation as an artist. When he first joined his brother Theo, an art dealer working in Paris, in March, 1886, he was still painting in the dark, heavy style of his early masterwork *The Potato Eaters*. But in Paris he began experimenting with light-filled Impressionism and colorful pointillist brushwork.

Though Gauguin, too, came late to art (he was 25 when he started painting), he had been doing Impressionist canvases since the late 1870s, and had worked with masters like Camille Pissarro. That, plus his adventuresome, knockabout background as a sailor who had cruised the world, a stockbroker who had left his wife and children to devote himself to painting, and a wanderer who had lived on the Caribbean island of Martinique, greatly impressed the unworldly van Gogh. The two quickly found they had much in common, as both were seeking new forms of expression and both had great regard for each other's work. Van Gogh praised the "high poetry" of Gauguin's painting, while Gauguin both admired van Gogh's passionate approach to art and, with cool calculation, saw that the Dutch artist's brother could be useful in promoting and selling his work.

As a token of friendship, they exchanged paintings in late 1887: van Gogh gave Gauguin two studies of cut sunflowers, while Gauguin reciprocated with a canvas done in Martinique of a woman, boy and cow on the bank of a dried-up river. Gauguin then went to Pont Aven, in Brittany, where he joined an artists' colony. Van Gogh, in turn, was drawn by the clarity of the light of southern France, wishing to see nature under a brighter sky, because, he wrote Theo, "One feels that the colors of the prism are veiled in the mist of the North." On February 20, 1888, he arrived by train in Arles.

He was a man reborn. Responding to the brilliance and warmth of Provence, he threw himself into one of the most productive periods of his life, painting landscapes, flowering trees, haystacks, virtually anything that caught his eye. "I have a terrible lucidity at moments, when nature is so glorious that I am hardly conscious of myself and the picture comes to me as in a dream," he wrote Theo ecstatically. Already he was leaving behind the delicate, evanescent Impressionist approach he had picked up in Paris, and starting to use strong, pure color arbitrarily to express himself more forcefully.

But, longing for the companionship that his difficult, stubborn character had always prevented him from finding with others, he had a dream of a brotherhood of painters of similar beliefs, living and working together. Now was the time to realize it. In May, with Theo's financial help, he rented a small house on Arles's Place Lamartine, near the train station. The color of fresh butter, it had two rooms on the ground floor and two above, with lavatory privileges at the hotel behind it. He furnished it sparely with two beds, a dozen straw-bottom chairs, and a few other necessities. The Yellow House, as he called it, would do nicely for his planned Studio of the South. At its head, in his idealized view, like an abbot among monks, would be his much-admired new friend, Paul Gauguin.

Van Gogh bombarded Theo and Gauguin with letters urging Theo to subsidize Gauguin in return for paintings. On June 5, two days before Gauguin's 40th birthday, a formal invitation was extended to the near-penniless artist; 50 francs were enclosed. Although still hesitant, Gauguin accepted in late June, but kept putting off his departure.

With Gauguin in mind, van Gogh worked feverishly to decorate the house with several paintings of his signature sunflowers. In October, Gauguin exchanged self-portraits with Vincent. Van Gogh's was a starkly austere work, the gauntness of his face emphasized by almost shaven hair, intense eyes vaguely staring into the distance—the character, he explained in a letter, of a Buddhist monk. Gauguin sent van Gogh a written description of his own portrait before the work itself arrived in Arles. It was, he said with typical swagger, "the face of an outlaw, ill-clad and powerful like Jean Valjean—with an inner nobility and gentleness…the eyes suggest the volcanic flames that animate the soul of the artist." But when van Gogh saw the portrait, he was disappointed by the pessimism and desperation he divined there. "What

Gauguin's portrait tells me above all is that he cannot go on like this," he concluded.

Finally Gauguin decided to go. With Theo underwriting his living expenses and paying for the train ticket, it was a sweet, no-risk deal, to which he brought considerably less commitment than van Gogh. As Gauguin wrote to his estranged wife, he simply planned to spend "six months with a painter who will provide me with food and lodging in exchange for drawings."

Now that his friend's arrival was imminent, Vincent worked himself practically to exhaustion, often painting from 7 a.m. to 6 p.m. non-stop, to have as much as possible to show him. Although casting himself in his own thinking as a sort of disciple of Gauguin's, he wanted to assert his individuality before being subjected to Gauguin's influence. "I am sufficiently proud to want to impress Gauguin to some extent with my work," he wrote Theo. The resulting series of paintings includes some of his best known: *The Yellow House, The Bedroom,* and *The Poet's Garden.*

The intensive work took its toll; van Gogh was overwrought when Gauguin arrived on October 23. Still, the pair began sorting out living arrangements. Gauguin bought a chest of drawers and various household utensils, but, confronted with his partner's untidy living habits, the old bohemian began to act positively bourgeois. "Everywhere and in everything I found a disorder that shocked me," he later related. "His paint box could hardly contain all those tubes, crowded together and never closed." And money! "From the very first month, I saw that our common finances were taking on the same appearance of disorder…I was obliged to speak, at the risk of wounding that very great touchiness of his."

Gauguin set up a strict budget, with fixed sums for rent, food, incidentals, and tobacco. A certain amount was also set aside for "hygienic" brothel visits, which, they reasoned, would promote productivity by discouraging entangling amorous relationships. All the while, Gauguin was regaling van Gogh with tales of his adventurous life as a sailor and traveler in the tropics, presenting a virile, macho persona that only increased van Gogh's wide-eyed hero worship. "This gives me an enormous respect for him and a still more absolute confidence in him as a man," he wrote Theo. But Gauguin had a premonition of looming trouble. "Between two such beings as he and I," he later reflected, "the one a perfect volcano, the other boiling too, inwardly, a sort of struggle was brewing."

Gauguin liked to get accustomed to a new place before painting, but the day after his arrival, the eager van Gogh pushed him out of the Yellow House to do landscapes. Technical research reveals that they both painted, that first workday, on the same pre-primed linen support van Gogh habitually used at the time; apparently van Gogh was so impatient to get going on the Studio of the South that he gave the canvas to his partner rather than wait for him to buy and prepare his own. In any case, the results show profound differences: van Gogh's *The Sower* and *The Old Yew Tree* are done with his usual impetuous, pell-mell brush strokes, and the latter features his trademark yellow sky; Gauguin, however, used an almost Cézannesque approach, carefully planning and executing his *Farmhouse in Arles* with studied composition and deft, discreet strokes.

They tried an experiment, buying 20 yards of coarse jute cloth to use instead of canvas. The hairy, absorbent fabric, similar to burlap, forced them to alter their habitual painting methods: Gauguin, used to painting deliberately with delicate strokes, began using a rougher application, while van Gogh's gestural strokes and characteristic impasto became less important than color.

That can be seen in their second foray to do landscapes, which took them to Arles's Alyscamps area, a burial ground dating to Roman times that had become a tourist attraction and lovers lane. Gauguin's deliberate technique captured a more decorative, imaginative view of the locale. Van Gogh's paintings, rendered in a quick, agitated style, were based more on the actual scene. In another new departure, he showed willingness to adapt to Gauguin's habit of doing studies outdoors and the finished work in the studio; research shows that he finished his *Falling Leaves* back in the Yellow House.

That was an important concession, for van Gogh maintained stoutly that he needed to work directly from his model. Gauguin tried to persuade him to do it his way, which was to work from memory. As Vincent put it as delicately as possible, "Gauguin…has more or less indicated to me that it is time for me to vary my style a little bit." He tried conscientiously in several works, notably in his *Spectators at the Arena, A Novel Reader,* and other versions of *The Sower,* all painted from his head. But the results are stilted and heavy, far from the powerful vitality of his more typical works.

Gauguin, too, showed signs of his partner's influence. When they painted a vineyard, he transformed it from a bustling scene of grape pickers at work (as van Gogh showed it in his *The Red Vineyard*) to a somber, melancholy study called *Human Miseries.* In this he seems to be appropriating his friend's frequent theme of human suffering. Technically, too, he changed, troweling paint on thickly with a palette knife in a style resembling van Gogh's. But the stylistic influence in both cases was slight and temporary. "Their ideas on art differed greatly," says Andreas Blühm, head of exhibits at the van Gogh Museum in Amsterdam. "They influenced each other to a degree, and then went back to their original styles." Douglas W. Druick, curator at the Art Institute of Chicago, agrees. "The influence on each other was formative and motivational rather than in technique as such," he says. "For example, Gauguin picked up the idea of the painter as pilgrim and missionary from van Gogh."

Their differences in approach and style are again clear in their portraits of Madame Ginoux, owner of the Café de la Gare near the Yellow House. Vincent dashed off his in the single hour she sat for them in early November, seeming to reject deliberately any imitation of his partner's slow, studied methods. Gauguin, on the other hand, first did a chalk and charcoal study on paper, then over the following days transposed her portrait to the foreground of a bar scene. In his *Night*

Café she appears to give the viewer a sly look while proffering a glass of absinthe. Although they placed their easels side-by-side and worked from the same model at exactly the same moment, the results could not have been more different.

Van Gogh's perception of the deep personality differences between himself and Gauguin show up in his paintings of his and his friend's chairs in the Yellow House. He chose to depict his as a sturdy, rush-bottom chair standing on simple red floor tiles, a pipe and tobacco lying on the seat. But he pictured Gauguin's as a much more elaborate armchair standing on an exotic carpet, with a lighted candle and two books on the seat—witty metaphors for the pair, contrasting Vincent's rough simplicity with Gauguin's perceived refinement.

When not painting, the two artists were talking. Besides art, they discussed novels, history, the Bible, physiognomy, graphology and evangelism. The conversations were stimulating, acrimonious, and grueling. "Our arguments are terribly electric," van Gogh told Theo. "We come out of them sometimes with our heads as exhausted as an electric battery after it has run down."

Increasingly they saw their fundamental discord. Vincent insisted that painting should be from nature and offer a poetic dimension, while Gauguin called for art to have intellectual strength and be based on what happened in his "wild imagination." Ultimately Gauguin contemptuously ascribed Vincent's views to "a disordered brain" and "absence of reasoned logic." Writing to his friend and fellow painter Emile Bernard, who van Gogh had hoped would join them in Arles, Gauguin said, "In general, Vincent and I do not see eye to eye, especially as regards painting.... He is a romantic and I am rather inclined to a primitive state."

By mid-November, Theo had sold some of Gauguin's paintings in Paris, giving him more money than he had had in years. He thus began thinking of leaving Arles for Martinique, where he would start a Studio of the Tropics, which he and van Gogh had discussed. Van Gogh sensed this and his anxiety grew as he realized that his dream of a community of painters in Arles was doomed. The tension between them is graphically portrayed in the odd, unfriendly portraits they did of each other in early December. Van Gogh painted Gauguin from the strange perspective of right-rear, in an awkward, roughly finished work, *Man in a Red Beret*, which seems to suggest he was watching his friend cautiously. Gauguin did a similarly disturbing image of van Gogh, in *The Painter of Sunflowers*, in which van Gogh's head is distorted, his eyes lost in a trancelike gaze, the overall impression loaded with aggression.

Tension like that would trouble even a man with stronger nerves than van Gogh. After he snapped on December 23 and ended up in the hospital, Gauguin took the train for Paris. They never met again. His dream of a Studio of the South was over, but van Gogh went on to paint brilliant works while in the asylum at St. Rémy, including *The Reaper*, *Cypresses*, and his famous *Starry Night*. In May 1890, he left St. Rémy for the town of Auvers-sur-Oise, near Paris, to consult the physician Paul Gachet, an amateur painter and collector who apparently suffered from a similar nervous disorder.

Although van Gogh wrote to his brother that "I feel a failure," he produced dozens of paintings and drawings during his two months there, including his renowned portrait of Dr. Gachet. (The work sold for $82.5 million in 1990, making it at the time the most expensive painting ever sold at auction.) But of his entire production of some 870 paintings and 1,050 drawings, van Gogh sold just one—*The Red Vineyard* now in Moscow's Pushkin Museum—before he shot himself on July 29, 1890. He was 37.

Update: *Paul Gauguin went on to paint for another 13 years in Brittany and the South Pacific. Fearing that van Gogh's reputation was rising faster than his, he insistently used the word "crazy" to describe him, and claimed he could not remember how long they had spent together. "When I arrived at Arles, Vincent was trying to find himself," he later wrote with condescension. "I undertook the task of enlightening him…From that day on, my van Gogh made astonishing progress." Still, his experiences in the Studio of* *the South stayed with Gauguin, perhaps hauntingly. In Tahiti, ill and broke in 1898 at age 50, he did a series of still lifes featuring sunflowers. Earlier, he had done another work that may have been an implicit salute to his friend and their tense time together in the Studio of the South. A self-portrait in the form of a stoneware jug, it is an excellent likeness. But Gauguin portrayed himself without ears.*

Paul Guillaume: First of the Avant-Garde

Context: *Many of those who made Paris the creative center of the Western World in the early 20th century were foreigners. Even the French who early on recognized the value of modern art tended to view it with a foreign, or at least atypical, eye. Paul Guillaume, the first gallery owner in France to encourage many avant-garde artists and to put together a collection of truly great modern art was an outsider, therefore free of the prejudices of the French art Establishment. Indeed, he would eventually chide the French government for what he considered its shameful neglect of modern art. Guillaume was a loner rather than the scion of a wealthy family or son of a well-known Paris art dealer, a failed artist from a modest family. He had to rely on his own love of art, his "assertively impertinent" taste, and good luck.*

It was a bright spring day in the year 1900. A top-hatted French President Émile Loubet was being ceremoniously shown around the 1900 Paris Exposition Universelle, the largest of the great world's fairs that gave the city such monuments as the Eiffel Tower in 1889 and now, 11 years later, the immense, glass-roofed Grand Palais off the Champs Élysées. Just as Loubet turned to enter the section devoted to Impressionist painting, he was prevented from doing so by Jean-Léon Gérome, an officious member of the august French Academy, supreme arbiter in matters cultural. "Stop, Monsieur le Président!" Gérome ordered abruptly, as if the president's very life were in danger. "This is the dishonor of France!"

Such was still the French art establishment's rigid hostility toward modern painting when a young man of 23 opened a Paris gallery in 1914. But Paul Guillaume, driven by ambition though he had little formal art training and only the most limited means, was undeterred. As he made his way in the catty Paris art scene, he had to dodge the slings and arrows of tart-tongued critics who found him daringly avant-garde, or maybe merely threatening. "A dealer in extremists," snorted one. "His canvases by Derain, Picasso, and Matisse are chosen with assertively impertinent taste," wrote another. "He is in harmony with the iconoclasm of modern art, itself symptomatic of the 'decline of the West.'"

Strong stuff. But besides the courage of his convictions, Guillaume had taste and luck. During the 20 years he was active as a dealer and champion of modern art, he amassed not only a tidy fortune, but also created one of the world's finest collections of late 19th-and early 20th century masterpieces. Many of the paintings he bought and sold have found their way into art museums across Europe and America. Most of his own cherished private collection of 145 works went after his death to Paris's charming little Orangerie museum in the Tuilleries Gardens near the Louvre.

More than simply a collection of masterpieces, the collection also shows how an individual of exceptional prescience and flair put together a collection in real time, not after-the-fact, the way most early 20th-century museums did. Guillaume was an actor on the scene, scouting new talent, nurturing it, and shouting from the rooftops to get it the appreciation it deserved. The collection shows a consensus about who were the great figures of modern art, including works by its four main pillars, Cézanne, Renoir, Picasso and Matisse.

The whole collection is a delight to the eye. But one big favorite is inevitably the world-famous *Young Girls at the Piano* by Pierre-August Renoir, with its two graceful girls in long, flowing dresses absorbed in a page of sheet music, the whole scene immersed in Renoir's shimmering color. It's so light and fluid it looks as if Renoir dashed it off easily. In fact, he wrestled long and hard with the painting, starting over five or six times, the color seeming to him to veer toward the yellow each time. No sooner had he delivered it than he decided *that* version was the least successful. For the last century, most viewers have disagreed with him.

Other great items in Guillaume's collection necessarily include Soutine's *The Room-service Waiter* with the waiter's smeared sneer and raw-meat ears illustrating the artist's technique of distorting his subjects to get at their essence; Douanier Rousseau's *Old Man Juniet's Trap*, a delightful naïf vision of a simple peasant family out for a carriage ride under a sunny sky; Cézanne's *Apples and Biscuits*, one of the 10 or so works bought not by Guillaume but by his wife Dominica after his death; and Picasso's Junoesque, extravagantly modeled *Large Bather* from his neo-classical period.

Then there's the unforgettable portrait of Paul Guillaume himself by Amedeo Modigliani. Other artists he worked with, including André Derain, Giorgio De Chirico, and Kees van Dongen, also did his portrait. But this is the most original, perceptive, and penetrating: Guillaume is shown as a 23-year-old dandy in a high collar and trilby hat, his head slightly back in an attitude of hauteur, eyes shrewdly half-closed, one eyebrow raised skeptically, lips parted as if to exhale smoke from the cigarette in his left hand. Modigliani, who got his start thanks to Guillaume, has playfully scrawled phrases like "Stella Maris" ("Star of the Sea") and "Nova Pilota" ("New Helmsman") on the canvas, gently mocking hyperbolic praise for the cocky young dealer. It's one of the great portraits of the 20th century, with great depth and tenderness but also a trace of subtle irony, showing Guillaume as a slightly arrogant dreamer.

Although extremely social, Guillaume was intensely private, not given to talking about himself, and cloaking his life and dealings in an opaque smoke screen. The staff of the Orangerie is still trying to determine how many paintings he bought and sold during his career; the latest, incomplete, count is more than 1,300. His reticence was possibly due to his being a self-made man in a country where that was very much the exception. Most of the other great Paris art dealers of his time, like Bernheim, Rosenberg, and Kahnweiler, were all scions of dealers or descendents of wealthy families. Guillaume, however, was the son of a modest Paris tax collector. He wanted to be an artist and briefly tried his hand at it, but realized he could never succeed professionally.

His first job, at 18, was a menial position in an automobile garage near the Arc de Triomphe. He saved his sous and began buying his first paintings: a Picasso for about 50 francs, a De Chirico for even less. The garage imported raw rubber from Gabon to make tires. Some of the shipments contained gifts of African tribal statuettes that Guillaume found fascinating. Excited by the esthetic qualities of *art nègre* at a time when it was generally considered only an ethnographic curiosity, he soon developed a network of suppliers in France's African colonies. By 1914 he was well enough established to lend 18 objects from Ivory Coast and Gabon to New York's first exhibit of African art, "Statuary in Wood by African Savages: The Root of Modern Art."

It was also the root of Guillaume's budding success. Opening a minuscule gallery, he financed purchases of paintings with his sales of African statuettes. Modern art came cheap in those days: he bought up dozens of paintings by Montmartre artists from a shopkeeper who sold them for next to nothing to augment his regular trade in mattress coverings. When paintings hanging in a cabaret called La Belle Gabrielle caught his eye, he scooped them up for about 45 francs apiece from the owner, who had taken them from a penniless fellow named Maurice Utrillo in exchange for meals. A few years later, Guillaume was selling them for some 20,000 francs each. He himself had little cash on hand. As his wife, Dominica, recalled later, "He never had a cent in the bank. When he needed a little money to pay the rent or buy a suit, he just sold a painting."

Living in Montmartre, home to experimental painters like Pablo Picasso, Georges Braque, and Juan Gris, and avant-garde writers like the surrealist Guillaume Apollinaire and poet Max Jacob, Guillaume drank in their ideas along with apéritifs at the Café Cyrano or the bistrot Chez Azon. He pumped his intellectual friends for tips on who were the coming artists. Apollinaire introduced him to numerous painters like Picasso, Picabia, and De Chirico, while Jacob put him in touch with Modigliani at a time when nobody wanted his work. Guillaume was virtually his only buyer from 1914 to 1916, even renting an atelier for him. He also discovered and supported Chaim Soutine, writing the first serious text on the young Lithuanian fresh from Vilnius whose agitated brushwork, thick impasto and bizarre vision shocked most dealers and bewildered the public.

His first gallery was so small that Guillaume rented three maid's rooms on the top floor of an apartment building to store his stock. One day when he called on the building's concierge, he was surprised to see a familiar painting hanging on her wall. "*Mais monsieur*," she explained, "it's only one of those things you threw away in the maid's room upstairs." He had forgotten to lock the door to one of the rooms, and several of the building's occupants had helped themselves to what they considered worthless, if decorative, bric-a-brac. Guillaume politely asked the concierge for his Modigliani back, then climbed the stairs to reclaim several Picassos, Derains and Utrillos.

Success seems to have come quickly and easily to this Pygmalion of the avant-garde. At one Paris show in 1916, he made his then-controversial point about the relationship between tribal art and modern Western painting by juxtaposing 25 African statuettes with works by his stable of artists. The fashionable young poet Jean Cocteau wrote the preface to the catalogue, the ultra-modern composer Erik Satie played the piano, and *le tout Paris* loved it. As a contemporary press report described a typical scene in his gallery, "All the avant-garde gentry were there: many chic women, covered with ochre-colored powder, wearing satin turbans and many-hued necklaces." As for Guillaume himself, a photo taken about this time shows him in an elegant tweed suit and gray, buttoned-up spats, sitting somewhat imperially in his apartment—now no longer in Montmartre but in the expensive 17th arrondissement—surrounded by a plethora of paintings.

Before long, he would meet the most important client in his career. Albert C. Barnes, the Philadelphia physician who made a fast fortune with his formula for an antiseptic, had been prospecting the Paris art market for several years for the private art foundation he was creating in Merion, Pennsylvania. By the early1920s, Guillaume was Barnes's main dealer, adviser and confident, selling him scores of paintings by day, accompanying him to his favorite Paris show, the Folies Bergère, by night. So impressed was Barnes by the vibrant cultural atmosphere in Guillaume's gallery that he called it "the temple." "Practically all the important French painters and sculptors visit the temple with regularity," he wrote. "I have visited the temple a hundred times and nearly always found interesting people there." When the Barnes Foundation officially opened in March 1925, a bronze plaque bearing Guillaume's name was over the door of room 14, testimony to the role he played in creating the foundation's important collection of modern painting and African tribal art.

Guillaume was surely pleased by that gesture. He had long fought to be accepted not only as a merchant, but also as an art patron and private collector who often kept the best paintings for himself—a hard sell in a France where lowly business was considered tainted with money and thus incompatible with art. When a noted French art writer, Maurice Sachs, visited Guillaume's apartment in the late 1920s, with its wall-to-wall masterpieces, he was bowled over: "What a collection of treasures, what perfection in their display! This is how the palaces of the great princely patrons of the arts looked!"

In the Paris auction rooms too, he now cut quite a figure. He and his retinue would disembark from two superb Hispano-Suiza limousines with chauffeurs in livery and sweep into the room. As one awed description had it, "When he enters majestically draped in a fur coat, there is a vast murmur among the crowd of art lovers and patrons, and even the auctioneers themselves suddenly suspend the sale, stopping their hammers in mid-air. A small bisexual army of secretaries is suspended on his slightest word, moving around with military discipline on a sign from him."

To consolidate his claim to being a serious collector, Guillaume began planning to create a private art museum that would be open to the public. In a slap at what he considered the French government's shameful neglect of modern art, he wrote in an essay that the collection might even be donated to France, "if the state shows itself worthy of it." But he never carried out the plan. His sudden death of peritonitis in 1934, at the age of 42, hit the Paris art world like a thunderclap.

His wife, Dominica, a headstrong lady used to having her way (she once casually asked the French minister of the interior how much it would cost to close a nearby Paris street to annoying automobile traffic), kept the collection relatively intact. She sold some paintings and purchased a few like a Monet and several Cézannes. She remarried to a wealthy architect and industrialist named Jean Walter. After his accidental death in 1957, she began negotiating with the French government, finally selling it the collection for a fraction of its real value in 1963. She retained it until her death in 1977, and after the Orangerie added an extra floor for it, the collection—known officially as the Jean Walter and Paul Guillaume Collection, although Walter had no hand in creating it—opened to the public in 1984, joining Monet's monumental *Water Lilies* as the museum's only other exhibit.

Update: *Today the Guillaume collection at the Orangerie enjoys a far better presentation, thanks to a three-year, $11-million renovation completed in 2002. The museum now has a more rational, user-friendly layout. Paul Guillaume's beloved masterpieces are easier to appreciate, and two new rooms show the collection's history and put it in the context of modern art. The dealer-collector is finally receiving the status he craved. Pierre Geogel, the museum's curator, is convinced that Guillaume succeeded handsomely in both roles. "He was not only a master dealer," he says, "he really did love art."*

Master Class at the Louvre

Context: *For more than two centuries, copyists have flocked to the Louvre museum to learn from the masters by copying them from the original. "Going to the Louvre is like reading the Bible or Shakespeare," said Marc Chagall, who went straight there when he arrived in Paris. Paul Cézanne said, "The Louvre is the book where we learn to read." Today's copyists from around the world are a varied group of artists.*

The Louvre has been open only a few minutes, but already crowds are ambling through its vast galleries. Up on the second floor, in a long, red-walled room devoted to 19th-century French paintings, a group is gathering around a young woman wearing a black velvet tunic and a floor-length silk skirt. Her glossy auburn hair braided and coiled around her head, she sits on a stool before an easel, deftly applying paint to a canvas. Some of the visitors hang back at a distance, stare dubiously, then wander off. Others crowd in for a better look, glancing up at the famous painting on the wall, *Les Femmes d'Alger* by Eugène Delacroix, and back at the copy on the easel, gauging and comparing. "Boy, she's really good," whispers one to his companion. "Aw, I bet she's doing it by the numbers," comes the skeptical reply.

Sorrel Smith, a 25-year-old artist from California, is in fact performing that difficult paradox, an original, fully creative copy. She is also carrying on a venerable tradition. Ever since the museum opened its treasures to public view on November 18, 1793—one of the indisputable benefits of the French Revolution—it has encouraged artists to hone their technique by copying the masterpieces in its collection. Thousands have done so, including great classical painters from Turner to Ingres, Impressionists from Manet to Degas, and modernists like Chagall and Giacometti. "You have to copy and recopy the masters," insisted Degas, "and it's only after having proved oneself as a good copyist that you can reasonably try to do a still life of a radish."

The Louvre's pull on artists is legendary. When 23-year-old Marc Chagall arrived in Paris in 1910 from his native Russia, he literally couldn't wait to get to the museum: he went there directly from the train station, suitcase in hand. "Going to the Louvre is like reading the Bible or Shakespeare," he later said. Post-Impressionist Paul Cézanne, who regularly trekked there to copy Michelangelo, Rubens and classical Greek and Roman statuary, agreed. "The Louvre is the book where we learn to read," he declared.

Though most of them are women, today's copyists are a varied lot. Of the 150 who did 269 copies in a recent year, 72 percent were art students or in artistic professions. But one was a psychoanalyst, one a surgeon, one a midwife, and 13 were retired. Nearly three-quarters were French, with the American contingent of 20 the largest single foreign nationality, followed by Japan with six. Maïten de Ferrier, the helpful, enthusiastic head of the Louvre's Bureau des Copistes, which runs the museum's copy program, believes a stint at the Louvre is a rite of passage for many. "These artists like to follow in the footsteps of all the great painters who have copied here," she explains. "And of course they also come to improve their technique, to find solutions to their artistic problems."

Some, however, like the eccentric Surrealist Salvador Dali, who created several provocative renderings of Jean-Francois Millet's pious *The Angelus,* prefer to use the masterworks simply as a point of departure for their own artistic explorations. Picasso, who liked to copy at the Louvre to recharge his creative batteries, painted there frequently in the 1950s. He produced a series of singular interpretations of Delacroix's *Les Femmes d'Alger* after noticing a marked resemblance between one of the women in the painting and his then companion, Jacqueline Roque.

At the moment, Sorrel Smith's problem is getting Delacroix's composition and colors just right. An accomplished technician who loves 19th-century painting and poetry, designs theatrical costumes and likes to do miniature portraits on ivory, Smith came to Paris with the Wells College Program for the Arts in Aurora, New York, where she learned to mix colors and stretch canvases. This is her third Louvre copy. "Making my own paints with earth pigments means I don't have to search for the colors the Old Masters used, because I'm starting from the same point they did," she explains. "It's a pity that most art students today don't learn the old painting techniques; a lot of golden rules of painting have been lost at art schools. In this painting the colors are very vibrant and at the same time muted, creating a difficult balance. It's the hardest copy I've ever done."

Louvre copyists clearly are marching to a different drummer in today's culture of quick 'n' easy. Difficulty is what most of them are looking for. "It's a challenge to try to reach the level of the old masters, and to meet it you have to extend yourself," says Mary Chavance, a French artist who studied at Paris's Ecole des Beaux-Arts and does mainly Impressionist-style landscapes in her Left Bank studio. But here, on the other side of the Seine in the Louvre's bustling Grande Galerie (covering slightly more than one acre and devoted to French, Italian and Spanish classical paintings), she is grappling with an aristocrat in gleaming dark armor by Caravaggio. The painting, *Alof de Wignacourt*, is typical of the Baroque master's Tenebrism, the depiction of dramatically illuminated form emerging from shadow. Her copy looks perfect, but she is not quite satisfied. "If you don't copy you'll never really improve," she says. "But you can't do it passively, you have to involve yourself deeply in creating something that is more than just a reproduction of a painting."

That seems to have been the original idea when the museum opened its doors two centuries ago. "Each visitor should be able to put his easel in front of any painting or statue to draw, paint or model as he likes," declared an early official. Louvre access at first was reserved primarily for artists, with only limited time allotted to the public. But it was soon so flooded with artists that officials had to suspend free access, issuing authorizations and limiting hours for copyists. (That continues today, with copying permitted from 9 a.m. to 1:30 p.m. from September through June, except Tuesdays, Sundays and holidays.) Art students, never known for their decorum, often had to be reminded to refrain from games, singing and horsing around, in what was supposed to be "a sanctuary of silence and meditation."

Not all the self-styled copyists came to the Louvre for purely esthetic reasons. In the mid-19th century, mothers began accompanying their daughters, worried that classical statues and paintings showing scantily clad bodies might be a bad influence. They brought their knitting and fended off young males offering artistic advice. The 19th-century novelist and art critic Champfleury wrote tongue-in-cheek directions on how to meet a demoiselle at the Louvre. "Copy a painting next to hers, then ask to borrow some cadmium or cobalt," he advised. "Then correct the odious mess of colors she calls a painting (they're always glad to get advice) and talk about the old masters until the Louvre closes and you have to continue the conversation in the street. Improvise the rest."

By the middle of the 19th century, 400 to 500 artists were busily copying masterpieces, mainly to satisfy orders from clients in this era before photographic reproduction. Many visitors, wending through a veritable forest of easels, ordered copies on the spot. Thus copying came to offer advantages besides improving technique: the Louvre was dry and heated, unlike the garrets and ateliers many artists lived and worked in, and sales of copies were a welcome source of income. But by the 1890s, photography had begun to erode the financial rewards of copying.

Still, many of today's Louvre copyists continue the tradition of selling their work. Art galleries near the museum occasionally market them for the artists, and some copyists, such as Amal Dagher, sell directly to visitors who offer to buy what they're working on. The affable 62-year-old Dagher, the unofficial doyen of Louvre copyists by virtue of coming there regularly for 30 years, was born in Lebanon and studied for four years at Beirut's School of Fine Arts and later in India, Thailand and Japan, before settling in Paris. He is currently working on the *Portrait of Mademoiselle Caroline Rivière* by French Neoclassicist

Jean-Auguste-Dominique Ingres, along with Delacroix one of the most copied of the Louvre's masters because of his firm, clear line, rigorous composition and subtle coloring. (Paradoxically, one of the world's most famous paintings, Leonardo's Mona Lisa, is one of the least copied works—in part because the crowds that flock to the painting make it difficult for an artist to set up an easel, and partly because, according to Maïten de Ferrier, its fame intimidates artists.)

"Caroline Rivière is almost an Italian Madonna, and the challenge here is to achieve the form that Ingres gave her, making her seem to float above the background," Dagher explains as he jabs lightly at the canvas where the copy is taking shape. "She was mentally handicapped and died at 14, and I believe he was trying to console her parents with this idealized vision of her." Despite his many years of painting and copying, Dagher admits to feeling a sort of stage fright every time he starts a new copy on a blank canvas. "That's a good sign," he says. "If you're too satisfied with yourself you can't continue to improve."

Besides copying to improve, Dagher also likes working at the Louvre because of the chance it affords to meet the public. "Not many people passing through actually buy my copies," he says, "but often they will ask me to do something else for them." Some want him to make copies of portraits of their ancestors to give to other family members. And one American visitor, liking what he saw on Dagher's easel, asked him to reproduce a ceiling fresco from the Palace of Versailles at his home in Connecticut. "The gold leaf molding around the fresco alone cost nearly $60,000," he recalls wistfully. "That was a lot more than I asked for the painting."

But selling their canvases is the furthest thing from the minds of many Louvre copyists. Gilles Malézieux, for instance, does it as a sort of busman's holiday and to create his own collection. In the corner of a quiet room he is peering closely at a small seascape, *The Ferry*, by 17th-century Dutch landscape painter Salomon van Ruysdael. He knows the Louvre better than any of the other copyists for good reason: he's a security officer at the museum. When not keeping an eye on problems like pickpockets, he returns to the Louvre with brushes and paint. "I take days off from my vacation time to do this," he says. "I'd rather copy than go to the beach."

The 45-year-old began copying six years ago because he loved paintings but could not afford to buy them. "I would have liked to collect art, but you need a fortune to be a collector today. So this lets me hang paintings I like at home, mainly genre scenes and landscapes." Self-taught, Malezieux does four or five copies a year. Pointing out the flattish composition of the original, he explains, "I chose this one because it's a seascape with a river and oceanfront, mostly transparent, a glaze without much detail. That lets me dream a little, and that's enough vacation for me."

Not far from him in another room given over to 17th-century Dutch painting, Tsutomu Daitoku is working on a meticulous copy of Jan Vermeer's famous *The Lacemaker*, with its assiduous young lady bending to her delicate handiwork. Tall, thin and earnest looking, the 25-year-old Japanese amateur taught himself to paint by reading books and frequenting museums. "I came to Paris just so I could copy here at the Louvre," he says. "I plan to become a professional artist when I return to Japan, moving around the country and doing all kinds of paintings. This one by Vermeer is very difficult, especially the—he takes out a Japanese-English pocket dictionary and checks the word—'coloring.'"

The museum provides each artist with an easel and a stool. Besides requiring that the copy be one-fifth smaller than the original, the museum protects against any temptation to produce a forgery by carefully checking the copyists' canvases at the beginning and end of each session. De Ferrier and other Louvre officials continually pass through the rooms for further checks. "It's not a problem we have here," says De Ferrier. "If someone really wants to make a forgery, it's much simpler to work from a good color photograph in the secrecy of their own studio."

The Louvre is more liberal than, say, Washington's National Gallery of Art, which requires four reference letters on character and artistic proficiency, original samples of paintings done, a personal written statement about how past artistic training relates to the Gallery's collection, and an interview. And its list of rules and regulations runs on for pages. "I think we should leave the artists as free as possible," says Maïten de Ferrier. "There was a time when applicants needed references from an art teacher, but today we're much more open to requests. Sometimes we have a small waiting list, but in recent years nearly everyone who has applied has been accepted because the number of applicants has just about corresponded to the 87 easels available."

One American artist who has benefitted from the Louvre's liberal attitude is Will H.G. Thompson, a tall, slim man of 30 with a shock of thick dark hair. A professional artist who won an award for a painting at Paris's Salon des Beaux Arts and has shown his work twice at the city's Salon des Independents, Thompson is a cosmopolite born while his parents were living in Geneva. He grew up in France, Belgium and Germany before studying art at the Pennsylvania Academy of Fine Arts in Philadelphia, and now makes his home in Paris. In a small, dimly lit room devoted to Spanish classical painting at the extreme end of the Grande Galerie, he is copying Francisco de Goya's *Young Woman with a Fan,* a full-length portrait of a proud, poised, stiffly elegant young lady holding a fan with a dreamy gaze.

"I got a good foundation at the Pennsylvania Academy, but you never stop learning to paint," he says as he orients his easel to catch the light better. "I'm basically an Expressionist, but I also do Impressionist and other styles. When I copy a masterpiece, I get a sort of mental trip out of it, applying the paint differently, studying different bone structures, using light and dark the way the artist did. It's like taking a lesson from an old master."

Like most Louvre copyists, Thompson often chats with some of the average 18,000 visitors who enter the museum each day. "There's a real exchange between the copyists and the public that we consider very positive and profitable for everyone," says Maïten de Ferrier. "Copyists working amid the visitors enhances the way the public sees paintings, inciting them to look more closely with a more active and analytical approach. They start noticing how the artist actually did the work."

Those who frequent the museum have come to know a wispy little man of 77 with pale blue eyes, soft voice and gentle manner. Bruno Nini has been copying nearly every day since 1990, when he retired as maitre d' at the restaurant in Paris's Austerlitz train station, where he began his days at 5 a.m. by taking delivery of 5,000 croissants. Now he is working on his excellent copy of *Gabrielle d'Estrées and One of Her Sisters*, a symbolic portrait of the mistress of Henri IV by an anonymous 16th-century painter of the School of Fontainebleau.

"I learned most of my technique from books," he says with obvious pride. "After realizing I wanted to paint, I sought out street artists and tried to get tips from them. Then one day I came here and saw copyists at work. I knew that was what I wanted to do." Nini figures he has done more than 100 copies, about half of which he has sold, while the others hang on the crowded walls of his Paris apartment. He's an amateur in the true sense of the term, someone who passionately loves what he's doing. "Sometimes, when I see the figures in a painting coming to life under my brush strokes," he says, "tears come to my eyes."

Update: *In order to copy at the Louvre, non-French artists must attach to their application a photocopy of their passport and a recommendation from their embassy or consulate. But otherwise the procedure is the same as for French citizens, a simple form specifying the desired starting date and the work to be copied. (For American applicants, the Louvre has an understanding with the Franco-American Commission for Educational Exchange in Paris, which handles their requests.) No samples of work are requested. Except for the requirement that copies be one-fifth smaller than the original and that the artist's signature not be reproduced, the Louvre* *imposes few rules on copyists, whose permits are good for three months. Copyists can then reapply for another permit.*

Mona Lisa, Mythic Parisienne

Context: *Temptress or icon of innocence, cult figure or cultural archetype, Leonardo's mysterious Madonna has intrigued art historians and the public for 500 years. The painting holds pride of place at the Louvre museum, where it is by far the most popular exhibit. It is perhaps the best example of how France readily appropriates foreign art and smoothly associates it with its own artistic heritage.*

Going with the flow, I follow the body heat from the cavernous crypt beneath the Louvre's glass pyramid up past a dying Italian slave and a nude Greek warrior, a diminutive French general directing troops and a carelessly draped lady with wings. On the second floor, in a room where you could comfortably play tennis, the background murmur grows to a clamor and the air, on this warm August day, is distinctly ripe. Harried tour leaders waving striped sticks or colorful scarves try to corral their polyglot charges. But most of them are busy jockeying and elbowing as close as they can get to a bulletproof, air-conditioned showcase for a glimpse of Leonardo da Vinci's 500-year-old portrait of a preternaturally poised Florentine lady.

Largely ignoring the room's other masterpieces of Italian classical painting, its splendid Raphaels, Tintorettos, Veroneses and Titians, the throng aims high-performance cameras at the showcase and lets fly a fusillade of flashes, pinpoints of light bouncing back from its window. Many stand beside it to be photographed as if they were in front of the Eiffel Tower. It all reminds me of when, as a young reporter, I occasionally had to cover chaotic, shoving, celebrity press conferences. Except here the superstar says nothing. She merely gazes back with a cool, appraising smile.

The Mona Lisa is the most famous work in the entire 40,000-year history of the visual arts. And if you don't agree with that, your argument is not with me but with the respected art historian Roy McMullen, who has studied the phenomenon extensively. "It provokes instant shocks of recognition on every continent from Asia to America," he observes, "reduces the Venus of Milo and the Sistine Chapel to the level of merely local marvels, sells as many postcards as a tropical resort, and stimulates as many amateur detectives as an unsolved international murder mystery." Like many celebrities, the Mona Lisa today is famous for being famous.

Louvre officials estimate that most of the museum's first-time visitors come mainly to stare at this cross between a cultural archetype and an icon of kitsch that has somehow become part of our collective subconscious. What they are looking for is the picture that has provoked, and been the object of, more crazy reactions, addled adulation, arcane analysis, gross imitations, scandalous take-offs, and crass commercialization than any other work of art in history.

The painting's status as a world-class superstar was confirmed beyond any doubt when, in 1963, French Minister of Culture André Malraux—who called the painting "the most subtle homage that genius has ever paid to a living face"—sent it to the United States and Japan as a sort of itinerant ambassador of French culture, its Italian origins notwithstanding. On arriving in America in January of that year in its own first-class cabin aboard the passenger liner *France,* the Mona Lisa was received more like a potentate than a painting. A tuxedoed John F. Kennedy and an evening-gowned Jacqueline Kennedy formally welcomed it to Washington's National Gallery of Art, where its director, John Walker, hailed it as "the most famous single work of art ever to cross the ocean."

White-gloved U.S. Marines guarded the painting around the clock. Even though the museum was kept open evenings for the first time in its history, crowds waited for up to two hours to get a look at the famous face; one man asked a guard, in passing, what the grand building was used for when the Mona Lisa wasn't there. It was the same mob scene in February and March at New York's Metropolitan Museum, with lines down Fifth Avenue for blocks in severe winter weather. In all, more than 1 million Americans ogled the Mona Lisa.

But Mona mania in America paled beside the frenzy in Japan, to the hand-wringing despair of some French aesthetes who complained that the work was being exhibited like Brigitte Bardot or a Folies Bergère danseuse. When it arrived at Tokyo's National Museum in April 1974, visitors totaling 1.5 million stormed the building and were hustled past the painting, rigidly three abreast, for a 10-second look, a uniformed guard atop a podium directing traffic. Outside, the hype approached hysteria. Dozens of bars and nightclubs changed their names to Mona Lisa, one staging a Mona Lisa Nude Revue. A telephone number yielded a recording of the lady saying, in Italian, how happy she was to be in Japan. Japanese girls wore décolleté dark dresses with long sleeves, hair parted in the middle; some fashion victims even had plastic surgery for a more convincing Lisa Look.

The look that inspires such bizarre behavior is defined by the enigmatic, tight-lipped smile that has launched a thousand learned interpretations, lucid explanations, and loony analyses. The renowned art critic Bernard Berenson set the tone for serious appreciation in the early 20th century when he proclaimed that Leonardo's subtle *sfumato* technique of modeling light and shade reached its apex with the Mona Lisa, carrying "facial expression perilously close to the brink of the endurable." For centuries many an artist has tried to equal it as a sort of ultimate challenge, the Everest of oil painting. One, the French artist Luc Maspero, threw himself from the fourth-floor window of his Paris hotel in the mid-19th century, leaving a farewell note: "For years I have grappled desperately with her smile. I prefer to die."

When not mortal, the smile has often generated perplexity. Is it "more divine than human," as a 16th-century Italian writer had it, or "worldly, watchful and self-satisfied," according to the British art historian Kenneth Clark? The 19th-century French Positivist thinker Hippolyte Taine seemed unable to make up his mind, variously calling it "doubting, licentious, Epicurean, deliciously tender, ardent, sad," while novelist Lawrence Durrel puckishly dubbed it "the smile of a woman who has just eaten her husband." Feminist Camille Paglia went further: "What Mona Lisa is ultimately saying is that males are unnecessary," she opined. Salvador Dali, ever provocative, even attributed the 1956 attack on the painting, when a young Bolivian threw a rock that put a small scar on the left elbow, to the smile. "Subconsciously in love with his mother, ravaged by the Oedipus complex," Dali mischievously theorized, the young man was "stupefied to discover a portrait of his own mother, transfigured by the maximum female idealization. His own mother, here! And worse, his mother smiles ambiguously at him....Attack is his one possible response to such a smile."

In our less poetic age, the trend has been more to physiological explanations for the smile. Was Mona Lisa, whoever she was, asthmatic? Simply a contented pregnant housewife? Some researchers have concluded that she probably smiled with her mouth closed because she was undergoing 16th-century-style mercury treatment for syphilis; the mercury would have turned her teeth an ugly black, as well as leaving her with a sorely inflamed mouth. A Danish doctor found that the model had congenital palsy affecting the left side of her face, backing up his theory by pointing out that she had the typically large hands of such patients. For an Australian doctor the problem was a defective muscle in the upper lip, making her smile asymmetrical. After due study, an orthopedic surgeon in Lyons decided that Mona Lisa's semi-smile resulted from her being half-paralyzed either from birth or a stroke; one indication of this, he argued, was that her right hand looks relaxed but her left hand is strangely tense.

But more intriguing than why the model is smiling is the mystery of exactly *who* is doing the smiling. The only real link to a woman named Lisa comes from the 16th-century Italian art historian Giorgio Vasari, who himself never actually saw the painting. Writing around 1550, a good 40 years after it was supposed to have been done, Vasari says, "Leonardo undertook to paint for Francesco del Giocondo a portrait of Mona [a variation of Madonna, Lady] Lisa his wife." Historians know that a Lisa Gherardini of Florence was married in 1495, at the age of 16, to Francesco di Bartolommeo di Zanobi del Giocondo, a 35-year-old Florentine official already twice a widower. But there is no evidence at all that Del Giocondo commissioned the portrait from Leonardo, no sign he paid the artist for it, and, most important, certainly no sign that the painting was delivered to him, since Leonardo kept it with him until his death in Amboise, France, in 1519. Nor does Leonardo mention the project anywhere in his voluminous notebooks.

Thus art historians have had a field day trying to guess whose portrait it is. Some plump for Isabella d'Este, who knew Leonardo well in Milan and whose portrait he did in crayon, perhaps as a study for an oil painting. Others hold for Costanza d'Avalos, Duchess of Francaville, who is mentioned in a contemporary poem as having been painted in mourning by Leonardo, "under the lovely black veil." There's also the unnamed mistress of Giuliano de' Medici. Evidence exists that he asked Leonardo to paint her, leading to the intriguing possibility that the artist did two Mona Lisas, one for her husband, Francesco, and one for her lover, Giuliano. Now *there's* something to smile secretly about.

Then there's the computerized approach. Researcher Lillian Schwartz, a computer graphics consultant at the Lucent Technologies Bell Labs in New Jersey, has applied computer-based techniques to the mystery. After reversing Leonardo's self-portrait so the artist is facing to the left, then scaling it and superimposing it over the Mona Lisa (whose subject also faces left) on the computer screen, Schwartz found that the noses, mouths, foreheads, chins, eyes and brows all line up. Conclusion: Leonardo started with an earlier portrait of a woman, then, finding himself without the sitter, used himself as the model, sans beard. She ties it all together with the knotted patterns, like basketwork, on the bodice of Mona Lisa's dress. Noting that Leonardo, like many Renaissance poets and artists, loved riddles and puns, she makes the connection between his name, Vinci, and *vinco*, the Italian word for the osier branches used in basketry. Voilà, case made. "That famous smile, so tantalizing for so many centuries, is the mirrored smile of Da Vinci himself," she says confidently.

Not everyone is convinced. But the possibility of a pun lying at the heart of Leonardo's mystery painting is taken seriously at the Louvre. Giocondo, Lisa Gherardini's married name, means, in Italian, cheerful, merry, joyous, as does "jocund" in English. (A variant of the word supplies the French title for the painting, *La Joconde*.) Leonardo had already played with a sitter's name by incorporating a juniper bush in his portrait of Ginevra (related to juniper, *ginepro* in Italian) de Benci that hangs in Washington's National Gallery of Art. "He was punning on Mona Lisa's married name when he gave her a subtle smile in *La Joconde*," says Cécile Scailliérez, curator of 16th-century French and Italian painting at the Louvre. "He made it emblematic of her. What we really have here is an idea, more than a realistic portrait, the idea of a smile expressed in the form of a painting." She adds with a verbal shudder, "That picture always makes me feel uneasy when I look at it."

As it has many others over the centuries, and not just because of the smile. For at least the past 150 years, appreciation of the Mona Lisa has veered back and forth between awed Giocondolatry and burlesque Giocondoclasm.

The overwrought school of heated, romantic interpretation might have begun, oddly enough, with the Marquis de Sade, who found Mona Lisa full of "seduction and devoted tenderness," and "the very essence of femininity," though given his tastes one wonders exactly what he meant. A bit later the great French historian Jules Michelet admitted, "This painting attracts me, calls me, invades me, absorbs me; I go to it in spite of myself, as the bird goes to the serpent."

The idea of Mona Lisa as femme fatale was launched. Walter Pater, leader of the 19th-century English Aestheticism movement and ardent advocate of art for art's sake, followed up turgidly. "She is older than the rocks among which she sits," he swooned, "like the vampire, she has been dead many times, and learned the secrets of the grave; and has been a diver in deep seas." Not only that, but for him this exotic beauty expressed "the animalism of Greece, the lust of Rome, the mysticism of the middle age...the return of the Pagan world, the sins of the Borgias." Pater seemed badly in need of a cold shower, as was the French writer of the same period, Arsène Houssaye, who called her "treacherously and deliciously a woman, with 6,000 years of experience, a virgin with an angelic brow who knows more than all the knowing rakes of Boccaccio."

Sigmund Freud, too, pulled out all the stops when trying to figure out "the beautiful Florentine lady." Neatly pigeonholing Leonardo as an obsessive neurotic in his book-length study, *Leonardo da Vinci, A Study in Psychosexuality*, Freud decided that Mona Lisa's expression must have resembled the lost, mysterious smile of the artist's mother: "This picture contains the synthesis of the history of Leonardo's childhood." As for Mona Lisa herself, he proclaimed her nothing less than "the most perfect representation of the contrasts dominating the love-life of woman, namely reserve and seduction, most submissive tenderness and the indifferent craving, which confront the man as a strange and consuming sensuality." (On second thought, maybe we'd better not take the kids to the Louvre after all.)

Twentieth-century ideas on art became more down-to-earth—like how much is it worth? King François I added the Mona Lisa to France's royal collections for 4,000 gold écus, or about $105,000, after Leonardo's death. Today Louvre officials say simply that the Mona Lisa's monetary value is inestimable. In 1911, however, it was somewhere in between: precious but not yet such a superstar on the world art market that it couldn't be sold. That made it worth stealing.

The biggest art heist in history occurred that year, with Parisians waking up on August 23 to screaming headlines like the one in Paris's daily *Excelsior*: "The Louvre's Joconde Stolen: When? How? Who?" The answers were a long time coming, as an army of French, German, Russian, Greek and Italian detectives went on a merry, futile chase for two years. Then, when the public was becoming resigned to the loss of the Mona Lisa, an Italian laborer named Vincenzo Perugia got tired of keeping the original in the false bottom of a trunk.

Perugia, who had worked in the museum, used his knowledge of it to lift the painting. He was put up to it by an Argentine con man named Eduardo de Valfierno, who had a skilled art forger knock off six copies. Valfierno then sold the copies to eager if unscrupulous collectors, five in North America, one in Brazil, who thought they were getting the real thing straight from the Louvre. The scam made him the equivalent today of $67 million. When Valfierno didn't claim the original—ironically, he didn't need it for the scam—Perugia naively offered it for sale to a Florence art dealer and was promptly pinched. The Mona Lisa returned to France on December 31, 1913, riding like royalty in a special compartment of the Milan-Paris express, escorted by a squadron of policemen, politicians, museum officials, and artists. Incredibly, the painting itself had suffered no physical damage.

The damage was to the blind veneration and respect in which the portrait had been held for centuries. Somehow the caper and its familiar, irreverent press coverage rubbed off some of the Mona Lisa's mystique. The age of Giocondoclasm had begun.

Even Bernard Berenson admitted a change of heart. "To my amazement," he wrote after the theft was announced, "I found myself saying softly: 'If only it were true!' And when the news was confirmed I heaved a sigh of relief....She had simply become an incubus, and I was glad to be rid of her." For this eminent connoisseur of Western art, as surely for many others, all the bowing and scraping over the Mona Lisa had become a pain in the neck.

Suddenly the public couldn't get enough of jokey Giocondiana. One postcard showed a grinning, toothy Mona Lisa thumbing her nose at the public and saying, "I'm off to see my Vinci. Thanks and good-bye, all you gawkers." Paris newspapers published photos of music hall stars like Mistinguette in the Gioconda pose, while another postcard, after the return, showed her holding a baby with Perugia's picture in the background, as if she had been on a romantic escapade.

With irreverence and reaction against "bourgeois" values the new order of the day, the painting that had been the image of perfect, inac-

cessible beauty became the ideal target for desperately modern iconoclastic artists like the Dadaists who were sick of the very idea of a
masterpiece. Marcel Duchamp, unofficial leader of the Dada anti-art
movement, summed up the new zeitgeist in 1919 with a few strokes of
his brush. Taking a standard postcard reproduction of the Mona Lisa,
he painted a pointy mustache and goatee on the sacred face, and added
a naughty caption. Now it looks like no more than a childish prank.
But an Art Establishment raised on the likes of Pater and academic
painting was shocked, *shocked*.

Today the Mona Lisa is in the paradoxical situation of being both
the symbol of Art and the ultimate in kitsch. Artists vie to see who can
do the most outrageous parody, advertising studios labor to come up
with the funniest way to sell everything from aperitifs to airlines, golf
clubs to strips that hold your nasal passages open. Collectors of Giocondiana have catalogued nearly 400 advertising uses of the image and
counting, along with at least 61 products called Mona Lisa, made in 14
countries. The goods bearing her smile range from rosé wine and chocolate to cigars, cheese, hairpins, potatoes, corsets and beer.

Want to mock Salvador Dali's commercialism? Do a collage with
his eyes and upraised mustache on Mona Lisa's face, put his hands
overflowing with money in place of hers. Touché! Want to make light
of a weighty public figure, from Stalin to De Gaulle to Prince Charles?
Caricature him as Mona Lisa. Funn*eee*! The portrait also has become
the favorite of computer-age digitizers of images. In Paris, Jean-Pierre
Yvaral has done over 150 synthesized Mona Lisas composed of hundreds of geometric patterns that look abstract up close but become
Herself from afar. One gigantic such composition covered a wall in,
appropriately, rue du Louvre. "I work with Mona Lisa because such an
image has to be immediately recognizable so the viewer can participate
in the work," Yvaral explains. Next big project: digital images of her on
the tails of British Airways jetliners.

Though he's no high-flying art critic or historian, Jean Margat has
his own answer to the painting's mythic hold on the imagination. A

retired geologist, Margat from his home near Orléans, France, presides over The Friends of Mona Lisa, a club of serious collectors of Giocondiana, of which the Louvre Director Pierre Rosenberg is a member, along with a lady in far-away Ann Arbor, Michigan. "There's no way you can get away from it today," Margat says, confessing to being a bit of a Giocondoclast. "The Mona Lisa has an enormous recognition factor, like a monument or a top model. I'm afraid it still symbolizes Western art."

Margat and other Friends get together once in a while for a convivial lunch in Paris—accompanied, of course, by Mona Lisa-brand champagne—where they discuss and compare their collections. His own takes up a good part of his two-story house. It ranges from Mona Lisa T-shirts, posters, ball-point pens, coffee mugs, drink coasters, condoms, panty hose, clocks, matchbooks and thimbles bearing The Face, to truly rare, and expensive, items like a beaded curtain from Vietnam, a Persian rug, and a life-size Mona Lisa sculptured in two kinds of marble that he paid a pretty penny for in an antique shop in Switzerland. His latest enthusiasm is for a bit of kitsch known as the Giggling Mona Lisa Pillow, which squeals with glee when squeezed in the middle and comes from Brooklyn.

As it happens, the Mona Lisa leaves Margat cold. "Frankly, I don't much like that painting," he says with a shrug. "To me it's not expressive and it doesn't look like a real person. But I guess it's timeless, *hélas*."

Update: *Mona Lisa now has a room of her own at the Louvre, the better to be admired—and keep the crowd away from the other museum goers—thanks to a $4.1 million grant from a Japanese television broadcaster. This biggest-ever act of cultural sponsorship in France leaves Louvre curators with mixed feelings. Already prisoners of the myth, they can't touch the Mona Lisa to clean it for fear of media and public outcry, although it's filthy and covered with thick yellowish varnish that would benefit from cleaning. "The room is an improvement," says a resigned*

Cécile Scailliérez, "but unfortunately it makes the Mona Lisa even more of a superstar by setting it apart."

SOURCES

The items in this book have been culled from my writings for a number of publications while based in Paris. Most were first published in *Smithsonian*, the *Dallas Morning News*, for which I did an editorial page foreign affairs column entitled "Europe Today," and *Time*. In the case of *Time*, it is important to recall that its stories used to be entirely written in New York from correspondents' dispatches, which were called "files." The work for *Time* that I include is based on my original files rather than the published stories, which were less comprehensive, and in any case not my own writing.

PART ONE: *La France Eternelle*

"Culture Heroes: The Immortal Members of the Académie Française," *Smithsonian*, January 1990.

"André Malraux Considers the State of the World," based on a *Time* file, October 1968.

"Solving the Mystery of Saint-Exupéry," *Air & Space Smithsonian*, September 2001.

"Quel est Votre Signe?" *Dallas Morning News*, 15 January 1985.

"Intellectuals in Crisis," *Dallas Morning News*, 12 February 1984.

"Schools of Thought: Ferment in French Philosophy," based on a *Time* file, November 1965.

"The Masterful, Medieval Brotherhood of the Compagnons," *Smithsonian*, June 1996.

"France Raises the Tallest Tower," excerpt from Harriss, Joseph, *The Tallest Tower: Eiffel and the Belle Epoque*, Unlimited Publishing, 2004.

"Concorde: A Plane for Prestige," *Air & Space Smithsonian*, September 2001.

"Rogues of Peace: Today's French Foreign Legion," uncondensed version of an article for *Reader's Digest* international editions, October 1997.

"The Divine Sarah," *Smithsonian*, August 2001.

"Champagne: The Brilliant Soul of France," *Oui*, July 1974.

"Oysters for Openers," *Asiaweek*, February 1980.

"How Fast Le Food?" *Dallas Morning News*, 24 June 1984.

"Taking Mustard Seriously," *Smithsonian*, June 2000.

"Vacations with a Vengeance," *Dallas Morning News*, 7 August 1983.

"The Grand Sport of Driving in France," *Dallas Morning News*, 28 August 1984.

"The Outrageous Crazy Horse Saloon," based on a *Time* file, January 1965.

PART TWO: *La Politique*

"The Great French Passion," *Dallas Morning News*, 5 March 1983.

"Politicizing Culture," *Dallas Morning News*, 27 February 1983.

"Testing the Myth of the Resistance," *Dallas Morning News*, 7 February 1984.

"Something Happened: May 1968," based on *Time* files on the dates indicated.

"Where are the Stones of Yesteryear?" based on a *Time* file, 1 August 1968.

"How They See Us," *Dallas Morning News*, 29 January 1985.

"Kerry Loses, Bonjour Tristesse," *The American Spectator*, December 2004.

"*Parlez-vous Franglais?*" based on a *Time* file, 3 April 1969.

"Napoléon Sells Louisiana for a Song," *Smithsonian*, April 2003.

PART THREE: *Le Bon Dieu*

"On Familiar Terms with the Deity," based on a *Time* file, 14 March 1966.

"Worker Priests: Infiltrating the Masses for God," based on a *Time* file, 27 October 1965.

"Victims of a Killer Cult," uncondensed version of an article for *Reader's Digest* international editions, December 1997.

PART FOUR: *Mère des Arts*

"The Prolific, Prodigious Georges Simenon," based on a *Time* file, 7 March 1969.

"Picasso Superstar," based on a *Time* file, 22 November 1966.

"Saul Steinberg, New Yorker in Paris," based on a *Time* file, 30 March 1966.

"The Free Spirit of Marc Chagall," *Smithsonian*, December 2003.

"Van Gogh and Gauguin: Creative Tension in the South of France," *Smithsonian*, December 2001.

"Paul Guillaume: First of the Avant-Garde," *Smithsonian*, November 2000.

"Master Class at the Louvre," *Smithsonian,* October 2002.

"Mona Lisa, Mythic Parisienne," *Smithsonian,* May 1999.

Index

978-0-595-34695-0
0-595-34695-2

16514923R00180

Printed in Great Britain
by Amazon